Development-induced Displacement

STUDIES IN FORCED MIGRATION
General Editors: Stephen Castles and Dawn Chatty

Development-induced Displacement

PROBLEMS, POLICIES AND PEOPLE

Edited by
Chris de Wet

Berghahn Books
New York • Oxford

First published in 2006 by

Berghahn Books
www.berghahnbooks.com

© 2006 Chris de Wet

Library of Congress Cataloging-in-Publication Data
Development-induced displacement : Problems, policies and
people / edited by Chris de Wet.
 p. cm. – (Studies in forced migration ; v. 18)
 includes bibliographical references and index.
 ISBN 1-84545-095-7 (hb. : alk. Paper) – ISBN 1-84545-096-5 (pbk)
  1. Economic development projects—Developing countries. 2. Land
Settlement—Developing countries. 3. Forced migration—Developing
countries. I. De Wet, C. J. II. Series.

HC59.72.E44D48 2005
304.8'09712'4—dc22   2005041202

British Library Cataloguing in Publication Data

A catalogue record for this book is available
from the British Library

Printed in the United States on acid-free paper

ISBN 1-84545-095-7 (hardback)

Contents

Preface

This book represents the outcome of a project undertaken by the Refugee Studies Centre at the University of Oxford and funded by the U.K. Department for International Development (DfID). The project addressed itself to the fact that every year some ten million people worldwide are displaced as a result of development projects of one sort or another, and that, in the great majority of cases, those people are left economically and socially worse off. Considerable progress has been made over the last two decades with regard first to the formulation, and then to the refinement, of resettlement policy frameworks and guidelines – most notably, by the World Bank. However, many countries do not have such policies, and where the policies are applied, their goals are often not realised in practice.

This project therefore sought to examine more closely the factors hindering attempts to improve outcomes in resettlement projects and, in the light of its analyses, to offer suggestions as to how those obstacles might be more effectively dealt with and outcomes improved.

The project, conducted in two phases between 1998 and 2002, consisted of four thematic studies, which were submitted to DfID as reports, together with synthesising reports by Chris de Wet, the overall project coordinator. These reports were:

(1) Addressing Policy Constraints and Improving Outcomes in Development-induced Displacement and Resettlement Projects, by Alan Rew, Eleanor Fisher and Balaji Pandey
(2) Addressing Legal Constraints and Improving Outcomes in Development-induced Resettlement Projects, by Michael Barutciski
(3) Towards Local Development and Mitigating Impoverishment in Development-induced Displacement and Resettlement, by Dolores Koenig
(4) Displacement, Resistance and the Critique of Development: From the Grassroots to the Global, by Anthony Oliver-Smith

These reports have been reworked as chapters 3, 4, 5 and 6 in this book, which also includes chapters by Chris de Wet and David Turton, who served as Director of the Refugee Studies Centre for the duration of most of the project. A concluding chapter dealing with policy recommendations and suggestions for future research, although written by Chris de Wet, pulls together suggestions made by the authors of the thematic studies in their reports and in their book chapters.

Chris de Wet

Acknowledgements

It is my pleasure, on behalf of all the members of the project, to record our sincere thanks to the following institutions and people: the Department for International Development (U.K.), for funding the project; the Refugee Studies Centre at the University of Oxford, for providing the institutional base for the project; Elizabeth Colson, Dawn Chatty, Ted Downing, Patricia Feeney, Sean Loughna, S. Parasuraman and Warren Waters, for their valuable input into the workshops held during the course of the project, and/or for commenting on the project proposals; Helen Hacksley, for her expert help in getting the final manuscript ready to send off to Berghahn Books; those people who consented to be interviewed by members of the project and who shared their knowledge and insights about resettlement with us; all our colleagues in academe, especially those working more directly in the field of resettlement, for their encouragement and comments on our work; and our families, for their ongoing support and tolerance of the demands the project made upon our family situations.

List of Contributors

Michael Barutciski is Assistant Professor in the International Studies Programme at Glendon College, York University, Canada.

Chris de Wet is Professor of Anthropology at Rhodes University in Grahamstown, South Africa.

Eleanor Fisher is Lecturer in International Development at the Centre for Development Studies at the University of Wales in Swansea, Wales.

Dolores Koenig is Professor of Anthropology at the American University in Washington, United States of America.

Anthony Oliver-Smith is Professor of Anthropology at the University of Florida in Gainesville, United States of America.

Balaji Pandey is Director of the Institute for Socio-Economic Development in Bhubaneswar, Orissa, India.

Alan Rew is Director of the Centre for Development Studies and Professor of Development Policy and Planning, at the University of Wales in Swansea, Wales.

David Turton, formerly Director of the Refugee Studies Centre at the University of Oxford, is now a Senior Research Associate at the Refugee Studies Centre.

1

Introducing the Issues

Chris de Wet

The last twenty years have seen the displacement or resettlement of some two hundred million people as a result of development projects (Cernea 2000: 11). In the overwhelming majority of cases, this movement has been forced, in the sense that the affected people have been compelled by the authorities to move, whether they wanted to or not, and, short of resisting, they have effectively had no say in the matter. The last two decades have also seen the generation of resettlement guidelines and resettlement policies in a number of countries and states, which have in some cases – most notably, in some projects in China (e.g. Trembath et al. 1999; Shi et al. 2000a; Shuikou and Xiaolangdi – see Picciottio et al. 2001) – led to an improvement in outcomes in Development-induced displacement and resettlement (DIDR) projects. Successful resettlement (which would seem to require making planned provision for people who have to move, but which does not necessarily have to involve people moving to planned new resettlement areas as such) would seem to require resettled people being economically better off and living in socially stable and institutionally functional communities, in a sustainable manner. However, in the overwhelming majority of cases, most of the people displaced or resettled by development projects are still left worse off than before and suffer socio-economic impoverishment.

This would seem to suggest that successful resettlement is not simply – or even predominantly – a matter of getting the 'right inputs' lined up, such as sound legal and policy frameworks, sufficient political will, and the necessary financial and administrative capacity. A number of resettlement schemes in China, where all the above ingredients for successful resettlement would appear to have been present at a national level, have in fact not been successful with regard to income generation and a number of other issues (Shi et al. 2000b). Although there is no denying that successful resettlement is not possible without the necessary 'inputs', it would seem that those 'inputs', while necessary, are not sufficient.

The contributors to this volume would all broadly be in agreement with the argument put forward by the World Commission on Dams (WCD) that

> At the heart of the dams debate are issues of equity, governance, justice and power – issues that underlie the many intractable problems faced by humanity ... [and that while] dams have made an important and significant contribution to human development, and the benefits derived from them have been considerable ... in too many cases an unacceptable and often unnecessary price has been paid to secure those benefits, especially in social and environmental terms, by people displaced, by communities downstream, by taxpayers and by the natural environment. (World Commission on Dams 2000: xxviii)

They would further agree that 'by bringing to the table all those whose rights are involved and who bear the risks associated with different options for water and energy resources development, the conditions for a positive resolution of competing interests and conflicts are created' (loc. cit.).

While many of the findings and recommendations in this volume resonate with those put forward by the WCD, they range more widely than those of the WCD, which concerned itself exclusively with dams, whereas this volume also deals with resettlement arising from other causes. The WCD focused on a range of dam-related issues much wider than only resettlement, which is the principal focus of this volume. The approach of this volume is also somewhat different from that of the WCD, which is designed as a 'New Framework for Decision-Making' concerning dams. While the current volume is concerned with policy issues relating to resettlement, its contributors argue, from different perspectives, that there is a complexity – and a tension – inherent in the situation where we try to reconcile ordering people to move, often to a specified resettlement area, with leaving them in a socio-economically viable and sustainable situation afterwards. The failure to come to terms with this complexity is one of the main reasons why resettlement projects keep coming out wrong. Although policy recommendations are made, the perspective in this current volume is predominantly analytical, as opposed to its being a 'framework for decision-making' that seeks to arrive at the formulation of a set of 'strategic priorities' and 'guidelines for good practice' (World Commission on Dams 2000: ch. 8 and 9).

Turton suggests that academics and practitioners in the broader field of forced migration have tended to behave in a very compartmentalised fashion, with refugee studies 'fundamentalists' (Adelman 2001: 9) seeking to distinguish their field of interest from that of 'internally displaced persons' (IDPs), as well as 'development-induced displaced persons' (DIDPs)

– and vice versa. At first glance, this may appear to be somewhat irra-
tional, since, as instances of forced migration, they should presumably
have a significant amount in common and have much to learn from each
other. While there may well be issues of academics wishing to protect
their turf and jobs, Turton suggests that there may be more practical and
policy-based motivations for this separatist behaviour, with policy considerations influencing academic conceptualisation. The argument for
keeping refugees separate from IDPs relates to their different status in
terms of international law, as well as the fear that blurring the distinction
and referring to IDPs as 'refugees' may lead to a lessening of the protection currently extended to 'real', i.e. cross-border, refugees. Refugee policy is seen as properly concerned with issues of asylum *in other countries,*
whereas IDP policy is about the rendering of humanitarian assistance to
people fleeing from violence or threat of persecution *within their own countries.* Both of these are again different from DIDR, where Cernea argues
that the principal policy objective is seen as *'restoring the income-generating
capacity of resettlers'* (Cernea 1996: 314, my emphasis), and where the state
is seen as having an obligation to protect their rights as citizens it has displaced in terms of the legal provisions of eminent domain.

It would thus appear to be concerns for policy turf at least as much as
for academic turf that are keeping the various areas of forced migration
artificially apart, with policy seeming to influence the way we craft our
concepts – instead of the other way around. For Turton, this raises the disturbing question as to whether the terms 'refugee' and 'IDP' have any
conceptual substance, leading him to make the claim that 'the term [i.e.
"refugee"] does not distinguish a "subset" of forced migrants that can
meaningfully be compared to other subsets'. By the same token, we in the
field of DIDR forced migration may be 'deconceptualising' our subject in
a similar way: if our policy concern is with income restoration, then we
may be tempted to conceptualise resettlement in those terms, and only to
think about it in ways that are relevant to income restoration. Hence
Koenig's concern that we have focused on the economic aspect of resettlement at the cost of the political, and Oliver-Smith's and de Wet's concerns that a unidimensional, cost-benefit analysis approach and a policy
based on a set of operational procedures designed to deal with particular
risks are unable to do justice to the cultural dimension, with all its complexity and multidimensionality. We need temporarily to stand back from
the undisputed need to restore incomes and improve outcomes, and from
a policy-driven conceptualisation of the phenomenon of resettlement. We
need to look afresh at what constitutes resettlement and what it involves
– and why, *in strictly sociological terms,* that should be the case.

Rew, Fisher and Pandey put forward the concept of 'policy practice' to
capture the idea that the translation of policy into practice is an essentially problematic and often messy process, in which policy and implemen-

tation should not be seen as two separate stages, where we need to get from one to the other, but rather as two interacting and mutually influencing aspects of the same thing. Policy is actually modified in the process of implementation, leading to what might be called policy slippage or 'implementation deficit'.

In their chapter they develop a three-tier model of what they call the 'policy landscape', showing how policy is modified as it finds its way 'down' the institutional landscape, to the actual resettlement projects on the ground. At the 'top of the hill', in the capital, are the high-level policy makers, who formulate policy at a normative level, rather than in any detailed manner. Such normative policy frames are of necessity fairly general and open to various interpretations, as they have to accommodate trade-offs and compromises between various government departments and interest groups. The middle or 'plateau' level relates to state or regional administrative centres or district towns, where resettlement and rehabilitation and other policy directives are co-ordinated and implemented. This level is usually characterised by weak decision-making structures, poor communication, and lack of co-ordination (if not outright competition) between various departments and agencies. The bottom of the hill, or the 'swamp', is where actual project implementation and service delivery takes place. Officials are poorly paid, seriously understaffed and thus under tremendous work pressure and poorly motivated – as well as having considerable discretion as to how they go about their jobs. This results in them cutting corners and developing their own operational routines in order to deal with their workload, and allows considerable scope for corruption. Resettlement policy effectively becomes what the resettlement officer on the ground makes of it.

The key to understanding why resettlement projects go wrong thus lies in understanding the way the various levels of the policy landscape function and are interrelated (or, as is perhaps more commonly the case, very poorly interrelated) and how this effectively rules out an orderly and uncorrupted passage from policy to implementation. Any attempt to improve policy and outcomes must squarely confront those realities, or fail.

Koenig and Oliver-Smith both argue that planners fail to recognise the inherent complexity of the pre-resettlement social and economic systems that they are trying to plan and provide for in the post-resettlement situation. Because they fail to see this complexity, they cannot take all the relevant factors into account, let alone deal with unexpected developments. For reasons of efficiency and cost-effectiveness, planners are also predisposed to simplify complexity down to manageable dimensions, which effectively means deciding beforehand which social factors are important and what their significance really is. More often than not, this will result in operationally motivated outsider categories at best skimming over the top of insider complexities and ambiguities, and at worst getting them fundamentally wrong. This kind of misfit can only be compounded when it takes place in the context of displacing and relocating people in terms of outsider conceptions of settlement and land use.

One area in which local complexity is misunderstood and misrepresented is in the area of compensation, where a value is attached to local resources in order to be able to compensate affected people for losses arising from displacement. To calculate compensation, resources are evaluated in terms of assumed uses, productive value and apparent patterns of access. However, resources have multiple uses, both more directly economic and otherwise, and patterns of access to resources are notoriously complex, ambiguous and dynamic. What the outside implementers think they are taking away and compensating for may bear little resemblance to the multiple uses and meanings the affected people see themselves as losing, and to whether they consider that such loss can in principle be made good through compensation. The attempt to secure and impose a process of commensurability of evaluation necessarily requires a process of simplification, which is likely to give rise to confusion, anger and resistance. Such oversimplification reaches its height with cost-benefit analysis, which seeks to put a numerical type value, and more particularly, a monetary value, on resources. Outsider ability to impose itself dictates that not only are people's complex relationships to resources subjected to a process of evaluation in the first place, but that this also takes place in terms of an outsider set of categories and system of exchange.

Koenig suggests that this failure to take the complexity of local systems into account is directly related to the fact that insufficient attention has been paid to the political aspects of DIDR. Forced resettlement impoverishes people, in part because it takes away their power to make decisions about where and how they are to live, the conditions under which they are to have access to and use productive resources, and the autonomy they are to exercise over the running and reproduction of their own socio-political institutions. In situations where social, spatial, economic and political relations are intimately intertwined, where resources have multiple uses and meanings, and where livelihoods are multi-stranded, complexity is not simply an aesthetic or intellectual value – it is the key to socio-economic viability and sustainability. To overlook that complexity is to undermine the basis of both livelihood and community. Koenig suggests that planners do not take all the relevant factors into account because they effectively do not have to – they are not constrained to undertake planning in a sufficiently democratic manner. Until genuine local-level participation is achieved, for all stages of the development project as a whole and not just its resettlement component, local complexities will not be properly articulated, understood or taken into account. Local tensions and conflicts will be exacerbated and access to resources compromised.

While clearly a complex issue with all sorts of trade-offs, a substantial case can be made that displacement (which is here understood to be compulsory) constitutes a prima facie case of a violation of, or at the least an assault on, basic human rights, at two levels. First, a number of international treaties (such as those discussed by Barutciski in his chapter) specify freedom of movement, choice of residence, and ownership and possession of the land peoples traditionally occupy, as general human rights. This raises the fundamental question of the relationship between human rights and development, with Rew, Fisher and Pandey arguing that a failure on the human rights front signals a failure for a development project. Economic 'development' that comes at the price of a lessening of the human rights of the affected people does not qualify as development. A failure to provide an alternative for entitlements such as livelihood, food security, home or socio-cultural heritage, which are lost as a result of displacement, amounts to a violation of human rights, as well as a disregard of the principles of equity. As Cernea (2000: 12) argues: 'The outcome is an unjustifiable repartition of development's costs and benefits: some people enjoy the gains of development, while others bear its pains'.

Second, as Turton argues, displacement raises rights issues at the level of the nation-state, in which all citizens are held to be equal. But people who are displaced clearly do not enjoy equal rights when it is held to be expedient that some should suffer for the collective good, such as when a dam brings water and electricity to large cities, but at the cost of the displacement of others.

The 'limited good' argument, that all cannot benefit because of the limited nature of resources, does not hold because directly as a result of the project, there are more resources (water, electricity, irrigated fields, better roads, etc.) available. The wider society therefore cannot be made worse off by making the affected people beneficiaries of the increased resources flowing from the project. Who gets what from the new resource base is therefore unambiguously a political question and as such, a question about rights.

The problem for DIDPs (i.e. development-induced displaced persons, who may or may not be resettled) is that there does not seem to be either effective international protection for, or national consensus on, their rights and entitlements. Barutciski argues that neither international law relating to refugees nor documentation relating to internally displaced persons apply to DIDPs, as the former is concerned with issues of asylum in foreign countries and the latter with humanitarian intervention in situations of violence or persecution, whereas DIDR relates to DIDPs' governments having an obligation to compensate people for damages incurred as a result of displacement in terms of the law of eminent domain. Using the example of India, Rew shows how there is no common vision of the rights and entitlements of DIDPs, or of the view that compensation is basically a human rights issue. This lack of national-level consensus renders the position of DIDPs all the more precarious as the nation or the state is effectively both player and referee, as it makes the laws that are supposed to protect the rights of all its citizens, while at the same time assuming the right to interpret and implement those laws in displacing its citizens.

But unless laws, treaties, guidelines and policies are enforceable, they serve little purpose. Barutciski shows us how, in spite of the fact that international general human rights treaties and EU development policies may be important in contributing to the terms in which the debate around the rights of displaced people is couched, and may act as a kind of moral court of appeal, they actually offer DIDPs only limited protection. The most promising development for the protection of DIDPs would seem to be the resettlement guidelines developed by international banks – and particularly those of the World Bank – in which they impose restrictions on themselves and their clients. However, such guidelines operate under various limitations. Firstly, international banks such as the World Bank have an explicitly non-political mandate and therefore, short of withdrawing from funding a project – with all that involves, lack the means to enforce their guidelines. They are therefore also in something of an ethical dilemma: if they insist on borrower countries scrupulously obeying their guidelines, such countries may turn to sources of funding that are not bound by such guidelines and have less scruples. Alternatively, if such banks lower their standards, they may keep the borrower countries from going elsewhere for funds, and exercise at least some scrutiny and control over the resettlement process.

One of the more promising vehicles for the monitoring and enforcement of resettlement standards is the World Bank's Inspection Panel, which enables individuals to bring complaints against the World Bank if they feel it is not keeping to its own policies and procedures. However, Barutciski argues that, while the Inspection Panel could exercise a very positive influence in the development of international human rights law, there has seemingly been a move on the part of the Executive Directors of the World Bank to limit the activities of the Panel, as well as access to it. Investigations have been refused on a regular basis, on the grounds that they were unnecessary because 'action plans' had been agreed between the Bank and the borrowing country. This change of approach does raise questions about the potential viability of such mechanisms. Here again, the tensions raised by international banks having nonpolitical mandates come to the fore: the effectiveness of such mechanisms for enforcement will hinge on the willingness of banking institutions to put projects at risk for the sake of human rights – which in turn would involve compromising their nonpolitical mandate. Enforcement mechanisms are more likely to be effective when implemented by governments making bilateral loans which are not subject to such restrictions.

In the end, enforcement would seem to be a function of two things: the financial and administrative capacity to implement such enforcement and the political will to do so. Political will is responsive to pressure, which can come from a range of sources, such as court judgements, public protest and resistance to resettlement, particularly when this is assisted by international non-governmental organisations (NGOs) and by coverage in the world media. But principled, consistent and transparent enforcement – whether by the courts, governments or international banking organisations – is notoriously difficult to achieve, and this must remain the Achilles heel of attempts to secure the rights of DIDPs.

Resistance to resettlement is directly related to the issue of the rights of those threatened with, or affected by, displacement, to make their voice heard and to have a say in what happens to them. Increasingly, alternative visions of development are being voiced across particularly 'the Third World', which has for decades been subjected to Western models of development, often involving dramatic transformations of the physical and socio-economic environment. Resistance to resettlement has become one of the contexts in which the top-down, capital-intensive, infrastructure-based approach is being contested, and in which 'alternative developments' are being put forward. This counter-movement has taken on significance in the context of an emerging transnational civil society, fuelled by the conjunction of global-level concerns about human rights, the environment and indigenous peoples, and facilitated by the communication revolution of the last few decades.

At stake is who has the right to promote their particular vision of development: the state and/or capital, or the people targeted for resettlement and environmental transformation; for those under threat, what is at stake is the autonomy, together with the complexity and multidimensionality, of their local social and economic systems, which they perceive as directly under threat from externally imposed development combined with resettlement. Resistance seeks to assert their rights in this regard.

As a venture that is fraught with both personal and economic risk, resistance provides us with a very useful barometer of the way people under threat see what is at risk in resettlement. Using Dwivedi's conceptualisation of risk, Oliver-Smith suggests that resistance occurs when people judge that displacement and resettlement pose risks that they regard as culturally unacceptable, and/or when they evaluate the potential rewards, in the form of compensation or new opportunities, as insufficient. The occurrence of resistance is thus a strong indicator that issues of development, human rights and equity are out of kilter, and that people are divided as to how they should be brought into alignment. Resistance is also a very good measure of lines of differentiation and vulnerability within a community, as not everybody will feel equally at risk, or equally able to resist. Resettlement plans that do not cater for this kind of intra-community diversity cannot succeed.

Oliver-Smith suggests that, while resistance usually does not succeed in preventing that which it opposes, such as a dam, irrigation scheme or conservation area, that does not mean that it has been a failure. Resistance may succeed in getting the terms or conditions of resettlement improved; it may also give the resisting local community valuable experience of dealing with wider-level political and administrative structures, as well as enabling them to acquire valuable allies in that wider context – which can only stand them in good stead in any future development undertaking in which they become involved. While it may well tear communities apart, resistance can also give them a sense of cohesion and identity, generating new leadership and energy for future undertakings. At its widest level, local-level resistance can become part of the wider struggle against infra-structure- and capital-based models of development, contributing to the ongoing debate about development alternatives. That connection to wider struggles and issues is, however, often a two-edged sword, with local-level struggles becoming dependent upon or manipulated by wider, more powerful and articulate interests – with communities seeking to defend their autonomy from one master, only to cede it to another.

As with policy and implementation, so with resistance and resettle-ment – they are best seen not as discrete entities, but as part of the same process. It is only reasonable to expect that people are going to oppose, and even resist, being forcibly moved. If they are listened to and their grievances fed back into an open-ended process of resettlement planning and implementation, the result can only be a better resettlement outcome. Here the affected people have to tread a very difficult tightrope. People resist in order to have their grievances taken seriously – but, if the price of being taken seriously at the level of planning details is to lose one's moral or political authority for resisting the very kind of development that leads to one's displacement in the first place, then one is truly caught up in very difficult trade-offs.

De Wet attempts to develop a systematic analysis of the complexities involved in the resettlement process by trying to understand why things so often turn out badly. He argues that there are problems inherent in the nature of forced resettlement, as well as in the nature of the resettlement project as an institutional process. Forced resettlement involves several processes of change taking place simultaneously, feeding into each other, in such a way that the process takes on a life of its own. It involves: imposed spatial change; a sudden realignment of social relationships; a change (often a diminution) in patterns of access to resources; incorpora-tion into larger, more heterogeneous settlements (often resulting in con-flict over resources and leadership) and involvement in wider adminis-trative and political structures (usually involving a lessening of local autonomy). It is the combination of these factors, in the context of a process of accelerated socio-economic change, that results in a process over which neither planners nor people have very much control, which takes on a dynamic of its own.

In addition to the problems of policy practice, resettlement projects often suffer from a number of mutually reinforcing critical shortages, such as participation, money, manpower, skills and time. Resettlement is all too often seen as an external cost, and is accordingly not planned as a development exercise, with the result that, by default, what should be resettlement with development becomes reduced to relocation with minimal (if any) development. Resettlement projects are also characterised by a number of aspects that are not readily amenable to rational planning procedures. They are seen as part of wider political programmes, and are also subject to conflicting time frames and to competing visions as to the nature and process of development. A range of risks hits the affected people all at the same time, constituting a crisis for them (Cernea 2000). The same applies to the planners of resettlement. De Wet develops a typology of interacting risks involved in forced resettlement, from the local level of the individual or household, to the affected community, to the resettlement project itself, to the national and international levels. Both planners and people find themselves having to respond in an ad hoc way to unfolding events, and their responses feed back into the process, but often in an unplanned manner – all of which renders rational planning and procedures, and positive outcomes, increasingly unlikely. Looking at what characterises the more successful cases of resettlement in China, as well as cases of voluntary resettlement and ways in which people involved in forced resettlement schemes have been able to turn events to their own advantage in ways not anticipated by the schemes, de Wet argues that we need to develop a flexibility and open-endedness in the way we go about planning and implementing resettlement that allows us to cater for and counter the complexities that it inevitably generates.

Good policy has to be grounded in an adequate understanding of the phenomenon with which the policy seeks to deal. An enhanced understanding of displacement and resettlement should logically lead to better policy. Indeed, that has been one of the principal intentions of the research programme that has led to this book.

Having stepped back from policy in our thinking about DIDR, we are now free to cross the policy-patrolled boundaries between the various kinds of forced migration, such as refugees, IDPs and DIDPs – and, indeed, in this book we have not even considered people having to move as a result of natural disasters – and systematically to consider differences and similarities between them. In this way, we can develop a comparative discipline of forced migration. Cernea (1996), Scudder (1993) and Turton (infra) have all argued for the political and experiential similarities between different kinds of forced migration. Sharing research findings, insights and experiences in trying to develop policy will lead to better policy across the board. The more solidly such policy is grounded in a systematically and comparatively based understanding of the *sociology* of forced migration, the better that policy will be. To echo Turton's invocation of Louis Pasteur: 'There is no such thing as applied science: there is only the application of science'. With this approach in mind, the concluding chapter makes various policy recommendations and suggestions for further research.

Note

1. In this volume we have chosen to use the term 'forced', rather than 'involuntary' or 'compulsory', to describe situations where people migrate or are resettled against their will. The reasons for this are explained by David Turton in Chapter Two.

References

Adelman, H. 2001. 'From Refugees to Forced Migration: The UNHCR and Human Security'. *International Migration Review*, 35(1): 7–32.

Cernea, M.M. 1996. 'Bridging the Research Divide: Studying Refugees and Development Oustees'. In T. Allen (ed.). *In Search of Cool Ground: War, Flight and Homecoming in North-East Africa*, pp. 293–317. London, Trenton: James Currey/Africa World Press.

_____ 2000. 'Risks, Safeguards and Reconstruction: A Model for Population Displacement and Resettlement'. In M.M. Cernea and C. McDowell (eds). *Risks and Reconstruction: Experiences of Resettlers and Refugees*, pp. 11–55. Washington DC: The World Bank.

Picciotto, R., W. van Wicklin and E. Rice (eds). 2001. *Involuntary Resettlement: Comparative Perspectives*. New Brunswick: Transaction Publishers.

Scudder, T. 1993. 'Development-induced Relocation and Refugee Studies: 37 Years of Change and Continuity among Zambia's Gwembe Tonga'. *Journal of Refugee Studies*, 6(3): 123–52.

Shi, G., Q. Su and S. Yuan. 2000a. *Policy, Planning and Implementation of Resettlement and Rehabilitation of Reservoir Projects in China*. Unpublished conference paper, Tenth conference of the International Rural Sociology Association, Rio de Janeiro, Brazil.

Shi, G., Z. Wu, S. Chen and W. Zhu. 2000b. *Policy, Planning and Implementation of Resettlement and Rehabilitation of Reservoir Projects in China*. Unpublished conference paper, Tenth conference of the International Rural Sociology Association, Rio de Janeiro, Brazil.

Trembath, B., M. Ter Woordt and Y. Zhu. 1999. *The Shuikou Hydroelectric Project in China: A Case Study of Successful Resettlement*. Washington DC: The World Bank. (This report is a summarised version of a larger report entitled 'Successful

Reservoir Resettlement in China: Shuikou Hydroelectric Project': EASES Discussion Paper Series.)

World Commission on Dams (WCD). 2000. *Dams and Development: A New Framework for Decision-making.* London, Sterling VA: Earthscan.

2

Who is a Forced Migrant?

David Turton

The term 'forced migrant' has emerged in recent years, in both academic and policy circles, as a catch-all label for a person who has been forced to leave his or her home, or homeland, for whatever reason. 'Forced migration' has become, in effect, the name of a new problem-oriented field of academic enquiry, potentially combining the study of political, environmental and developmental displacement. And yet research on different categories of displaced people tends to proceed as though on parallel tracks, a good example of this being the so-called 'research divide' which Michael Cernea (1996) has identified between the study of refugees and the study of forced resettlers. It shall be argued later that the main reason for the fragmentation of research on displacement is the heavy dependence of this research on categories and concepts that are the product of policy considerations rather than of scientific ones (Hansen 1996: 8, Black 2001). If this is correct, then it becomes important to ask how 'forced migration' can be conceptualised as a unitary, scientifically coherent and yet 'policy-relevant' field of academic enquiry. This chapter is an attempt to think through some of the main issues that need to be addressed if a satisfactory answer to this question is to be found.

It begins by considering the empirical and conceptual similarities between people who are classified as refugees and those who are classified as forced resettlers. It then approaches the subject from a wider viewpoint and discusses the difficulty of separating out a category of *forced* migrants from migrants in general. This difficulty rests on the logical awkwardness, not to say contradiction, of combining 'forced', which implies a lack of alternatives, with 'migration', which implies choice and human agency. It is suggested that the best way out of this difficulty is always to think of forced migrants as 'ordinary people', or 'purposive actors', embedded in particular social, political and historical situations.

The third part of the chapter considers the main categorical distinctions that the broader category of 'forced migrant' has come to include, namely 'refugee', 'internally displaced person' and 'development-induced displaced person'. Because these distinctions are artefacts of political and policy concerns, rather than of empirical observation and sociological analysis, they work against two fundamental requirements of the scientific method: the comparison of sub-classes within a class of related phenomena and the revision of categories and concepts in the light of empirical observation.

Finally, the implications of this argument for the general issue of 'relevance' within a problem-oriented field of study are discussed. On the one hand, the categories and concepts employed by policy makers may not be helpful – indeed they may be downright unhelpful – when it comes to the pursuit of scientific understanding. This, after all, is not their main purpose. On the other hand, we must assume that the more rigorous the science, both theoretically and methodologically, the more likely it is to have a beneficial impact on policy (Jacobsen and Landau 2003). It will be suggested that, in order to find a way through this dilemma, we need to distinguish, not between two kinds of professional activity, research and policy making, or between two kinds of people, the 'academic' and the 'practitioner', but between two kinds of knowledge, 'practical' and 'scientific'. Practical knowledge is produced by 'doing' and is necessarily unreflective and unself-conscious, though not necessarily false. Scientific knowledge is produced by the application of scientific method and is necessarily reflective and self-conscious, though not necessarily true. It follows that scientific knowledge will be most relevant to policy when it is used to reflect critically on the practical knowledge upon which policy is based. Paradoxically, therefore, research on human displacement is less likely to be 'relevant' to policy, the more closely it follows policy-related categories and concepts in defining its subject matter and in setting its research priorities.

Refugees and Forced Resettlers: Tracing the Connections

'Refugees', for the purpose of this discussion, are people who have left their own country because of persecution and violence and who are unable or unwilling to return to it. 'Forced resettlers' are 'development-induced displaced persons' who have been allocated a specific area within their own country in which to resettle and who have been provided with at least a minimum of resources and services in order to re-establish their lives. The term may also apply to those who are resettled by government-sponsored programmes that use resettlement as a method of rural development and/or political control.

The connections between refugees and forced resettlers can be traced on an empirical as well as on a conceptual level. Empirically, one can focus on the experiences of those who are forced to move, rather than on the causes of their movement, and on the challenges they face in re-establishing themselves in a new place. Here this chapter will rely mainly on Cernea's own writings and on an unpublished essay by Elizabeth Colson, 'Coping in Adversity' (1991). This is a rare example of an attempt to achieve precisely the kind of 'bridging' between two bodies of 'research literature' that Cernea has been calling for. Second, the chapter will move from the empirical to the conceptual level and suggest that both the figure of the refugee and the figure of the forced resettler can be seen as revealing underlying contradictions in the ideology of the nation-state as the dominant political organising principle of the modern world.

Both Colson and Cernea emphasise the 'commonalities of experience ... among the uprooted, however they are set in motion' (Colson 1991: 1). Colson focuses on the psychological stress caused by the experience of being forcibly displaced. She notes that, while all migrants are liable to increased levels of stress, this is compounded for those who are forced to move against their will by bereavement at the loss of their homes and anger and resentment towards the agents and institutions that forced them to move. This is likely to lead, for both refugees and forced resettlers, to a loss of trust in society generally and to the expression of opposition and antagonism towards the administrative authorities and the staff of humanitarian organisations who have power over their lives. For refugees, this is seen most obviously in a critical and resentful attitude towards camp personnel, as reported, for example, in Barbara Harrell-Bond's (1986) account of Ugandan refugees in Sudanese camps. In a similar vein, Liisa Malkki reports that Burundian refugees in Mishamo refugee settlement in Tanzania regularly described themselves as the 'slaves' of the Tanzanian authorities (1995a: 120).

Unlike most refugees, forced resettlers (this refers specifically to those displaced by infrastructural projects) have no choice about leaving their homes and cannot entertain the slightest hope of returning to them. Also unlike refugees, it is possible for their move to be planned well in advance. The authorities can therefore take steps to ensure that the disruptive impact of the move is minimised and that the standard of living of the resettlers is improved, or at least maintained. In practice, however, this hardly ever happens: those displaced by development projects are not only (like refugees), typically, amongst the poorest and politically most marginal members of a society, but they are also likely to become even more impoverished as a result of the move. Forced resettlers, therefore, may end up 'as alienated from their governments as the refugees who have fled their countries' (Colson 1991: 15).

Based initially on her study of the forced displacement of the Gwembe Tonga of Zambia by the Kariba Dam in 1957/58, Colson has attempted, in conjunction with Thayer Scudder, to demarcate phases in the process of forced displacement, which are also found to apply to refugee populations. The first two of these phases are particularly applicable to refugees. First there is a stage of denial, when 'the possibility of removal is too stressful to acknowledge' (Scudder and Colson 1982: 271). After the move has taken place there is likely to be a phase during which people will cling to old certainties and take no risks, even if this prevents them from taking advantage of new economic opportunities: 'Following removal, the majority of relocatees, including refugees, can be expected to follow a conservative strategy. They cope with the stress of removal by clinging to the familiar and changing no more than is necessary' (Scudder and Colson 1982: 272). Here we may see a clear illustration of the difference that force, or the relative lack of choice in deciding whether, when and where to move, makes to the behaviour of migrants. The greater the area of choice available to them, even though they may be escaping from difficult or even life-threatening circumstances, the more likely they are to show high levels of innovation and adaptation in taking advantage of the opportunities offered by their new environment (Turton 1996).

The fact that forced resettlement, unlike the flight of refugees, can be planned in advance, and the fact that it is, in many cases, a seemingly inescapable consequence of economic development, has provided both the motive and the opportunity for social scientists to study its long term consequences. This research, much of it carried out by social anthropologists, has produced a huge amount of detailed information that has been used in efforts to promote improvements in the design and implementation of resettlement projects. Michael Cernea, who was formerly Senior Adviser for Sociology and Social Policy at the World Bank and the main architect of the Bank's policy on 'involuntary resettlement', has been at the forefront of these efforts. His 'impoverishment, risks and reconstruction model' of forced resettlement is intended to act as a guide to the actions needed if the potentially impoverishing effects of forced resettlement are to be avoided or minimised. Two of these effects are particularly relevant to the comparison of forced resettlers with refugees: landlessness and loss of 'social capital'.[1]

According to Cernea, empirical evidence shows that loss of land 'is the principal form of decapitalization and pauperisation' of forced resettlers (2000: 23) and that 'settling displaced people back on cultivable land ... is the heart of the matter in reconstructing livelihoods' (2000: 35). Loss of social capital refers to the disruption and disintegration of the informal social support networks which are vital to economic survival in communities where individuals and households are vulnerable to short-term and unpredictable fluctuations in income. Both of these potentially impoverishing effects of forced migration clearly apply to those forced to move by conflict, whether across international borders or not, at least as much as they do to those forced to move by development projects.

On an empirical level, then, it is clear that refugees and forced resettlers 'confront strikingly similar social and economic problems' (Cernea 2000: 17). But it is also possible to trace a connection between them at the conceptual level, by considering their relationship to the nation-state, or to what Malkki (1992) has called 'the national order of things'.[2] The refugee, as a person who is unable or unwilling to obtain the protection of his or her own government, makes visible a contradiction between citizenship, as the universal source of all individual rights, and nationhood, as an identity ascribed by birth and entailing a sentimental attachment to a specific community and territory.

> The twentieth century became the century of refugees, not because it was extraordinary in forcing people to flee, but because of the division of the globe into nation-states in which states were assigned the role of protectors of rights, but also that of exclusive protectors of their own citizens. When the globe was totally divided into states, those fleeing persecution in one state had nowhere to go but to another state, and required the permission of the other state to enter it. (Adelman 1999: 9)

The figure of the refugee exposes a contradiction in the idea of the nation-state, as both a culturally homogeneous political community and as the universal principle of political organisation. The refugee is 'out of place' in a conceptual as well as an empirical sense. He or she is an anomaly produced by the universalisation of the nation-state as a principle of political organisation.

The forced resettler, displaced in the 'national interest' to make way for a development project, exposes a contradiction between the nation-state, as the ultimate source of legitimate political control and the principal agent of development in a given territory, and as a community of equal citizens. The official objective of a project involving forced resettlement is, of course, to benefit a much wider population than that of the displaced themselves. And the key characteristic of this wider population is that it shares with the displaced population membership of the same nation-state. Co-membership of the nation-state, therefore, makes legally and morally legitimate a situation in which, as Cernea has put it, 'some people enjoy the gains of development, while others bear its pains' (2000: 12). But who are these 'others' who are also fellow citizens? In what sense are they 'other'? Is it just that they are 'not us' or is it, more fundamentally, that they are 'not like us', that they have a different and systematically inferior relationship to the sources of state power?

The empirical evidence suggests the latter answer is correct. In case after case of forced resettlement, we see the state exercising its right to expropriate property for public use against a relatively impoverished and powerless group of its own citizens, with typically disastrous consequences for their economic, physical, psychological and social well-being. In many cases, the displaced people are members of an indigenous minority who are forced out of their home territory or part of it. They are economically and politically marginal to the nation-state within which they were incorporated in the process of nation building and their forced displacement can be seen as a continuation of that same process. Writing about the contribution of forced resettlers to the 'greater common good' in India, Arundhati Roy notes that well over half those due to be displaced by the Sardar Sarovar Dam on the Narmada River belong to ethnic minorities that make up only 8 percent of the Indian population as a whole. She comments: 'this opens up a whole new dimension to the story. The ethnic "otherness" of their victims takes some of the pressure off the Nation Builders. It's like having an expense account. Someone else pays the bills, people from another country, another world. India's poorest people are subsidising the lifestyles of her richest' (Roy 1999: 18–19). In other words, forced resettlement is a 'price worth paying' for the good of the nation, provided somebody else pays it, where 'somebody else' refers to fellow citizens whose relationship to the state is different from, and inferior to, one's own. It follows that, when affected populations form themselves into campaigning organisations to resist resettlement, they are challenging, not just a particular project, or the development policy of a particular state, but also the idea that underpins the state's claim to sovereign power over its territory: that it is a 'nation'-state, a national community of equal citizens. They are challenging, in other words, the legitimacy of state power. On this basis, the forced resettler has an equal claim, along with the refugee, to being considered the 'Achilles heel' of the nation-state system (Adelman 1999: 93): both expose underlying contradictions in the ideology of the nation-state.

Given the empirical and conceptual connections that can be traced between refugees and forced resettlers it is, on the face of it, puzzling that those who write and teach about refugees should show so little interest in the substantial literature on forced resettlers which now exists. According to Cernea, the disinterest is mutual.

> The literature on 'refugees' coexists side by side with a literature on 'oustees' or on 'development caused involuntary displacement'. There is little communication and mutual enrichment between them. Concepts and propositions are not inter-linked, and empirical findings are rarely compared and integrated. For instance, most of the writings on refugees omit oustee groups from the typology of displaced populations. In turn, research on oustees forgoes the opportunity of doing comparative analysis by studying refugees. As a result, the chance for more in depth treatment is being missed. (Cernea 1996: 294)

Four years later he returned to the same argument, repeating the summary he gave in his 1996 chapter of the benefits to be gained from 'bridging the research divide'.

> This potential for gain is fourfold. *Empirically*, the two bodies of research could enrich each other by comparing their factual findings. *Theoretically*, they could broaden their conceptualizations by exploring links and similarities between their sets of variables. *Methodologically*, they could sharpen their inquiry by borrowing and exchanging research techniques. And *politically*, they could influence the public arena more strongly by mutually reinforcing their policy advocacy and operational recommendations. (Cernea 2000: 17, emphasis in the original)

The main benefit Cernea sees coming from the bridging of this divide is intellectual – it will improve the quality of research, theoretically and methodologically, in both areas. But, as the above quotation illustrates, he also hopes that this will, in turn, help policy makers to recognise, and then to prevent or minimise, the risks of impoverishment that are faced by both refugees and forced resettlers.

Paradoxically, however, there are good reasons to believe that it is precisely the close relationship that already exists between research and policy in these two areas that has worked against the interchange of ideas and research findings between them. This point will be revisited later, as part of a discussion of the various subcategories into which the overall category of 'forced migrant' has been divided. Before this, the practical and conceptual difficulties involved in separating out 'forced' from 'unforced' migration, as a field of academic enquiry, will be considered.

When is a Migrant a Forced Migrant?

It seems logical to begin by asking why we need to attempt such a separation in the first place. At least three, mutually compatible but not equally persuasive, reasons come to mind.

First, people who have been forced to leave their homes may be seen as having a distinctive experience and distinctive needs. This is how Barry Stein attempted to define the 'parameters' of the new field of 'refugee studies' in the early 1980s (Stein 1981). But by emphasising the common experience and common needs of refugees, let alone of the whole gamut of forcibly displaced people, we risk seeing them as a homogeneous mass of needy and passive victims. The truth is that there is no such thing as 'the refugee experience' (the title Stein gave to his article), and there is therefore no such thing as 'the refugee voice': there are only the experiences, and the voices, of refugees.

There is no intrinsic paradigmatic refugee figure to be at once recognised and registered regardless of historical contingencies. Instead .... there are a thousand multifarious refugee experiences and a thousand refugee figures whose meanings and identities are negotiated in the process of displacement in time and place. (Soguk 1999: 4)

A United Nations High Commissioner for Refugees (UNHCR) document quoted by Soguk appears to go even further, on behalf of all migrants:

Behind the phenomena of moving lie deeper and often interrelated patterns of political, economic, ethnic, environmental, or human rights pressures which are further complicated by the interplay between domestic and international factors .... There are as many reasons for moving as there are migrants. (UNHCR 1993: 13, quoted in Soguk 1999: 3)

Second, population displacement may be seen as a product of wider processes of social and economic change, processes that are normally referred to under the rubric of 'globalisation', and which appear to be creating an ever increasing North-South divide in living standards, human security, and access to justice and human rights protection (Castles 2003: 16). The phenomena of economic migration and forced displacement can therefore provide a kind of window, through which these processes can be observed and analysed.

Third, those who have been forced out of their homes and home states may be seen as making a special claim on our concern. They require us to reflect on issues of membership, citizenship and democratic liberalism. They require us to ask what our responsibilities are to the stranger in distress, the stranger amongst us, on our doorstep, who is seeking a better life for himself or herself and for his or her children, and the stranger half way round the world who is brought into our homes by satellite TV channels. They require us, in other words, to consider who we are – what is or should be our moral community and, ultimately, what it means to be human.

For these reasons, and especially the last two, population displacement is a phenomenon of increasing significance in today's world of cross-border flows (of trade, investment and information as well as of people) and transnational networks. This is a world in which the difference between rich and poor can increasingly be seen as a difference between those who are able to travel freely about the 'space of flows', as Manuel Castells (1996) has characterised the contemporary global economy, and those who are condemned to suffer 'the discomforts of localised existence' (Bauman 1998: 2). These can include anything from threats to life and liberty to lack of educational and employment opportunities. It is clear from the harrowing accounts of the journeys made by asylum seekers and economic migrants into the rich industrialised countries that they are prepared to take tremendous risks (of suffocation, for example, in container lorries and of drowning in crowded and unseaworthy boats) in order to escape these 'discomforts'. From this point of view, the consideration of migration and displacement leads us, ultimately, to consider the gap between rich and poor countries, and to the question of how far rich countries are prepared to go to close that gap, by means of development aid, trade reform and, crucially, the liberalisation of migration policies (Rodrik 2002, Winters et al. 2002).

But while population displacement is certainly a subject worthy of academic research, when we try to separate out a class of 'forced migrants' from migrants in general, we are faced with a problem which is both methodological and ethical. The methodological problem is that it proves impossible to apply the term 'forced migration' to the real world in a way that enables us to separate out a discrete class of migrants. It turns out, on closer inspection, that most migrants make their decision to migrate in response to a complex set of external constraints and predisposing events. These constraints and events vary in their salience, significance and impact, but there are elements of both compulsion and choice, it seems, in the decision-making of all migrants. In order to deal with the fuzzy boundaries between 'forced' and 'unforced' migration, therefore, we have to resort to the familiar device of the continuum.

Two authors who have done this for us are Anthony Richmond (1994: 59) and Nicholas Van Hear (1998: 44). Richmond has what looks, at first sight, like a fearsomely complicated matrix in which he places all kinds of migratory movements in relation to various axes. He distinguishes between 'proactive' and 'reactive' migration as the opposite ends of a continuum. Towards the reactive end he places war victims and slaves and towards the proactive end retirees and returnees. He also tries to catch the reality that the causes of migration are political as well as economic, it being just as impossible to make categorical distinctions between the political and the economic causes and conditions of migration as it is to make categorical distinctions between proactive and reactive migrants. Van Hear has an equally challenging matrix, with one axis running from voluntary (meaning more choice and more options) to involuntary (meaning less choice and less options). Along the other axis he has four kinds of movement – inward, outward, return and onward – and 'staying put'. At the involuntary end of his continuum he has refugees, and people displaced by natural disasters and development projects and at the voluntary end he has tourists, students and business travellers.

The ethical problem follows from this use of the continuum as a device for separating out categories of migrants according to the amount of choice open to them – entirely free at one end and entirely constrained at the other. For, by classifying migrants in this way, we run the risk of ignoring or underestimating the most important quality they share with all human beings, namely their agency. Richmond's continuum between 'proactive' and 'reactive' migration makes this particularly clear, since he classifies migrants precisely according to the extent to which they exercise agency. There are at least two points to be made here.

First, even at the most 'reactive' or 'involuntary' end of the continuum, people probably have a lot more choice than we might think – or than these models allow us to think. They may have choices, for example, not only about whether but also about when, where, how and with whom to move – choices which cannot be encompassed by continua of this kind. Second, we know from studies that have been made of the behaviour of people in concentration and labour camps that, even in the most constrained of circumstances, human beings struggle to create and maintain some area of individual decision-making, and that those who succeed best in this are those who have the best chance of surviving relatively unscathed from the experience (Levi 1987, cited by Parkin 1999: 306). This effort to maintain agency 'against all odds' (Soguk 1999: 5), even in the most constrained of circumstances, can be seen as an example of the 'hard and regular work' of 'locality production' which human beings, always and everywhere, must engage in to keep at bay 'an endemic sense of anxiety and instability in social life' (Appadurai 1996: 179–80). Refugee camps, prisons, urban slums and ghettos are merely 'the starkest examples of the conditions of uncertainty, poverty, displacement and despair under which locality can be produced' (Appadurai 1996: 193).

The term 'forced migrant' obviously implies that there is such a thing as an 'unforced' migrant, but one hardly ever comes across this usage. What we usually find is a distinction between 'voluntary' and 'involuntary' migrants, the latter being treated as synonymous with 'forced migrants'. This is the terminology used by Van Hear, for example, in his representation of the continuum between force and choice in migration. Strictly speaking, though, 'involuntary' is not the correct English word to oppose to 'voluntary'. Commenting on the usual English translation of Aristotle's distinction between an act for which an agent can be held morally responsible ('voluntary') and an act for which he or she cannot be held responsible ('involuntary') the philosopher Antony Flew writes:

> This is certainly awkward, since in English the opposite of voluntary is not involuntary but compulsory: attendance at the rallies of the ruling party may – in different countries – be either voluntary or compulsory, but scarcely involuntary; whereas the cries, starts, and twitches which are so typically involuntary could scarcely in any normal circumstances be said to be compulsory – or even voluntary. (Flew 1971: 226)

If it is linguistically 'awkward' to talk about 'involuntary' human migration this is because to migrate, when applied to human beings, implies at least some degree of agency, some degree of independent will. To migrate is something a person does, not something that is done to him or her. People can be moved and displaced, in other words, but not 'migrated'. The term 'compulsory migration' is, for the same reason, no less awkward. Where there really is no reasonable alternative, as for example for the victims of the African slave trade, or for those forced to move because their homes are about to be inundated by the waters of a dam, it would be more appropriate, on linguistic and logical grounds, to speak of compulsory or forced displacement than of compulsory, forced or involuntary migration.

It should not be concluded from this that we should dispense with the term 'forced migrant' altogether and replace it with something else. For one thing, any other term we might use to encompass such a wide range of human behaviour would be bound to have its own problems. But we should be aware of the conceptual, logical and ethical difficulties raised by the term 'forced migration' and not assume that it refers to a clearly discriminable class of events and individuals, and a clearly demarcated sub-category of migrants. It is perhaps best to regard it as a more or less useful shorthand term which cannot be defined analytically but which allows us to bring together a whole range of overlapping ideas and events that resemble each other like the members of a family. 'Some of them have the same nose, others the same eyebrows and others again the same way of walking; and these likenesses overlap' (Wittgenstein 1969: 17, quoted in Kenny 1973: 153).

A second conclusion is that, while we should be interested in the factors that limit choice and the ways in which individuals, households and groups make decisions in the light of those limiting factors, we should not lump migrants together into categories, according to the extent of choice open to them. Different people who are forced to move, whatever the factors that led them to move, have different areas of choice and different alternatives available to them, depending not just on external constraining factors but also on such factors as their sex, age, wealth, social connections and networks. This means that we have to understand the point of view and experiences of the people making a decision about whether to move and/or where to move. We have to emphasise that they are 'embedded' in a particular social, political and historical situation.

In other words, we should see them as 'purposive actors' or 'ordinary people', and this for two reasons, one practical and one ethical. The practical reason is that this is how migratory processes actually work. Research and teaching in the field of refugee studies has tended to focus on policy issues on the one hand and on the needs – physical and psychological – of refugees on the other. As Jeff Crisp has pointed out, there has been a relative absence of research on how individuals, families and groups make the decision to leave their homes, what information they have when they make the decision, how their journey is financed and how far it is planned with a specific destination in mind.

> In terms of empirical enquiry (both in academic institutions and in operational agencies such as UNHCR) there has been a dearth of research on asylum seekers: how they reach the decision to leave their own country; what information is available to them when they make that decision; the way in which their journey is financed; the degree to which it is planned with a specific destination in mind; and the extent to which they had prior contact with that country. Rather than focusing on asylum seekers themselves ... the refugee discourse has focused far too narrowly on issues of public policy. (Crisp 1999: 4–5)

It is worth noting here that we are encouraged to think of displaced people as identical members of homogeneous categories, rather than as 'purposive actors', by the metaphors we habitually and unselfconsciously use in order to discuss and conceptualise them. The most pervasive of these are what Lakoff and Johnson (1980: 25–32) have called 'ontological metaphors', that is, metaphors which have to do with entities, substances and containers. We speak of flows, streams, waves and trickles of migrants. We speak of 'asylum capacity'. We speak of dams, channels and sluice gates. We speak of being flooded, inundated and swamped. This metaphorical language of migration is clearly not 'innocent'.

First, it is not a language that is spoken by migrants themselves – it is spoken from a sedentary, state-centric point of view. It is the language we use to talk about 'them', even if we, or our ancestors, were also migrants once. Second, this kind of language requires us to think of migration as an inexorable process with its own logic and force – something we did not bring about, but which we ignore at our peril. Third, the metaphors we use to talk about migration require us to think of migrants as an undifferentiated mass. By de-personalising and even de-humanising migrants, these metaphors make it easier for us to see them as a threat to our well-being.

The use of metaphor – understanding one kind of entity or experience in terms of another kind – is not something we can dispense with. It is fundamental to the way we understand and reason about the world.

> Understanding our experiences in terms of objects and substances allows us to pick out parts of our experience and treat them as discrete entities or substances of a *uniform* kind. Once we can identify our experiences as entities or substances we can refer to them, *categorise them, group them, and quantify them* – and, by this means, reason about them. (Lakoff and Johnson 1980: 25, emphasis added)

But, as Ulf Hannerz has put it, 'when you take an intellectual ride on a metaphor, it is important that you know where to get off' (2002: 6). To which one might add that it is even more important to know that you are riding on a metaphor in the first place. When we talk of 'migratory flows', then, we should recognise that we are talking metaphorically and that the metaphor encourages us to think of the people in question in a certain way – as passive victims of circumstances, carried along like identical molecules in a liquid – and 'get off' the metaphor before it is too late.

The ethical reason for focusing on forced migrants as 'purposive actors' or 'ordinary people' is that by emphasising what Soguk, writing of refugees, calls 'their capacity for agency against all odds' (1999: 5), we increase our imaginative ability to identify with the suffering of others, to see them as potential members of our own moral community. This is what the philosopher Richard Rorty describes as 'human solidarity'.

> Solidarity is not discovered by reflection but created. It is created by increasing our sensitivity to the *particular* details [emphasis added] of the pain and humiliation of other, unfamiliar sorts of people. Such increased sensitivity makes it more difficult to marginalise people different from ourselves by thinking, 'They do not feel it as we would', or 'There must always be suffering, so why not let *them* suffer?' (1989: xvi)

In short, the more we are able to see the refugee or the forced resettler as an ordinary person, embedded in a particular set of local circumstances, the more difficult it becomes to ignore his or her plight – to become, and remain, a bystander.

Refugees and 'Other Forced Migrants'

There has been a growing tendency, over the past few years, in both academic and policy circles, for refugees to be mentioned alongside, and almost in the same breath as, 'other forced migrants'. But who are these 'other forced migrants'? A brief look at four recent publications, which can be seen as falling squarely within the field of refugee studies, shows that the people referred to belong to a particular category of displaced people, defined, like refugees, in terms of the reasons for their flight and their status in international law, namely 'internally displaced persons' (IDPs).

In an edited collection, *Managing Migration: Time for a New International Regime?* (Ghosh 2000), Gil Loescher has written a chapter entitled 'Forced Migration in the Post-Cold War Era: The Need for a Comprehensive Approach'. This call for a 'comprehensive' approach to forced migration focuses overwhelmingly on refugees, defined as 'people who have fled from and are unable to return to their own country because of persecution and violence' (Loescher 2000: 190). There is a short section, however, on the 'internally displaced',[3] defined as 'people who have been uprooted because of persecution and violence but who remain in their own countries' (loc. cit.). Passing reference is made to 'people who have been uprooted by development projects', but only to point out that they are among the 'millions' of forced migrants 'who are outside UNHCR concern' (Loescher 2000: 191).

In his section on the 'internally displaced', which is headed 'Addressing the growing problem of internal displacement', Loescher notes that 'a new comprehensive international regime for forced migrants will necessarily have to place internally displaced persons at the centre of its concern' (Loescher 2000: 210). He also calls attention to the need to strengthen the international human rights regime, so that the international community can better 'monitor developments in human rights issues and intercede on behalf of forced migrants' (loc. cit.). It is here that one might reasonably have expected some reference to be made to the rights of forcibly resettled people, but it is clear that Loescher's sights remain firmly fixed on those who have been forced to move by conflict.

The lack of any reference to forced resettlers is more striking in a book edited by Ann Bayefski and Joan Fitzpatrick, *Human Rights and Forced Displacement* (2000), the entire purpose of which, as the title implies, is to discuss the human rights of forcibly displaced populations. The book does, however, include a chapter (by Roberta Cohen) on the 'internally displaced' (as defined by Loescher), which is discussed below.

In a UNHCR working paper entitled *Forced Migration and the Evolving Humanitarian Regime*, Susan Martin defines forced migrants, '[f]or the purpose of this paper', in the same way as Loescher, namely as 'persons who flee or are obliged to leave their homes or places of habitual residence because of events threatening their lives or safety' (Martin 2000: 3). She makes only passing reference to forced resettlers, although she does note that they could become 'of concern' to the international community if their governments were unable or unwilling to provide them with protection and assistance (Martin 2000: 6).

Finally, Howard Adelman, in an article entitled 'From Refugees to Forced Migration: The UNHCR and Human Security', sets out to examine the significance of the UNHCR's placing the refugee issue 'within the larger context of forced migration' (Adelman 2001: 7). But this 'larger context' turns out to be limited to the 'internally displaced'.

It cannot be denied that there are strong practical reasons for maintaining a clear distinction between refugees and the 'internally displaced' on the one hand, and forced resettlers on the other. The key point here is that both refugees and the 'internally displaced' are unable or unwilling to avail themselves of the protection of their governments, while forced resettlers have been deliberately moved by their own governments in the name of 'eminent domain' law, which allows property to be expropriated from its owners or traditional users for the sake of a wider public good. Forced resettlers, therefore, expect to be compensated for the land and property they have lost and it remains the theoretical responsibility of the government that moved them, under the national legal system, to provide them with protection and assistance.

> Development-induced displaced persons (DIDPs) generally remain in their country of origin and their legal protection should theoretically be guaranteed by the government. In terms of the international state system, the government is responsible for ensuring that the rights of people under its jurisdiction are respected ... The complexities of DIDR [development-induced displacement and resettlement] result specifically because the government that is responsible for the displacement is also responsible for ensuring the protection of DIDPs. (Barutciski 2000: 2)

There are also strong practical grounds for maintaining a clear distinction between refugees and the 'internally displaced', because of the different statuses of these two categories in international law. Refugee protection, for which there exists a strong body of legally binding norms and principles, 'is essentially about promoting asylum in foreign countries', while the protection of the 'internally displaced', for which there are no legally binding norms and principles, 'is basically about humanitarian intervention in troubled countries' (Barutciski, loc. cit.). There is, of course, much debate about how to address the needs of the 'internally displaced', given that there is no single international organisation with a mandate to protect and assist them. But what appears to be widely accepted is that the protection currently afforded to refugees under international law would be put at risk by extending the term (as would be perfectly meaningful in everyday speech) to others who have not crossed an international border and who do not, therefore, qualify for the same level of international protection.

For Cernea, '[t]he key policy objective in forced resettlement is restoring the income-generating capacity of resettlers' (1996: 314). According to Barutciski, this would be an 'overly ambitious' objective to entertain in the case of refugees.

> While conceptual models that emphasise the reconstruction of livelihoods are appropriate for DIDR situations which may or may not involve abuse on the part of local authorities, they are not necessarily appropriate for refugee emergencies that are by definition situations in which the victims' human rights are violated ... It would be overly ambitious to believe or insist that emergency refugee assistance is intended to restore the livelihoods of victims of persecution or conflict to levels before their flight. (Barutciski 2000: 2)

There was a time, of course, when such an objective would not have been seen as 'overly ambitious'. That was during the 1960s and 1970s, when the integration of refugees in the country of first asylum (usually in the developing world) was seen, along with voluntary repatriation, as the most viable and feasible 'durable solution' to the 'refugee problem'. During that phase in the history of the international refugee regime, agricultural settlement schemes for refugees were set up with the help of the UNHCR in several African countries, the aim being to help refugees re-establish themselves in a new country and become self-sufficient.

> Between 1961 and 1978, approximately 60 rural settlements have been installed, most of them in Burundi, Uganda and Tanzania ... In the 1990s, nearly a quarter of all refugees in sub-Saharan Africa were estimated to be living in 140 organized settlements, most in the eastern and southern regions ... Planned land resettlements have long been considered the best means for promoting refugee self-sufficiency and local integration. (Lassailly-Jacob 2000: 112)

It is here, in the planning of agricultural settlement schemes for refugees, that research on forced resettlement has, potentially, the greatest practical relevance to refugee policy (Kibreab 2000: 324–31). But this policy has significantly changed since the 1980s, to one which focuses on prevention and containment in countries and regions of origin, and on early repatriation, rather than on the reconstruction of refugee livelihoods in countries of asylum.[4]

> The days are past when many rural refugees could be assisted towards achieving self-sufficiency in exile. Going into exile now means hiding among locals or surviving in transit camps, where the living conditions are so poor that few wish to stay on. (Lassailly-Jacob 2000: 123)

There is consequently little incentive for policy-oriented research in refugee studies to concern itself with the findings of the equally policy-oriented research on forced resettlers.

But there is another, more fundamental, way in which the dominance of policy concerns in the study of human displacement can be seen as working against the integration of research findings on different displaced populations. The scientific point of distinguishing subsets within a class of related phenomena is to encourage and facilitate comparison between those subsets, in order to throw light on the wider class, and to aid (in the sense of make more acute) the observation, description and analysis of empirical data. These objectives are interdependent, since there must be a constant readiness to revise and sharpen abstract categories in the light of empirical observation. The trouble with the categories used in the study of displacement – refugees, forced resettlers, disaster displacees, returnees etc. – is that, being dictated by political and policy concerns rather than scientific ones, they actually discourage comparison between the situation and behaviour of people forced to move by different causes and in different circumstances. Nor are they amenable to revision in the light of empirical evidence.

Consider the term 'refugee' itself. This is the name of a legal category, based on the 1951 Convention Relating to the Status of Refugees, which was itself heavily based on the 'strategic political objectives' of the Western powers at that particular historical moment (Hathaway 1991, quoted in Chimni 2000: 14). Hathaway distinguishes 'five essential elements' in the Convention definition, of which the first is 'alienage': the claimant for refugee status must be outside his or her country of origin. But the exclusion of 'internal refugees' from the Convention definition was not 'so much a matter of conceptual principle, as it was a reflection of the limited reach of international law' (Hathaway 1991, quoted in Chimni 2000: 401). Hathaway quotes Shacknove's argument that 'alienage' is not a necessary condition for establishing refugee status, which depends rather on 'the physical access of the international community to the uprooted person' (Shacknove 1985: 277). It follows that

> the physical presence of the unprotected person outside her country of origin is not a constitutive element of her refugeehood, but is rather a practical condition precedent to placing her within the effective scope of international protection. (Hathaway 1991, quoted in Chimni 2000: 401)

The key criterion, then, that is used to distinguish 'refugee' from 'internally displaced person' – whether or not an international boundary has been crossed – is not based on 'conceptual principle' and is not a 'constitutive element' of refugeehood. It follows that the term 'refugee', as used in the language of refugee protection and of refugee studies, does not distinguish a 'subset' of displaced people that can be meaningfully compared to other subsets. As Malkki has put it, the term refugee is not 'a label for a special, generalisable "kind" or "type" of person or situation' but 'a descriptive rubric that includes within it a world of socio-economic statuses, personal histories, and psychological or spiritual situations' (1995b: 496).

The 'internally displaced' make up an even more hazy and imprecise category. They are defined, in the 'Guiding Principles on Internal Displacement' of the UN Office for the Coordination of Humanitarian Affairs (OCHA), as

> persons or groups of persons who have been forced or obliged to flee or to leave their homes or places of habitual residence, in particular as a result of or in order to avoid the effects of armed conflict, situations of generalised violence, violations of human rights or natural disasters, and who have not crossed an internationally recognised State border'. (Quoted in Chimni 2000: 242)

The 'essential' purpose of the definition is to 'help identify persons who should be of concern to the international community because they are basically in refugee-like situations within their own countries' (Cohen 1996, quoted in Chimni 2000: 407). The inclusion of people who have fled their homes because of 'natural disasters' (itself a highly ambiguous and imprecise concept) is intended to cater for cases where governments 'respond to such disasters by discriminating against or neglecting certain groups on political or ethnic grounds or by violating their human rights in other ways' (Cohen 2000: 82). Two points are worth making here.

First, on these grounds, it would be logical and understandable to prefer the term 'internal refugees' to 'internally displaced persons'. This would both recognise the 'refugee-like' situation of the people being referred to (i.e. that they were in some way outside the protection of their own government) and make clear the distinction between them and forced resettlers, who are also displaced within their own countries but who are not in a 'refugee-like' situation. As noted earlier, however, the logic that dictates the use of 'internally displaced' rather than 'internal refugee' is a practical, not a conceptual one: it has to do with a concern not to undermine the protection available to refugees under the 1951 Convention, which makes 'alienage' an 'essential element' of the legal definition of a refugee (Hathaway 1991, quoted in Chimni 2000: 15).

Second, the form of words used to justify the inclusion of those displaced by 'natural disasters' in the definition of 'internally displaced person' could easily be used to extend the definition to many if not most of today's forced resettlers, even though they are not mentioned in the formal definition. Indeed, Principle 6.2(c) states that all human beings have a right to be protected from 'arbitrary displacement', including cases of 'large scale development projects, which are not justified by compelling and overriding public interests' (quoted in Chimni 2000: 427). But this ignores the main issue in forced resettlement, which is not that people should be protected from 'arbitrary displacement' but that, however compelling the public interest reasons for displacing them, there remains an obligation on governments to protect their political, social and economic rights (Pettersson 2002). On the one hand, then, the definition is logically and empirically extendable to a huge variety of different situations, groups and individuals, and yet it is confined in practice to a relatively narrow range of displaced persons. It is therefore too vague and ambiguous to serve as a meaningful analytical category for comparative purposes.

For the same reason, these policy-related categories are also unhelpful when it comes to the observation, description and analysis of empirical data. In an unpublished address given at the 2001 meeting of the International Association for the Study of Forced Migration, the then head of the UNHCR's Evaluation and Policy Analysis Unit, Jeff Crisp, lamented the fact that the staff of the organisation 'seem to know less and less about the people and communities we work with' (2001: 9). He gave a number of explanations for this – security problems which keep UNHCR staff away from rural areas where refugees are mainly found, increased paperwork which ties staff to their computers and rapid staff turnover 'in remote locations'. He also complained that researchers in refugee studies are spending too much time in libraries and not enough in the field. By way of illustration, he mentioned having met several postgraduate students in the recent past who wanted to write dissertations about the international community's responsibilities towards the 'internally displaced', but none who wanted to investigate their situation 'on the ground'.

This call for more in-depth empirical research on displaced populations goes to the heart of the matter discussed in this chapter, because it puts the focus on the experiences of refugees and 'other forced migrants', rather than on the causes of their flight or their status in international law. But the argument presented here suggests that the explanation for this lack of knowledge of the everyday lives and preoccupations of refugees 'and other forced migrants' goes deeper than mere lack of time and/or interest amongst UNHCR staff and academic researchers respectively.

Empirical research, as opposed to mere random observation, cannot proceed except in the light of general propositions which, among other things, identify the phenomena to be investigated and group them into meaningful categories. These categories must, in turn, be open to refinement and revision in the light of particular observation. But this condition cannot be met by categories that are designed to meet the needs of practical politics and humanitarian assistance rather than of scientific enquiry. The category distinctions that have been discussed here are tenaciously upheld by academics, policy makers and activists alike, on the grounds that they are vital, given the current 'reach' of international law, for the protection and assistance of refugees. But they would not stand up to the close scrutiny that would inevitably result from the kind of field-based, empirical research that Crisp is calling for (Allen and Turton 1996: 5–9). If taken seriously, therefore, such research could lead to a wholesale questioning of the category distinctions upon which the current international regime of refugee protection and humanitarian assistance – and possibly much else – is based.

I believe that such questioning could only be to the long term advantage of those – the majority of the world's population – who are currently suffering the 'discomforts of localised existence', including those whom the international refugee regime is mandated to protect. But when knowledge could have radical and disturbing consequences for established thought and practice, ignorance may well be considered bliss. This raises an issue that dogs every problem-oriented field of study: how to combine scientific rigour with 'relevance'.

The Problem of Relevance: Practical versus Scientific Knowledge

We can surely all agree that there is no justification for studying, and attempting to understand, the causes of human suffering if the purpose of one's study is not, ultimately, to find ways of relieving and preventing that suffering. This clearly applies to the study of human displacement, given the scale of the phenomenon and the level of suffering that must be observed, documented and analysed by anyone wishing to carry out empirical research on it. We can also agree, on a priori grounds alone, that the only kind of science that is going to make a positive and lasting contribution to the improvement of human well-being is science that meets the highest standards of theoretical sophistication and methodological rigour. This is borne out, empirically, by the history of those improvements in human well-being that have resulted from the application of scientific method to the prevention of suffering, whether in the natural or social sciences. One thinks, for example, of the 'relevance' of the work of the chemist Louis Pasteur to the control of bacterial diseases and of the work of the economist Amartya Sen (1981) to the prevention and relief of famine.

This issue is usually debated by asking such questions as 'How can we make academic research relevant to the real world?', or 'How can we bridge the research-practice divide?' Judging from the persistence of this debate, and the apparent lack of a satisfactory resolution to it, we should consider the possibility that it is not a 'real' debate at all: that it is not capable of a satisfactory resolution, if conducted in its current terms.

Perhaps the most common way of characterising the 'gap' between research and practice is to distinguish between two different categories of people, academics and practitioners, each engaged in different kinds of professional activity and each with a different objective: academics, it is sometimes said, want to understand the world, while practitioners want to change it. This apparently clear distinction soon becomes blurred, however, when one seeks to give it empirical content. For, on the one hand, it turns out to be no easy matter to sort individuals unambiguously into the two categories (academics often want to change the world too) and, on the other, understanding the world is obviously a prerequisite for deliberately, systematically and beneficially changing it.

A more productive way of approaching the issue might be to distinguish, not between two kinds of people or professional activities, each focused on a different objective, but between two kinds of knowledge, scientific (or academic) and practical, which the same person can happily combine and make selective use of, depending on context and situation. Since all knowledge is socially produced, an obvious basis on which to distinguish between different kinds of knowledge is to focus on differences in their modes of production and reproduction. Because practical knowledge is produced 'by doing' – that is, through the very performance of a task or activity that is not aimed primarily at producing knowledge – it is necessarily unreflective and unselfconscious, although this does not mean that it is necessarily false. Because scientific knowledge is the result of the deliberate application of the hypothetico-deductive method, it is necessarily reflective and selfconscious, though this does not mean that it is necessarily true.

Looked at in this way, scientific knowledge becomes 'relevant' to practice when it is used to scrutinise what practical knowledge takes for granted. It follows that the application of scientific knowledge to a specific practical task is not necessarily conducive to its effective implementation. Indeed, by raising doubts about the legitimacy and/or desirability of the proposed objective and/or the methods chosen to achieve it, such knowledge may suggest that the task should be either given up altogether or radically rethought. Some degree of tension, or even conflict, between scientific and practical knowledge is therefore to be both expected and welcomed.

In this sense, there is indeed a 'research-practice divide', but the tension that is symptomatic of this divide will disappear only when yesterday's science has become today's common sense – and is therefore no longer thought of as science. It follows that we should at least consider the possibility that, when public policy relating to migration and displacement fails to meet its objectives, this may be at least partly because the assumptions that guide research in this area have been tied too closely to short-term policy concerns and preoccupations. According to Stephen Castles, this could account for the spectacular ability of Western governments' immigration policies to bring about the opposite of what they intend.[5]

> The key point is that policy-driven research can lead not only to poor sociology but also to bad policy. This is because narrowly focussed empirical research, often designed to provide an answer to an immediate bureaucratic problem, tends to follow a circular logic. It accepts the problem definitions built into its terms of reference, and does not look for more fundamental causes, nor for more challenging solutions. (Castles 2003: 26)

This presents a twofold challenge for all those involved in the study of human displacement. First, we need to adopt a unitary and inclusive approach to the definition of the field, which means encouraging empirical research that is aimed at understanding the situation of displaced people at the local level, irrespective of the causes of their flight. This focus on the local is not, of course, intended to rule out consideration of the global. On the contrary, failure to recognise global connections in the study of local-level events and processes arises only when there has been a failure to specify the local in sufficient detail – that is, when it is not situated with sufficient clarity and precision within a particular place at a particular time. Second, we need to recognise that research of this kind will inevitably call into question the adequacy and usefulness of existing generalisations, assumptions and categories and that it is by such questioning that academic research can play its most effective and beneficial part in the general improvement of human welfare. Above all, we should remember the words of Louis Pasteur, a scientist whose practical contribution to the improvement of human welfare it is difficult to exaggerate: 'Il n'existe pas de sciences appliquées mais seulement des applications de la science' (There is no such thing as applied science; there is only the application of science) (cited in Oxford Dictionary of Quotations 1979: 369).

Notes

An earlier version of this chapter appeared as Working Paper No. 94, in the series 'New Issues in Refugee Research', published by the Evaluation and Policy Analysis Unit, UNHCR, Geneva, 2003.

1. The others are 'joblessness', 'homelessness', 'marginalization', 'food insecurity', 'increased morbidity' and 'loss of access to common property resources' (Cernea 2000: 20).

2. The argument that follows is set out at greater length in Turton (2002: 25–27).

3. I shall continue to place inverted commas around 'internally displaced' in order to emphasise that this category is normally not intended to include those like forced resettlers, who have been displaced within their own countries for reasons other than violence and persecution.

4. This was the result of the dramatic increase in the numbers of refugees and 'others of concern' to the UNHCR that occurred during the 1980s, coupled with geopolitical changes that coincided roughly with the end of the Cold War (Turton 2002: 34).

5. Among other examples, Castles cites the U.S. Immigration Reform and Control Act (1986), which was intended to reduce illegal immigration but which led to an upsurge in both legal and illegal immigration, and the efforts of Western European countries in the 1990s to prevent the entry of asylum seekers, which gave a powerful impetus to the transnational 'migration industry' of people smuggling and trafficking.

References

Adelman, H. 1999. 'Modernity, Globalization, Refugees and Displacement'. In A. Ager (ed.). *Refugees: Perspectives on the Experience of Forced Migrants*. London, New York: Pinter.

———— 2001. 'From Refugees to Forced Migration: The UNHCR and Human Security'. *International Migration Review*, 35(1): 7–32.

Allen, T. and D. Turton. 1996. 'Introduction: In Search of Cool Ground'. In T. Allen (ed.). *In Search of Cool Ground: War, Flight and Homecoming in North-East Africa.* London, Trenton: James Currey / Africa World Press.

Appadurai, A. 1996. *Modernity at Large: Cultural Dimensions of Globalization.* Minneapolis, London: University of Minnesota Press.

Barutciski, M. 2000. *Addressing Legal Constraints and Improving Outcomes in Development-induced Resettlement Projects.* Desk Study funded by the Department for International Development (U.K.), Project Grant R7305, Refugee Studies Centre, University of Oxford.

Bauman, Z. 1998. *Globalization: The Human Consequences.* Cambridge: Polity Press.

Bayefski, A. and J. Fitzpatrick (eds). 2000. *Human Rights and Forced Displacement.* The Hague, Boston, London: Martinus Nijhoff Publishers.

Black, R. 2001. 'Fifty Years of Refugee Studies: From Theory to Policy'. *International Migration Review*, 35(1): 57–78.

Castells, M. 1996. *The Rise of the Network Society.* Oxford: Blackwell Publishers.

Castles, S. 2003. 'Towards a Sociology of Forced Migration and Social Transformation'. *Sociology*, 37(1): 13–34.

Cernea, M. 1996. 'Bridging the Research Divide: Studying Refugees and Development Oustees'. In T. Allen (ed.). *In Search of Cool Ground: War, Flight and Homecoming in North-East Africa.* pp. 293–317. London, Trenton: James Currey / Africa World Press.

———— 2000. 'Risks, Safeguards and Reconstruction: A Model for Population Displacement and Resettlement'. In M.M. Cernea and C. McDowell (eds). *Risks and Reconstruction: Experiences of Resettlers and Refugees*, pp. 11–55. Washington DC: The World Bank.

Chimni, B. 2000. *International Refugee Law: A Reader.* New Delhi, Thousand Oaks, London: Sage Publications.

Cohen, R. 1996. 'Protecting the Internally Displaced'. *World Refugee Survey 1996.* Washington DC: U.S. Committee for Refugees.

———— 2000. 'The Development of International Standards to Protect Internally Displaced Persons'. In A. Bayefski and J. Fitzpatrick (eds). *Human Rights and Forced Displacement*, pp. 76–85. The Hague, Boston, London: Martinus Nijhoff Publishers.

Colson, E. 1991. 'Coping in Adversity'. Unpublished paper presented at the Gwendolen Carter Lectures, Conference on Involuntary Migration and Resettlement in Africa, University of Florida (Gainesville), 21–23 March.

Crisp, J. 1999. *Policy Challenges of the New Diasporas: Migrant Networks and their Impact on Asylum Flows and Regimes.* Working paper No. 7, New Issues in Refugee Research. Geneva: UNHCR.

———— 2001. Closing Remarks, Biennial Meeting of the International Association for the Study of Forced Migration, Johannesburg (unpublished).

Flew, A. 1971. *An Introduction to Western Philosophy: Ideas and Argument from Plato to Sartre.* London: Thames and Hudson.

Ghosh, B. (ed.). 2000. *Managing Migration: Time for a New International Regime?.* Oxford: Oxford University Press.

Hannerz, U. 2002. 'Flows, Boundaries and Hybrids: Keywords in Transnational Anthropology', Working Paper WPTC-2K-02, ESRC Transnational Communities Programme, University of Oxford. (Previously published in

Portuguese (1997) as 'Fluxos, Fronteiras, Hibridos: Palavras-chave de Antropologia Transnacional', *Mana* (Rio de Janeiro), 3(1): 7–39.)

Hansen, A. 1996. 'Future Directions in the Study of Forced Migration'. Keynote Address, 5th International Research and Advisory Panel, Centre for Refugee Studies, Moi University, Eldoret, Kenya (unpublished).

Harrell-Bond, B. 1986. *Imposing Aid: Emergency Assistance to Refugees*. Oxford: Oxford University Press.

Hathaway, J. 1991. *The Law of Refugee Status*. Toronto: Butterworth.

Jacobsen, K., and L.B. Landau. 2003. 'The Dual Imperative in Refugee Research: Some Methodological Considerations in Social Science Research on Forced Migration'. *Disasters*, 27(3): 185–207.

Kenny, A. 1973. *Wittgenstein*. London: Allen Lane (division of Penguin Press).

Kibreab, G. 2000. 'Common Property Resources and Resettlement'. In M.M. Cernea and C. McDowell (eds). *Risks and Reconstruction: Experiences of Resettlers and Refugees*, pp. 293–331. Washington DC: The World Bank.

Lakoff, G. and M. Johnson. 1980. *Metaphors We Live By*. Chicago, London: University of Chicago Press.

Lassailly-Jacob, V. 2000. 'Reconstructing Livelihoods through Land Settlement Schemes: Comparative Reflections on Refugees and Oustees in Africa'. In M.M. Cernea and C. McDowell (eds). *Risks and Reconstruction: Experiences of Resettlers and Refugees*, pp. 108–23. Washington DC: The World Bank.

Levi, P. 1987 (1958). *If This is a Man*. London: Abacus/Sphere Books.

Loescher, G. 2000. 'Forced Migration in the Post-Cold War Era: The Need for a Comprehensive Approach'. In B. Ghosh (ed.). *Managing Migration: Time for a New International Regime?*, pp. 190–219. Oxford: Oxford University Press.

Malkki, L. 1992. 'National Geographic: The Rooting of Peoples and the Territorialization of National Identity Among Scholars and Refugees'. *Cultural Anthropology*, 7(1): 24–44.

_____ 1995a. *Purity and Exile: Violence, Memory and National Cosmology among Hutu Refugees in Tanzania*. Chicago, London: University of Chicago Press.

_____ 1995b. 'Refugees and Exile: From Refugee Studies to the National Order of Things'. *Annual Review of Anthropology*, 24: 495–523.

Martin, S.F. 2000. *Forced Migration and the Evolving Humanitarian Regime*. Working Paper No. 20, New Issues in Refugee Research. Geneva: UNHCR.

Oxford Dictionary of Quotations (3rd edn). 1979. Oxford: Oxford University Press.

Parkin, D. 1999. 'Momentoes as Transitional Objects in Human Displacement'. *Journal of Material Culture*, 4(3): 303–20.

Pasteur, L. Address, 11 September 1872, 'Comptes rendus des travaux du Congrès viticole et sericicole de Lyon'. Cited in *Oxford Dictionary of Quotations*, p. 369.

Pettersson, B. 2002. 'Development-induced Displacement: Internal Affair or International Human Rights Issue?'. *Forced Migration Review*, 12: 16–19.

Richmond, A. 1994. *Global Apartheid: Refugees, Racism and the New World Order*. Oxford: Oxford University Press.

Rodrik, D. 2002. 'Globalization for Whom? Time to Change the Rules – and Focus on Poor Workers'. *Harvard Magazine*, 104(6). www.harvard-magazine.com/online/ 070280.html (read 23/9/03).

Rorty, R. 1989. *Contingency, Irony and Solidarity*. Cambridge: Cambridge University Press.

Roy, A. 1999. *The Cost of Living.* New York: The Modern Library.

Scudder, T. and E. Colson. 1982. 'From Welfare to Development: A Conceptual Framework for the Analysis of Dislocated Peoples'. In A. Hansen and A. Oliver-Smith (eds). *Involuntary Migration and Resettlement: The Problems and Responses of Dislocated People*, pp. 267–87. Boulder CO: Westview Press.

Sen, A. 1981. *Poverty and Famines: An Essay on Entitlement and Deprivation.* Oxford: Oxford University Press.

Shacknove, A. 1985. 'Who is a Refugee?' *Ethics*, 95: 274–84.

Soguk, N. 1999. *States and Strangers: Refugees and Displacements of Statecraft.* Minneapolis, London: University of Minnesota Press.

Stein, B. 1981. 'The Refugee Experience: Defining the Parameters of a Field of Study'. *International Migration Review*, 15(1): 320–30.

Turton, D. 1996. 'Migrants and Refugees: A Mursi Case Study'. In T. Allen (ed.). *In Search of Cool Ground: War, Flight and Homecoming in North-East Africa*, pp. 96–110. London, Trenton: James Currey / Africa World Press,

―――― 2002. 'Forced Displacement and the Nation-state'. In J. Robinson (ed.). *Development and Displacement*, pp. 19–75. Oxford, Milton Keynes: Oxford University Press / The Open University.

UNHCR. 1993. *Information Paper*, p. 13. Geneva, March.

Van Hear, N. 1998. *New Diasporas: The Mass Exodus, Dispersal and Regrouping of Migrant Communities.* London: University College London Press.

Winters, L.A., T.L. Walmsley, Z.K. Wang and R. Grynberg. 2002. *Liberalising the Temporary Movement of Natural Persons.* Economics Discussion Paper No. 87. Brighton: University of Sussex.

Wittgenstein, L. 1969. *The Blue and Brown Books.* Oxford: Basil Blackwell.

3

Policy Practices in Development-induced Displacement and Rehabilitation

Alan Rew, Eleanor Fisher and Balaji Pandey[1]

The Problem and Its Setting

Comparatively little attention has been paid in the research literature to the policy practices which shape the restructuring of residence and livelihoods associated with development-induced displacement and resettlement (DIDR) programmes. Surveys of policy dynamics by Cernea (1993a, b), Oliver-Smith (1996) and Rew (1996) stand out as relatively unusual. The relative lack of attention to DIDR policy variation and the practices of its implementation is disconcerting for a number of reasons.

First, the possibility, even likelihood, of major adverse impacts from poorly handled DIDR and the need for governments to 'will' a measure of social protection for the vulnerable and displaced is increasingly recognised in public opinion. A 'bad' 'resettlement and rehabilitation (R&R) component' can tarnish the reputation of a project and/or lead to severe delays in a project's construction timetable. Why, then, is this growing recognition of the need to plan for R&R not catered for in supporting policy measures?

A second reason for surprise is that a significant body of *published* analysis and diagnosis of DIDR impacts, that also strongly advocates comprehensive R&R policies and guidelines, has been widely available for some time (since at least Cernea 1988). As this recognition grows, and published documentation of risk and adverse impact advances, there should be valuable lessons flowing from increasingly sensitive R&R policies and their implementation to be used in the design of succeeding projects. In East Africa, a large body of academic research was generated on resettlement issues in the 1960s and 1970s (particularly voluntary settlement as part of agricultural schemes). In Asia there is a large literature on the social impacts of displacement (see, for example, the reviews for India in Mathur and Marsden 1998) and on the reform of land acquisition laws through NGO and other advocacy (e.g. Fernandes and Paranjpye 1997). But the instances of lessons for policy implementation and operations being identified and acted on in this field are not, in fact, numerous.

There may be a third (although somewhat ambiguous) reason for scarcity in DIDR policy studies: increased economic liberalisation and global investment pressures stimulate the need for improved infrastructure and greater investment. These pressures may tend to increase the need to plan for further population displacement while, at the same time, increasingly bringing investment plans within the ambit of 'good governance', 'public accountability' and 'policy reform' norms. The consequences of increased globalisation and liberalisation *could* therefore lead to increased attention to DIDR and to the need for relevant policy reform. Yet the 'accountability' and 'policy reform' pressures are ambiguous since they are also likely to focus on macro-economic management and broad patterns of growth to combat poverty rather than on the specific social context of the livelihood entitlements of the excluded or on the basic needs and rights of the vulnerable in a particular locality. Policy advisors could therefore stress the mainstreaming of poverty reduction within public-sector budgets and seek the *rehabilitation* of any displaced persons through economic growth rather than through the 'dirty' detail of sectoral *resettlement* schemes in, for example, mining, thermal power development, dam construction and major road development.

Given the very rapid changes in the global economy, there is certainly an urgent need to consider the reactions of governments to fiscal crisis and to the broad balances to be struck between investments in productive capacity and in social and environmental protection. The concerns of project displacement and resettlement may risk seeming too particular and too geographically specific by comparison. This is one reason why the emphasis of this chapter is on *policy practice for the rehabilitation of the livelihoods of project-affected persons* (PAPs) rather than *only the physical relocation and resettlement of displaced communities*.

Lack of attention to the lessons of DIDR policy also arises from the sense that (in the words of a government evaluator we interviewed in Uganda as part of the research for the chapter) 'the job is not clean'. In Uganda, as in the rest of East Africa, R&R does not exist as a sphere of expertise within administration. Moreover, in the past, 'settlement schemes' were held to lead to social and economic improvement; therefore, the idea that displacement and resettlement could have negative consequences was not a central consideration for planners. In India we found that, on the whole, R&R managers lacked much long-term commitment to DIDR aims even if there were DIDR policies in place.

Managerial reluctance, and / or lack of definition of management responsibilities, circumscribes many of the organisational options for lessening
livelihood risks (Rew 1996 and 2003). DIDR has not been an area in which
to make a notable career as a policy maker or administrator.

International Influences on National Policy

Generation of an international policy framework pertinent to the human
costs of DIDR has had some influence on national policy statements in
Africa and state policy in eastern India, especially where international
development banks and donors are financing projects with land acquisition
implications. Three African countries formulated policy guidelines on
DIDR in the 1990s – Uganda, Cote d'Ivoire and the Central African
Republic (Cernea 1997a). Each country was strongly influenced by the
World Bank, which supported the policy design process and has been leading the drive for international policy frameworks for DIDR. It was the first
donor to adopt a comprehensive policy on population relocation (World
Bank 1980). Later World Bank guidelines (e.g. 1990) have confirmed the
DIDR policy benchmarks to be reached (see also Morse and Berger 1992,
Oxfam 1998). Many other donor institutions – including the Organisation
for Economic Co-operation and Development (OECD) (and its list of bilateral donor signatories), IMF and African Development Bank – have drawn
on the World Bank guidelines in formulating their own policies. The World
Bank has advocated an important policy standard, namely, that the impoverishment of a displaced population should not be considered inevitable.
As the World Bank has stated: 'good resettlement can prevent impoverishment and even reduce poverty by rebuilding sustainable livelihoods'
(World Bank 1994: vi). Nonetheless, it is recognised that the twin processes
of displacing people and rebuilding their livelihoods are among the most
difficult in development work (ibid. viii; see also Kurian 1996).

United Nations agencies are increasingly addressing DIDR-related
concerns through international legislation on the human rights of 'forced
evictions' – including what other agencies usually term 'involuntary
resettlement'. The UN agencies – especially the United Nations Centre of
Human Settlements (UNCHS/Habitat) and the United Nations
Commission on Human Rights (UNCHR), the World Food Programme
(WFP), the United Nations Children's Fund (UNICEF), the United
Nations Development Programme (UNDP) and the International Fund
for Agricultural Development (IFAD) – have extensive experience of
international legislation, policy and actions that relate to displacement.
The focus is usually on contexts of armed conflict, ethnic or religious per-
secution, and situations resulting in a breakdown of law and order.
Displacement as a result of planned development has been given far less
attention. However, in the 1990s this became an area of increasing con-

cern, with persons forced to vacate their homes as a result of large-scale development or construction projects being classified as a distinct group of persons requiring protection under international human rights law (UNCHR 1996: 3; see also Leckie 1994).

The Macro-social Consequences of DIDR

This chapter starts from the perspective that the central issues underlying governance and DIDR are those of human rights and people's entitlements as citizens in the context of global poverty reduction. Indeed, when human rights and entitlements are considered, DIDR becomes a test case of the scope and limits of development policy and its implementation. The threats and opportunities flowing from infrastructure projects for key entitlements to livelihoods, to rights to welfare, and the right to be consulted, can be very dramatic. In part the outrage often associated with forced displacement and resettlement comes from the contrast between the needs of 'distant strangers', who are also weak, and the further gains of already more privileged urban groups and richer peasants. The projects causing the maximum displacement and need for rehabilitation usually provide improved infrastructure for those already in the mainstream of industrial or agro-business production. Power, mining and irrigation developments usually take large areas of distant land used by marginal farmers and natural-resource collectors and turn them into products of use in the modern sectors of the economy. People's homes and livelihoods are lost and communities severely disrupted; the 'displaced persons' (DPs) risk failing to make the transition to the modern sectors of the society and economy. Government and corporations do sometimes attempt to provide compensatory social and economic assets for the DPs, but the results are only rarely successful because of lack of skills, low education levels and the poor quality of agency support.

The transformation from marginal land-use to modern industrial and intensive agricultural production creates human tragedy but can also be seen as inevitable if basic material needs are to be met in the face of growing population pressures. So, in this light, DIDR can be regarded with pathos rather than moral outrage and policy-designed accordingly. It is only when the huge scale of displacement is related to the impact on the most vulnerable and culturally distinct that we become aware of the major policy failures in the field. Bandyopadhyay (1999) calculates that, in India, for example, a number of people equivalent to 2 percent of the total population were displaced by development projects in the first forty years of independence (1951 to 1990). The impact on tribal people was far, far greater however, since some 40 percent of those displaced were tribal; and people of tribal origin are only 8 percent of the total population. The Government of India itself (India 1989) suggests that around 20 percent of the total tribal population of India may have been uprooted and displaced in that period. There is a growing incidence of multiple displacements. The beneficiaries of industrial and infrastructure development may be many but the costs are being born disproportionately by the poorest and ethnically most vulnerable in Indian society. Arundhati Roy (1999: 21) believes that: 'the ethnic "otherness" of their victims takes some of the pressure off the Nation Builders. It's like having an expense account. Someone else pays the bills'.

Population displacement caused by African development programmes appears, compared to the numbers involved in India and China, small-scale in terms of the numbers of people displaced. However, as Cernea underlines (1997a: 15), displacements such as those caused by the Akosombo, Kossou and Kariba Dams have affected a much higher proportion of the respective countries' population than displacement caused by even the largest dams in Asia vis-à-vis the total population of those countries. By implication, the human consequences of involuntary resettlement in Africa can also be enormous for both individuals and states.

Reasons for Weak DIDR Policy

The Sardar Sarovar Dam project in India showed that despite explicit resettlement guidelines within the World Bank, which were agreed to by the Government of India (GoI), the fundamental weaknesses in legal protection and institutional arrangements were not taken seriously enough at appraisal stage (Cernea 1999: 6). Protection is also lacking in the multitude of minor displacement actions which take place on a regular basis on all continents – our research shows this is particularly a concern in relation to urban upgrading in both Asia and Africa, and throughout sub-Saharan Africa in rural and urban areas. There are various explanations for the repeated instances of weakness. Key commentators stress the absence of national policy frameworks. Cernea, for example, notes a clear association between performance in resettlement work and the presence, or not, of an enabling policy. In an introduction to a monograph on R&R in India (written by Parasuraman), Cernea summarises the situation thus:

> Some governments prefer to maintain a policy vacuum rather than issue binding norms and legislation for activities they know are going to be problematic, difficult and controversial. But hard facts teach us that *the absence of policy is a policy by default.* (1999: 21) [National R&R policies are therefore needed to set] standards in the state and the private sector in involuntary displacement and relocation operations together with comprehensive legal frameworks defining the rights and obligations of the people affected [and] the obligations of the [relevant] agencies. (1999: 20)

Other commentators, including Parasuraman himself, are less certain about the importance of written policy standards and laws and refer to 'commitment' and 'political will' as at least as important. In an essay on Sardar Sarovar, for example, Parasuraman argues that:

> It may be easy to provide a good R&R policy framework like the policies that the state and central governments have evolved for the social and economic development of tribals, *harijans*, and other weaker sections. However, the solution rests on the willingness and capacity of the state to implement these policies ... Satisfactory R&R policies cannot be carried out by an *ad hoc* machinery. The government should have an appropriate R&R machinery to carry out the task on a long-term basis (1999: 59, 61).

In the same volume, Parasuraman again writes:

> All in all, the approach to displacement has been *ad hoc*. There is no policy and thus no commitment. Guidelines are interpreted variously, changed at will and applied, if at all, mechanically. (1999: 49)

There is a core level of agreement between these two experts. Both recognise that consistently applied policy and co-ordinated institutional frameworks are necessary. Both accept that DIDR responds to a large range of policy, bureaucratic, social and political influences. For Cernea the main problem is how to persuade borrower governments to draft and adopt comprehensive laws; the execution of the frameworks must be left in the hands of the borrower's own agencies. Donors can offer help through monitoring visits and training support – they cannot intervene directly. Parasuraman's view is an insider's one; it both captures the piecemeal and largely unhelpful assembly of national policy aims, guidelines and implementation arrangements and regrets the lack of any real commitment to implementation. The thrust of Parasuraman's comment is that DIDR continues to be problematic because of the weak link between policy and implementation.

A Review of DIDR Policy Practices

The research reported here set out, initially, to provide desk reviews of policies for DIDR.[2] We chose three (populous and very poor) states in eastern India (Orissa, Bihar and West Bengal) and three countries in east Africa (Uganda, Kenya and Tanzania) for our enquiries. All six countries/states have democratically elected governments and thus good scope (at least in theory) for consultation and public participation in the mitigation of displacement and the design of R&R project components. (In part, the selection of these six cases reflected the previous work and field experience of the senior author, previous research on conservation in East Africa (Fisher 2002) and the ability to build on previous in-country studies with only modest funds.)

All the cases selected for detailed study had been British colonies and continued to use land acquisition and compensation laws modelled on British law. In very broad terms 'policy by default' (see Cernea 1999: 21) was found in three of the chosen six cases. These broad results were not wholly unexpected. Cernea had warned that 'sorely missing in most African countries are explicit policies and legal frameworks to compel relevant state agencies to effectively address the vital issues of livelihood restoration and productive reestablishment of those displaced' (Cernea 1997a: 24). We also found major variations in DIDR policy practice between the three Indian states.

All six cases had land acquisition laws in place and compensation was being paid for land acquired, although the practices were variable. There had been some tentative movements towards more conscious policy formulation relevant to DIDR in two of the cases. These two cases might be thought of as representing 'proto-policy' for DIDR, showing some potential for the orderly planning of R&R operations but lacking comprehensive or strategic DIDR policy norms within the co-ordinating and sectoral ministries. In only one case – Orissa in India – were there reasonably comprehensive, almost government-wide, DIDR frameworks.

As the research developed from its original scope we focussed increasingly on the links between DIDR and/or land acquisition policy and implementation, and the actual practices of policy makers, planners and managers. We needed to address the extent to which policy practices were ad hoc or reflected, however imperfectly, a movement towards appropriate legal and technical standards. To do so we needed to move from desk to field studies and to concentrate on certain regions and 'country' cases. In part the selection of cases for further field study sought to follow up promising DIDR policy development work by World Bank teams in Orissa and Uganda and to put these two cases into regional contexts.[3]

Studies of Policy Practice in Two Regions

Uganda is a country whose institutions – government and civil society – are being rebuilt after three decades of political insecurity, national conflict and civil war. It is a country that has borne witness to state atrocities and human rights abuses, with large numbers of people displaced by conflict within Uganda and surrounding countries. The rebuilding process means that government capacity and institutions are weak, especially when not supported by donor funding. The foundations for DIDR policy are thus uncertain and complex. Furthermore, there has been considerable recent change and upheaval in the institutional environment in which development projects were being framed and claims for compensation made.

In Orissa we found that even comprehensive R&R policy design, and some accomplished work by senior administrators, could not make much impression on the inertia created by existing patterns of social and economic exclusion and the work patterns of private and public sector middle managers and lower-level officials. In other words, our research found numerous implementation failures to report; and few implementation successes, despite the skill and hard work of some dedicated R&R connoisseurs. We concluded that it is important to underline the multiple causes of implementation failure since single-factor solutions are likely to mislead with their simplicity or prove unconvincing when advocates and consultants are trying to influence policy makers to reform their policy practice. Attempts to advocate only 'more participation', 'better communication' or 'extensive training' may have little impact. Instead the research reported in the chapter used a concept of 'policy practice' to capture the many interacting processes of policy and implementation. These processes link the front-line field staff in the 'swampy' detail of specific R&R projects to the district and company towns, and on to the Olympian heights of policy formulation and framing in the national capitals.

'Policy' is Both 'Means' and 'Ends' – it is Practice

We have used the idea of 'policy practice' to distinguish the thrust of our research from much conventional thinking about implementation and policy. The language of 'implementation' used throughout India and east Africa presents the translation of policy into action as being, under normal circumstances, essentially unproblematic provided bureaucracies remain obedient to their political masters. According to this view all administrators are trained to believe that if ministers or presidents declare a public purpose or policy it will be their job to carry out the policy and that civil servants not doing so will be brought to heel. In this view good DIDR policy requires the initial consent and commitment of heads of state or ministers; the rest will, over time, follow. In fact, the reality is often very different. Many informants can readily agree that ministers are omnipotent and able to force through policy, while also simultaneously agreeing that civil servants are rarely called to account for poor performance. They seem able to hold both beliefs simultaneously without worrying about the contradiction!

The idea of a guiding politics and a compliant administration has much to do with nineteenth century thought. The distinction follows the set of concepts developed by Weber (1947), with politics as a goal-setting process and bureaucratic decision-making proceeding, on a legal-rational basis, to carry out the requirements of policy/politics. The extent to which the creativity and coping behaviours of administrators would tend to transform policy, often fundamentally, was not appreciated in those early years. From the early 1970s onwards 'implementation studies' (e.g. Pressman and Wildavsky 1973, Gow and Morss 1988, Thomas and Grindle 1990, Stewart 1996, Jain 1997) have seriously questioned this view of implementation as unproblematic. Indeed cumulative research (see Hill 1993) has concluded that there will always be an irreducible 'implementation deficit' limiting the ambitions of those planners who believe there should be a very direct link between the concepts stated in a plan and the way it is realised on the ground. The size of implementation deficit will vary but perfect implementation is impossible because of communication chains, different interests and organisational attenuation.

Our own detailed research on DIDR has identified at least three different levels of difficulty with the view of DIDR policy-implementation relations as unproblematic. First, it is not at all clear that high-level policy makers are able to set clear policy goals. Policy options are usually 'framed' in such a way that they include a medley of aims, hypotheses and assumptions justified by broad ideological themes as much as by precise policy analysis. The inability of the project specialists assisting them to offer realistic policy alternatives for livelihood protection or new livelihood creation in keeping with displacement pressures is in part to blame. Interviews with the key policy makers themselves, carried out as part of this research, show how much they are also prisoners of completely contradictory pressures, juggling modernist and welfarist views without much ability to resolve the puzzles or to state clear recommendations. This means that R&R or DIDR 'policy' is more a set of 'frames' and broad global themes than any valid theory of cause and effect (see Rein and Schon 1994). R&R 'policy' is often too vague to be thought of, even, as 'bad' policy.

The status of DIDR policy in Uganda at the time of our research can serve to illustrate the general point. Policy guidelines on DIDR in Uganda were produced in the mid-1990s but were not taken forward. In 1995 a new constitution of the Republic of Uganda was brought into effect. This heralded a change in land rights as established in the Land Act (1998), although mechanisms for its implementation were still being considered at the time of our research (Purcell and Babumba-Kyeyune 1999). In 1997 the Local Government Act had instituted a process of government reform through a policy of decentralisation (see Villadsen and Lubanga 1996). These various developments raise new questions concerning how much influence local and central governments have on development planning. In 1995 the Office of the Prime Minister drafted policy guidelines and a study funded by the World Bank was undertaken, entitled 'Resettlement Policy and Institutional Capacity for Resettlement Planning in Uganda'

(Sengindo 1995, Uganda 1995). In essence, the policy guidelines are in keeping with those of the World Bank (1990).

Perhaps because a policy had been drafted, Cernea (1997a: 24) identified Uganda as a country in which 'remarkable progress has been made' in the DIDR policy sphere. However, the view from the ground in mid-1999 did not reflect such optimism. Those responsible for the report have since moved to new positions, while present incumbents have little knowledge of its existence. According to a local consultant involved in drafting the policy, it was subsequently given a low priority and thwarted by internal politics. This reception contrasts markedly with the high-priority attention given to the development of refugee policy. In addition, because of the restructuring of government ministries that took place in 1998, some of the DIDR report's recommendations were already out of date. The National Environment Management Authority (NEMA) also plays a role in enabling DIDR projects to go ahead by assessing their environmental impact. A senior official described them as being 'harmonised with the World Bank'. Draft guidelines for Environmental Impact Assessment were produced in 1995. However, they do not include guidelines for resettlement and compensation. In general in Uganda it is left to a line-ministry to take a lead on resettlement when a project falls into the sector over which it has responsibility. It uses land acquisition and 'fair' compensation methods, and those rehabilitation measures of which it is aware or deems appropriate, to implement the displacement operations.

Most research into organisations suggests that, in real life, the objectives of programmes and organisations are often difficult to identify or are couched in vague and evasive terms. Even if aims are 'cleared' and widely agreed at the beginning, it is likely that goals will be susceptible to the usual problems of succession, multiplication and replacement as implementation proceeds. Interviews with senior decision-makers in Orissa show that they worry about a great range of problems. These include the relatively minor details of the categories of PAPs to be included, to the imponderables of administrators' attitudes, NGO reactions, lack of clarity in economic rehabilitation policy and lack of a management system or thought-through implementation system. In this context and set of pressures it is very hard for policy work to stick to a logical sequence; it will rather jump from implementation contexts to new policy opportunities and fresh social and political constraints. Political pressures and sensitivities add to and maintain the complexity of the overlapping frames and practices. Officials who try to reorganise these complexities need to tread carefully if they are to avoid being subject to the threat and reality of re-posting to less desirable posts.

Second, apparent 'implementation failures' in DIDR may simply stem from the influence of other features in prevailing policy practice and in organisational routines. Where goals are set they are pulled through to implementation in such potentially contradictory ways. New policies, typically layered on top of older ones, are implemented only partially and with different components proceeding at different speeds, and abut and overlap many other policies from a range of sectors. A key problem is the number of organisational 'dependency' relations (see Borzel 1998) the policy maker faces with other participant agencies. Four ministries are usually needed to progress R&R schemes in Uganda. The Ministry of Water, Lands and Environment plays an important role in valuation, land administration and physical planning. The Ministry of Agriculture, Animal Husbandry and Fisheries is responsible for rural development, and the Ministry of Gender, Labour and Social Development holds responsibility for the social and economic welfare of the population. In principle, these ministries should play a (co-ordinated?) part in long-term planning for projects involving population displacement and resettlement. At the time of our research an overarching Ministry of Disaster Preparedness had recently been created with a remit encompassing DIDR. In principle it has the role of carrying out the resettlement action in the case of development projects. This includes procurement of food and relief items, linkage to NGOs and donors, transport, and provision of field officers. DIDR administration in Uganda also contrasts markedly with the way Uganda manages refugees. Since refugee problems in Uganda have a well developed policy context and large amounts of international aid there are, unsurprisingly, many refugee officers and sharper definitions of their roles. In terms of DIDR, there are conflicting accounts of the role the Ministry plays; one observer went so far as to suggest that 'a disaster' first needs to occur before intervention is considered.

In *rural* India, on the other hand, the number of agencies is usually kept quite small and dependency relations are not much of a problem. There is usually only the project-implementing authority (often an engineering unit of a company or parastatal) dealing with the district administration under a single head (the Resident Magistrate, District Commissioner or 'Collector') – although the two authorities do tend to pass responsibility between them without always settling the problem. 'Dependency' relations seem far worse for the R&R administrator in *metropolitan* India, partly because of the very real interest of many different levels of local and state government.

In practice, in East Africa and urban eastern India at least, implementation requires not only a complex series of decisions about events and linkages but also agreement about each event among a large number of participants, many from different branches of government, from within a single business corporation, and at grass-roots level. It is very easy in this context to exercise official power to gain early formal 'agreement' from weak and vulnerable PAPs in order to secure land for development, leaving the other necessary agreements to a later, often long deferred, stage.

This was the pattern seen in the planning of a 'best practice' industrial corporation in Orissa. Land was acquired, over-the-market-rate compensation paid and people displaced. But the corporation had no ability to complete the project and create compensating jobs in the economy because it was dependent on a whole series of environmental and other licences from government before it could begin construction.

Third, there is the argument that 'policy making' should not be viewed from 'the top' or even 'the middle' of the various organisational sets and fragments that dominate when the policy moves to state or district levels. Rather, policy is best 'negotiated' in the practices of routine administration at 'the bottom' between those who are expected to carry out the policy and those who are the PAPs. This front line in R&R projects is also the place at which the principal attributes of *all* bureaucratic organisations – discretionary decision-making and operational routines – can best be found. R&R policy makers in our Orissa case study have no alternative but to delegate priorities for DIDR to the District Collector/Resident Magistrate and he in turn to delegate them to a Resettlement Officer. The staff and offices of these two people have much scope to speed up or delay individual decisions, to invent formats and procedures, and to declare, as they confront the inevitable ambiguities and conflict in the detail of social and economic relations, this person eligible and that one not. In other words, they settle individual 'cases' very much as they see fit; they have considerable discretion because of the distance and gap between themselves and the PAPs. They can negotiate outcomes in terms of their priorities for the local setting and what they perceive as politically feasible. And it is these 'cases' that vitally concern the PAPs and the welfare outcomes, not the broad delineation of policy in the national or international capitals.

A Landscape of 'Policy Practice'

Indeed, far too much of the discussion of policy for R&R is 'on the hilltop' in the sense that it reviews lofty and normative policy frames rather than real systems of policy practice on the ground. We found it convenient as our research results emerged to think of a 'landscape' for policy practice. The landscape certainly had need of 'a hill' – where much of the top-level donor/investor, national government and executive agency discussions took place and where NGOs and parliaments debated national concerns. At the 'bottom of the hill' we found a rather messy 'swamp' of project detail and specific outcomes for PAPs. In the middle of the landscape was a 'plateau' on which officials and engineers in state capitals, company headquarters and district towns co-ordinated the administrative machinery for the implementation of R&R policy.

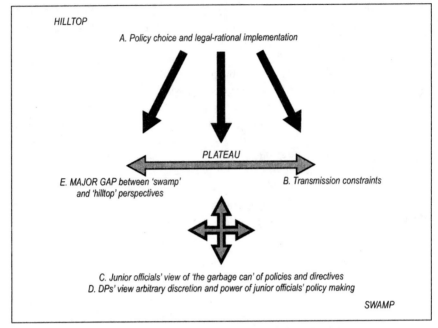

Figure 3.1. *Existing Landscape of Policy Practices*

At the 'hilltop' level the search for alternative policy formulations to displacement focuses on global issues, and on the broad distribution of power among government units. The global issues are generally 'policy frames' rather than any detailed policy that has been analysed for cause-and-effect linkages. Our results suggest strongly that there can be discussion about *the general need* for compensation and rehabilitation but usually no questioning of the realistic options for the protection of human rights or the creation of alternative livelihoods. The interests in implementation are often restricted to the importance of various ministries, and to recommendations that one or other be brought forward for greater responsibilities, that a further ministry be added to the co-ordinating group or, more rarely, that one be dropped from the list of key responsible ministries. For example, in Uganda the key administrative issues concern the relations between five (formerly four) main ministries. In India, the critical issues more usually concern the balance of power between state and central governments and the implementing (often parastatal or large corporate commercial) companies and authorities.

At the 'bottom' of the hill is the 'swampy' detail of the actual projects. Although complex and usually messy with a combination of human tragedy, stoic survival, some mendacity and corruption, and hard work under trying circumstances, the 'swampy' detail is often critical to the PAPs and to the actual outcomes and practice of policy making. It is here, at the project level, that the implementing organisations and PAPs come face to face with the irreducible discretion of even the lowliest administrator and with the local-level operational routines that officials and engineers develop to cope with the pressures of their jobs and social circumstances. These routines and discretionary decisions may seem of minor concern 'on the hill' but they appear as the key instruments of power and resource allocation to the (usually) socially highly vulnerable PAPs. Asif (2000) also recognises this point and argues that the discretionary abuse of official power is a major reason for people staying out of resettlement colonies.

Policies or policy intentions must typically travel 'down the hill', as well as from one public bureaucracy to another and through layers of hierarchy 'on the plateau', before they reach the point of contact with the PAP, the 'client' for service at the 'bottom of the hill'. It is frequently at this final stage of the process, the point of delivery, that the forces of discretionary decision-making and operational routine within the bureaucratic machinery are most difficult to reform. It is here that we confront the central problem of what is known in the organisational studies literature as 'street-level bureaucracy' (Lipsky 1980). Lower-level or 'street' bureaucrats shoulder virtually all responsibility for direct contact with the PAPs. They exercise a relatively high degree of discretion over detailed decisions about client treatment and thus have a major bearing on impact. In the Orissa cases, for example, it is they who decide whether or not an alternative livelihood for the displaced person is viable by granting or withholding project funds based on the certification of vouchers from local landlords, banks and businesses. The opportunities for abuses of power and the exaction of 'rent' are legion. From the perspective of the DIDR client in Orissa, the Resettlement Officer *is* the Government; his decisions *are* policy. And because of the frequency and immediacy of the contact between the local- level bureaucrat and his clients it is usually difficult if not impossible for higher-level administrators to monitor or control all aspects of his job performance.

Away from the lofty hilltop of policy formulation, and rising from the damp lowlands of project implementation, there is the broad plateau of state departments with sectoral responsibilities and the district towns within which R&R and other policy lines are co-ordinated and implemented. There is an opportunity here to both review and improve the chains of communication, real resource allocations and the 'notifications' and permissions that make up the (largely ad hoc?) institutional arrangements of which Parasuraman (1999: 49) complains. There is also an opportunity to examine the usually radical gap between the policy and operations spheres, from which many implementation problems flow. If there are 'big ideas' among the 'hilltop' policy makers they often fail to connect with operational routines and there is often little in the way of useful guidance based on 'swamp' realities available for the project-level administrator.

The weaknesses in the chains of decision-making 'on the plateau' are so many, we found in our case studies, that it is not difficult to agree with Parasuraman's description of them as essentially ad hoc. Even this description may be too kind. Some of the links in the chains of communication and allocation are so vulnerable that they could have been predicted to break or fail even under normal strain. For example, the Resettlement Officer is a key link in the chain of responsibilities for DIDR in Orissa. Yet he is so severely understaffed, and so overloaded with a myriad of responsibilities, that it is hardly possible his job was ever intended to function effectively. The great range of duties, which cover almost all DIDR tasks downstream of land acquisition, ensure that an adequate quality of implementation of DIDR plans is most unlikely. The duties include:

- compensation disbursement;
- follow-up to complaints about compensation made by DPs;
- enumeration of displaced individuals within the project-affected families;
- administering temporary income support during relocation;
- the co-ordination of DPs' transport and physical relocation;
- determining the eligibility of individuals for R&R assistance (for example, authorising assistance to the children of PAPs who have become adult during the project's implementation);
- implementing decisions and choices made for the disbursement of the project grants available to assist the rehabilitation of DPs;
- when DPs have purchased land and constructed their own houses, certifying the authenticity of the land purchase and advancing money for house construction; and
- managing the process to establish alternative livelihoods and income restoration, through (for example) verifying certificates of purchase of land or business assets.

Even if there were enough of them, rehabilitation officers usually lack the skills needed to help people suffering the stresses and disorders of displacement and rehabilitation. Typically, they have been posted to the job from an engineering or administrative background. They often lack any natural sympathy for the specific disruptions suffered by the DPs. They have only very rarely been asked to 'stand in the shoes of an oustee'. Their career orientation makes them more interested in the progression of the project's construction works or engineering; or they have the administrator's trained capacity to look mainly upwards for the key instructions on job performance.

In Uganda, many projects involve displacement by government officials not specialised in this function at all, for instance game wardens and game scouts. There are several examples of representatives of central government ministries ordering that people should be moved, but not saying how this should be done, and leaving it to minions in the field who have no relevant capacity or training whatsoever. Reliance on a 'proto' DIDR policy framework – consisting of streamlined land acquisition procedures, fair compensation and payment before land loss, and local-level consultations and dispute settlement with official and PAP stakeholders – settles official responsibilities far short of the ultimate goal of co-ordinated displacement management and postdisplacement rehabilitation. As already discussed, DIDR guidelines had been adopted but were largely forgotten, partly because policy and implementation development in this area had been supplanted by the pressing needs of disaster and refugee management. The lack of progress in DIDR policy also reflected the way that Uganda's land laws and local government structures had developed. Furthermore, although national institutions are correctly identified – by donors – as responsible for displacement management, some projects are so clearly identified with donor priorities that responsibility becomes uncertain and divided.

The 1995 Constitution vested title to land directly in the hands of Uganda citizens, away from the Uganda Land Commission, limiting the powers of the state in land ownership matters. According to the new constitution, both government and local authorities have power of compulsory acquisition. Established legal procedures in law require compensation to be paid promptly and fairly prior to displacing people. There is, however, some confusion over whether compensation has by law to be paid in advance, because this is not stated in the Land Acquisition Act of 1965, sections of which still apply. The constitution does not encompass any explicit resettlement or rehabilitation entitlements. Linked to the 1995 constitution, however, was a provision that parliament would enact a land law. This led to the Land Act of 1998, intended to strengthen the institution of formal land tenure in Uganda (Uganda 1998). The 1995 Constitution and the 1998 Land Act can be thought of as 'proto-vehicles' for government DIDR policy, as they have implications for people's involvement in decision-making concerning involuntary displacement; and they use 'fair' compensation as a norm to imply the limits to responsibility for the rehabilitation of displaced families and individuals.

The Land Act upholds the statutory power of compulsory acquisition conferred on the government and local authorities by the constitution. Somewhat confusingly (or predictably in our view) the Land Act does not repeal the 1965 Land Acquisition Act. Procedures for land acquisition include a number of acquisition and compensation procedures. They require a statutory declaration that the land is required for public use; and that copies of the declaration should be served on all stakeholders including district land boards, tribunals and local governments. An assessment of the value of the land rights and interests of the stakeholders must be made and 'fair and adequate' compensation must be paid for land acquired prior to the extinguishing of rights therein and any new rightholders taking possession. District land tribunals with the jurisdiction to determine any dispute relating to the amount of compensation to be paid for land acquired by the government are also established. In this way, the Land Act decentralises land administration and devolves decision-making about land management, tenure change and disputes. It has been argued, furthermore, that the Land Act represents an attempt to use legislation to lever economic and social change from below (Marsh and Kego Laker 1999: 7). Neither the 1965 nor the 1998 Act provides for the costs of resettlement and rehabilitation per se.

The provision, in India, that each individual resettlement site should be notified separately under a general enabling law is an instance of a seemingly deliberate attempt to emasculate rehabilitation policy requirements. The policy is there as an indication of good intention; but the notifications are never issued and so chain links in the policy process are 'sawn through' in practice before they can be implemented.

Prospects for Reform of Policy Practice

One major conclusion of our review is that weak policy frameworks centred on the failure to integrate policy and implementation systems. DIDR guidelines might appear as a set of potentially or actually enforceable laws or standards only for us to find, on closer examination in the field, that that they floated, without significant effect, above the everyday business of land acquisition and displacement. A major reason for these operational system failures was the apparent unwillingness to tackle each of the policy practice levels separately and then to integrate the solutions reached. For example, reluctance to clarify policy objectives about DIDR leads top officials to ignore the complexities, social exclusions and discriminations at local level and leads to cynicism at local levels about overall aims. If general policy discourse is vague to begin with, and any clarity remaining then evaporates in implementation, why subject lower-level administrative practice to closer scrutiny? If low-level practice is impossibly complex and messy with social detail, why bother to show exact cause-and-effect relations at national levels? Inertia in policy practice, that is, can be pervasive and affect all levels. The most effective means that donors and national-policy analysts have at their disposal to tackle problems at this level is to point to the lapses of planning, specification and control in the current execution and understanding of policy. Essential to this aim is that policy makers and senior administrators develop a common understanding of the necessary policy. It is also desirable that they have sufficient control of the implementation process to hold subordinates accountable to the common understanding. We will turn to this question of control in the next section, on 'chains' of control and co-ordination. The rest of the chapter will therefore try to identify the different 'policy practice' issues at each level and offer some suggestions for their overall integration.

Prospects for Strengthening Practices at Project Level

Visitors, especially those from 'the hilltop', tend to see the violence and impoverishment threats of DIDR more clearly than they see the social exclusions and structural violence of ethnicity, class and caste in the existing pre-project communities. 'Local' does not necessarily mean 'harmonious and equitable'. Decentralisation of decision-making to project levels can mean that most decisions are brought closer to the mass of people and that there is greater power for project-level staff and arbitrary or biased outcomes. Discussions with PAPs in Orissa and a review of resettlement colonies in India (Asif 2000) both show that the discretion – for good or evil – of junior project staff is considerable. A severe limit on reform therefore is set by the tension between the dead weight of necessary operating routines – routines imposed from 'on top', usually aimed at controlling lower-level officials' discretion – with the countervailing need to actively give or to concede discretion to project staff because of physical and communication distances. (This is not just a poor country or DIDR problem: there is a large literature showing the fate of poverty and social policy initiatives in the hands of street-level bureaucracy in the United States and in Britain.) The task of reorienting project staff in DIDR programmes and ensuring an effective voice for the weak and vulnerable is daunting but must be attempted if policy practice is to be changed. Our studies show that, from the perspective of local rural society, there are usually major social class and ethnic divisions between DPs and DIDR officials. In Orissa, for example, the officials can be stereotyped as the 'babus' (the white-collar workers); the DPs as 'the farmers' or 'the tribals'. Even though there are provisions in the Indian constitution for positive discrimination in favour of tribals and scheduled castes, the attitudes and exclusions of local officials are hard to alter. Moreover, the tasks and responsibilities of DIDR scheme officials are highly visible in a political sense. Opposition groups frequently use R&R issues to mount campaigns against the incumbent government; district officials then become exposed in unpredictable ways. Political visibility then stimulates much high-level interference as senior administrators try to adjust the systems to meet what they see as urgent management needs.

One way of ensuring that scheme officials are more accountable, and that they try to transcend local systems of ranking in their work for DPs and PAPs, is to ask civil society organisations to review field-level outcomes. The NGOs will need higher-level protection to ensure they can report on an independent basis. There could, for example, be parallel funding to civil society organisations to ensure that NGO-administered monitoring and evaluation (M&E) systems have a measure of autonomy from local and central government.

A further requirement is more socially sensitive training. The content of training must include skills in social diagnosis and there should be tests of competence after training for key staff such as resettlement officers. Training needs to be combined with major incentives in the workplace. Few officials we interviewed reported much job satisfaction. Some saw it as distasteful or unclean work. Many regarded it as a 'punishment posting'. DIDR tasks certainly involve enforcing loss of livelihood and home on some people and then assisting, under usually less than ideal circumstances, the adjustment of some DPs to that loss and to kinds of restitution, compensation and living they have not previously experienced. In some cases there is no apparent remedy for the loss of livelihood or for the distress and anger of PAPs – and officials can only receive complaints, perhaps promising to pass them on to a higher authority. Incentive schemes, including access to study tours and major training awards, are needed for staff serving at lower levels to help remove the 'punishment posting' culture from DIDR work.

Reform of project-level practice would also be achieved if DPs and PAPs were consulted more and allowed a stronger voice in project design and implementation. Not only would project arrangements be better adjusted to local circumstances, there would also be stronger formal checks on the use of officials' discretionary power. Unfortunately, the current provisions for 'participation' in policy practice are usually variable or uncertain. In Orissa provisions for public participation in project R&R components barely exist, although there is a very modest requirement that DPs should be shown resettlement sites and their views solicited. There is no provision for public consultation on project plans and designs as they are emerging.

Nonetheless, current policies in favour of local democracy in India and Uganda may, in time, be used to reform DIDR policy practice. In Uganda a new constitution, local councils and changes to the land laws mean that recognition of the human rights of DPs, and people's capacity to voice their own rights, have become more prominent. Whether this is translated into change in general, and DIDR practice in particular, is still an open question given that these changes were recent at the time of fieldwork. The equally recent local government (or *panchayati raj*) elections in Orissa also offer the distinct possibility that rural residents may choose to organise to protect themselves or to negotiate DIDR risks. This has been delayed in the case of local governments scheduled as 'tribal' because of

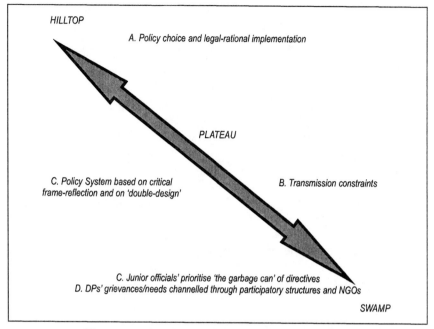

Figure 3.2. *Landscape of Reformed Policy Practice*

the way that the previous state government has responded to the implications of the amendments to the Indian constitution and the requirement of elections to tribal and non-tribal panchayats. In West Bengal the research found that panchayats, informal sector business associations, and trade unions are important channels available to residents through which to bring pressure to bear on land acquisition officers.

Prospects for Strengthening Chains of Decision-Making

We saw that one key problem 'on the plateau' could be organisational 'dependency' arising from multi-agency co-ordination needs. Regardless of how well focused or well organised an individual agency may be, its ability to implement programmes and projects successfully depends on its ability to influence agencies at other levels and in other sectors of government. Where more than one agency is involved in DIDR implementation, the lines of authority for policy are often blurred. A district administration and a sectoral engineering agency can each have very different agendas and links, pull in different ways, and tend to shift responsibility back and forth.

The studies in Orissa showed that considerable headway had been made (with much support from the World Bank) on these 'chain and linkage' issues for the water resources sector, with the production of compre-hensive written R&R guidelines (Orissa 1994). Guidelines such as these are crucial in reducing the gap between (usually underspecified) policy ends and project operations. Major weaknesses remain in this area in Uganda, both in terms of DIDR and for social and poverty reduction programmes in general. The research in Orissa highlighted that weaknesses in the water resources sector now lay elsewhere, in staffing levels, staff overload and unrealistic job specifications rather than in weaknesses in interdepartmen-tal procedure and linking. The written guidelines do hold departments more responsible. The weak point in the chain of capacity was found, in the Orissa research, to be the final link – that is, in the role of the Rehabilitation Officer. This role requires considerable liaison between the project engi-neers and the land administration, welfare and rehabilitation functions of government; yet there is almost always a shortage of staff available to do the work. The Rehabilitation Officer, who may be part of the District Collector's staff or of the project-implementing authority (PIA), is often a lone individual located at field level. Experience in Orissa shows that he may have initial responsibility for the displacement and rehabilitation of some 2,500 to 5,000 families. The sheer volume of displaced families and their traumas means the work is often carried out mechanically.

Given the low ranking of the R&R function and the lack of a compre-hensive development vision for DIDR, there are also few incentives in the bureaucracy for speedy decision-making or for the rapid co-ordination of work by officers at similar levels. The spirit of 'cautious concern' sur-rounding DIDR means that 'file movement' must follow the strict order of bureaucratic authority. Decisions can only be made 'on file' and files must first go 'up' then 'across' then 'down'. The chances of common-problem identification and speedy flexible solutions through local-level teamwork are thus very restricted.

There are many potential breaks in the chains of control and co-ordi-nation. We have seen that laws can be rendered impotent by refusal to issue notifications for individual sites. Draft policies are circulated for extensive discussion but never enacted. Responsibilities are shifted from provincial or state to national level and from ministry to ministry. Posts are agreed but never 'gazetted', 'posted' nor, finally, 'filled'; so initiatives founder because of inadequate real resources.

The Water Resource Guidelines in Orissa were referred to widely as examples of good practice, but it should also be noted that this is the only sector of the state where DIDR is controlled wholly within the State Government. The project authorities for mining and power there are India-wide parastatals; project authorities for industrial projects are usu-ally private-sector undertakings with all-India or global connections.

The cases in Orissa, indeed, show that, given pressures towards eco-nomic liberalisation and inward investment, perhaps the most urgent reforms in DIDR-related public administration were needed where it linked with the private sector. The power and wealth of major mining and industrial corporations can threaten the rights of the poor more effectively than underperforming bureaucrats. For example, there was some doubt about even the medium-term prospects of one industrial development project because key central-government clearances had not been obtained. Nonetheless, the R&R component had gone ahead very early on because of the industry's power in government circles. Some NGOs consulted took the view that major immediate losses to the livelihoods and welfare of the PAPs had been imposed for little gain. The industrial corporation took the view that national industrial capacity was being developed and that the R&R component has been implemented successfully. In one other highly publicised case of industrial development, the well known Council for Social Development based in Delhi reported, to the company and to the State Government, that the human rights of tribal residents may have been violated and that NGOs wishing to support them were being prosecuted and harassed unfairly.

There is a ready danger that private companies will try to ensure that where weak chains in government administration can be strengthened they are reformed to serve industrial interests. Tribal and other peoples' rights may suffer as a consequence. Private-sector investment in Uganda is very modest in comparison to the level of activity in eastern India. Nonetheless, progress towards the reform of DIDR in Uganda should seriously consider the regulation of private-sector investment and its impact on PAPs in order to establish best practice for the future.

To conclude this section on reform prospects at project level, we can see that the more ambitious the organisational links and the scale of the project in engineering terms, the greater the chance that the organisational abilities to implement the scheme effectively and in a balanced way will be undermined. The aim of project designers should be, therefore, to fit the scale of their engineering ambitions to the organisational capacity to implement. All too frequently, however, it is maximising engineering schedules that dominate in the implementation of R&R. Planners and appraisal experts should try to redress the balance and stress the time needed for human communities and the staff with implementing organisations to respond. The policy planning principle that should be adopted is 'double-design' (Rein and Schon 1994: 80), i.e. careful, and not overly ambitious, technical planning of activities, together with planned and resourced training programmes and incentives to increase people's skills and confidence in new methods of teamwork.

Prospects for Clarifying Policy Frames

Reform at the higher or 'hilltop' levels should aim at greater clarity and balance and at a closer specification of the ends of policy. Arundhati Roy (1999: 72) cites 'spurious shining stories' about project purposes as a major part of the problem. These give an upbeat 'modernist' view of the prospects without signalling the detailed implementation consequences and huge social costs incurred. National and state governments need to clarify competing policy frames and identify valid cause-and-effect relations. 'Policy frames' are essentially normative: they state and restate the problem(s) according to multiple existing assumptions and ideological themes and so provide an enabling 'frame' for policy advocacy or actual decision-making. They do not necessarily offer detailed analyses of specific behaviours in response to interventions, or of aims capable of realistic implementation (Rein and Schon 1994). DIDR policy, that is, should set realistic standards for performance in implementation rather than present impossible-to-achieve and necessarily controversial normative aims or 'shining stories'. Too frequently DIDR 'policy' is a jumble of frame confusions reflecting 'managerial' and 'movementist' positions at the extremes and many 'hazy' points in between these extremes, but managing, despite these frame controversies, to convey a sense of a unified field of study (Dwivedi 2002: 712). The frame controversies in the field of DIDR are maintained by a combination of gaps in information, mistrust and incommensurable knowledge systems. The chief of these are:

- representations of 'the project' as a unit of social order, minimising the importance of fundamental conflicts of interest over land acquisition;
- calculations of risk made by policy makers that are incommensurable with those made by displaced landholders;
- radical cynicism and mistrust between planners and the displaced;
- an official or semitechnical 'DIDR' and 'R&R' language that serves to obscure the interrelation of different knowledge systems and unequal power relations;
- gaps in information about existing resource rights and use;
- appraisal methods that are biased; and
- lack of agreed benchmarks or standards for rights, entitlements and sustainable assets.

Each of these seven sources of controversy, confusion and lack of clarity, and their inter-relationships, will now be discussed.

In the research interviews with policy makers in Orissa we found that infrastructure development projects were accepted as 'modern' and 'inevitable'. The policy makers agreed that displacement problems could be severe; but they also implied, despite their evident sympathy with DPs, that DIDR had to be resolved or tolerated as a second-order problem since projects are self-evidently 'needed' – that is, the projects themselves are 'first order'. The best that can happen to minimise disruption and displacement is to introduce modifications or delays in time. This was a general response of policy makers in all our studies. The discourse or policy frame about displacement is predominantly about the engineering of change and the match or mismatch between the engineering of concrete, earthworks and metal, and suitable social engineering remedies. *The discourse is about projects as units of social order with 'internalities' and 'externalities', and in which displacement's role is seen as a relatively powerless externality.*

The institutionalisation of contradictory policy frames leads to considerable cynicism, even if this is expressed in diplomatic terms. This was most evident in the case of schemes for non-land-based livelihood (NLBL) creation. One very senior GoI administrator we interviewed admitted that, at the time of agreeing to the project, it was always necessary to promise a range of alternative employment, income generation, new businesses and trades without knowing exactly how this would be achieved. Administrators have to rely on the passage of time to solve the problem through the progressive attenuation of the burden of DPs' complaints. He argued that there was no alternative since managers know that nonfarming jobs cannot easily be created, yet that they have to be promised.

The cynicism of planners and administrators may be matched by the reluctance of displaced people – whose skills, occupational experience and social status have hitherto been restricted to their sphere of life as cultivators – to engage in project-sponsored trade or manufacturing. In project planning terms the obvious solution to major land loss and land scarcity is to help create NLBLs. In the Orissa results we found that solutions and mechanisms were already there – in theory. Reasonably substantial grants can be made to DPs when they have identified alternative means of employment or business. Projects can help identify a list of possible NLBLs; and DPs are encouraged to make proposals and to request start-up grants for specific needs of equipment, premises or other start-up costs. Very few administrative problems or delays were encountered in processing the grant applications; almost anything that looked more or less practical could be funded on receipt of a certificate of intending or actual purchase.

We were greatly surprised, therefore, at the DPs' unwillingness to request support for NLBL grants or to express interest in NLBL activities. Discussion of the greater or lesser feasibility of particular individual NLBLs (for example, the profitability of a rickshaw hire business or a shop) did not even arise; very few initiatives emerged from the DPs, even when NGOs were promoting opportunities and ideas alongside the project-implementing agencies (PIAs). The only exception to this lack of DP initiative or response to PIA and NGO offers of help concerned the purchase of land; there is usually no reluctance to seek help with identifying alternative land, only a shortage of suitable purchases.

Initially, the research team was hard pressed to understand this lack of interest in taking up offers of help to secure alternative income-generating activity, especially as DPs do respond to their enforced unemployment as farmers by taking construction and other labouring jobs. We think the most likely explanation lies in the credibility gap between policy practitioners and the DPs in the context of *the many perceived risks, especially including the perceived uncertainty of planning and policy back-up, when moving from agricultural to nonfarming businesses and small enterprises.* In comparison, the movement from own-account farming to construction wage labour is seen as less risky. The many failures of the policy process have created such disbelief among the DPs that no solutions can be trusted, and so none emerge. In other words, *cynicism on the one side is matched by radical mistrust on the other.*

Moreover, there is often insufficient appreciation by project planners of the differences in timescale between the evolution of the engineering components and the emergence of new economic activity. DPs will not attempt to start NLBLs of any kind until they have re-established their houses and basic facilities. As they frequently experience such high levels of delay in the community resettlement process and in receiving specific facilities, their frustration and anger grow to the extent that they are unable to reconcile their survival priorities with the timescales of the R&R scheme. DPs, faced with the intense daily pressures of finding food and their other survival needs, do not want to take risks with their scarce time or possibly commit their own very limited financial resources, with the unacceptable partners that many project authorities have proved to be. Wage labour is often a less risky way of securing food supplies. Adventures by ex-small-scale cultivators into the relatively unknown and uncertain worlds of trade and transport business usually demand new skills and a substantial shift in social identity. This adventure can often only succeed, even with a grant, when an agency will help, quickly and flexibly, to smooth the transition so that the DP household does not starve as it adjusts to land loss.

The potential for linking economic growth in the specific sector creating, and ultimately responsible for, the infrastructure improvements causing the displacements on the one hand, with the linked economic rehabilitation of the DPs on the other, is often not realised, at least in eastern India.[4] For example, the considerable theoretical potential to build rental housing in order to accommodate employees of industrial plants requiring land acquisition has never been grasped (even though it is sometimes mentioned in consultations with those likely to be displaced), because the parastatals sponsoring the development quickly build their own 'housing colonies', acquiring further land to do so, and establish, in effect, a dual economy and society. The opportunity to develop intensive horticulture or dairying to feed the housing colonies or nearby towns using smaller, possibly irrigated, land plots has also not been seized, because of the combined inertia and credibility gaps experienced as a result of the poor relations between the PIA and the combination of DPs and other PAPs. The spirit of active partnership and joint participation in rehabilitating disrupted livelihoods is simply missing, even if it has been promised on paper to satisfy the funding body's procedures.

The gaps in understanding and credibility on both sides surface continually in the very *language of R&R* and rights to land. There are strong arguments – both in terms of equity and in terms of economic functioning and efficiency – in favour of incorporating, within PAP impacts and hence DIDR policy, both customary and formally legal rights in land on a comparable basis. In the communities of tribal people and others at greatest risk from displacement, formal legal tenure rights are not always privileged over customary tenure. Indeed, it is customary tenure that has the key place in terms of everyday access to, and use of, land and natural resources. Yet the language of project planning almost always uses the term 'encroachers' instead of 'customary right-holders' when there is prima facie evidence that the second term may be far more accurate. 'Encroacher' is privileged as a term in most policy frames for use as a pre-emptive assertion of actual or potential government and corporate claims on land. Unsubstantiated, and usually ill-founded, allegations of encroachment are made in India despite the fact that India was one of the first countries to ratify ILO Convention 107, which governs the protection of indigenous and tribal people and has measures protecting 'habitual territories' and removal of people from them. Research is continuing on the possible use of the ILO Convention and other human rights codes to create benchmarks for use in developing programme norms and in specifying the social protection tasks for junior DIDR staff. If policy makers at all levels could be taught to think in terms of overlapping systems of rights and entitlements, rather than of 'the government's domain' and of 'encroachers', the credibility gaps between them and DPs would reduce.

One obvious way of increasing the clarity of DIDR policy frames is through *more finely grained, locally specific knowledge,* especially when the knowledge gained directly taps the perspectives of the displaced people themselves. The emphasis in India on 'the government's domain' and the administrative fear of 'encroachments' of state property means that officials are reluctant to record what have been long-standing, tolerated, customary uses of 'vacant' state lands, or to calculate the likely costs arising from planned displacement of the livelihoods these lands have supported, lest local surveys help turn tolerated uses into 'rights'. We did find some cases, however – for example, in the Calcutta metropolitan area – where administrators settled land acquisition cases by tacitly recognising long-standing usage and livelihood entitlements through help with informal compensation but had to maintain, formally, that they were doing no such thing. This was hardly an issue in 1894 when the Land Acquisition Act was enacted. At that time major displacements were few and compensation payments could more readily be assumed to provide all necessary residential and livelihood alternatives by providing adequate purchasing power in nonpressured markets. Now there is a consistent gap between compensation levels and market prices for replacement land in contemporary eastern India. This arises in part because farmers try to avoid taxes and so consistently underdeclare land prices, but also because of the large scale of project displacements; the hunger, on the part of the PIAs, for residential as well as 'industrial' land; and the inflation of prices in surrounding areas immediately after a project is announced. Politicians and administrators have to hear many individual complaints as a result and, in effect, acknowledge in so doing that the probably valid entitlements of citizens cannot be met through compensation. Yet we lack any very precise information about the gaps in prices or entitlements involved. Administrators are usually more fearful of infringing the government's domain and entitlements than they are of the accuracy of just settlements.

Frame controversies are compounded by *unexamined assumptions in appraisal methods*. Pearce (1999) notes that the main manuals used for international project appraisal do not address compensation for displacement at all. Cost-benefit analysis theory requires only that project benefits more than compensate for losses; it does not require any actual transfers from gainers to losers. Scrutiny of costs tends to relate to *private* costs rather than the wider costs to livelihood and the disarticulation of communities and is, in the case of resettlement components, often made in haste or hope. Most importantly valuation methods in use do not take account of 'the fundamental asymmetry' between the value of the sudden and often irreversible losses of well-being experienced by DPs and the value of gains in well-being experienced by beneficiaries in the region or nation at large – for example, electricity consumers or established irrigation water users (Pearce 1999: 57, 69). Greater clarification of the policy here would involve a willingness to specify the value of aversions to loss of livelihood and home. At present we are left with frame controversies and conflicts between those who have a modernisation agenda and those who have an agenda of social protection, and *without benchmarks to use in clarifying the arguments*.

A key aim at the national or 'hilltop' level should be to create a single vision of the problem. The vision must be sufficiently broad to offer the chance of a single problem-solving system. If there is to be clear policy and concerted action there must also be a functioning, integrated collection of parts around a common purpose. This common vision must be capable of lifting the level of the debate beyond the initially inevitable policy controversies of, for example, 'projects versus people-centred development', 'efficiency versus disruption' or 'managerial DIDR' versus 'movementist DIDR'.

Cernea (1997b, 2000) advocates and details a 'risks and reconstruction' model capable of application to all cases of human displacement, whether development-induced or not. It has been applied to a large number of countries and project cases (Cernea and McDowell 2000), including DIDR in Orissa (Mahapatra 1999). It thus recommends itself as a potential reconciling framework for DIDR policy controversies. It takes the range of risks of impoverishment known to be associated with major land acquisition for development projects and makes a systematic categorisation and analytical review of them. The model is based on the proposition that the many risks can become cumulative and self-reinforcing if left unattended; that potential losses can vary greatly in degree; and that impoverishment risks are reversible if understood in time. Given the generally poor success rates in the sector, this last claim seems unduly optimistic. The model appears to imply that 'risks' are broadly commensurable and a more or less common ground of assessment is achievable. The 'fundamental asymmetry' in loss and gain referred to by Pearce (1999: 57) is not highlighted, although not ignored either. The emphasis on commensurable risks and reversibility may weaken the framework's appeal to community groups opposing displacement and to NGOs that support them or publicise their cause and that have many previous cases of implementation failure in mind.

'Sustainable development' is a vision that may generate an alternative benchmark. Intergenerational equity, and thus sustainability into the next generation, requires that the asset base of the poor should not decline as a result of development. Increasing the capital base of poor people gives them the ability to develop further. Sustainable development implies treating resettlement as a development opportunity. Pearce (1999: 59) notes that German environmental law requires the creation of equivalent environmental assets to replace any assets being lost through development. There is a theoretical possibility of creating equivalent social assets to replace those lost through community and household disruption. We suggest the comparable concept for compensatory social assets might be thought of as 'equivalent and safeguarded social assets' (ESSA). It may not only be a theoretical possibility. A very senior administrator in Orissa proposed such an idea to us, informally and in concrete terms, in our enquiries. He suggested that a project should, well ahead of its own construction works, acquire a bank of (a) small pocket(s) of rain-fed land, pay for the irrigation needed to convert it/them into viable arable land and then allocate small, intensively farmed plots and training to a group of selected DPs instead of monetary compensation. His experience as a district administrator told him that sufficient rain-fed land was available: lack of research into the feasibility of its development and the administrative mechanisms that would be needed was the key constraint. Without such prior, detailed, applied investigations, no one in the administration could risk adopting the idea. But if it succeeded it could provide a way of breaking though the current impasse. We were urged to examine the issue as a practical contribution to the questions raised by DIDR policy practices.

In both India and Uganda political and local contexts suggest that a human rights or entitlements approach may also be a suitable way to clarify DIDR policy. The Morse and Berger *Independent Review* (1992) for the Sardar Sarovar project drew attention to the need for recognition of human rights standards in the process of displacement and resettlement. The National Human Rights Commission (NHRC) in India called attention, in 2000, to 'the need to bring human rights centre-stage' (Justice M.N. Venkatachaliah) and recommended the study of human rights in the school curriculum. If the NHRC were able to review DIDR projects, the Commission could authoritatively judge the standards appropriate to the rights of tribal and other landholders and to the administration of criminal justice at the time of eviction by police and the PIAs. Their standards could be used, by civil society organisations, for example, to monitor implementation work. The UN institutions have increasingly turned to human rights perspectives when designing interventions to protect communities from the worst consequences of 'forced evictions'. The human and cultural rights benchmark starts from the asymmetry and initial likely incommensurability of land loss. For the communities losing land, there is loss of livelihood niches, some loss of food security, loss of home and loss of cultural continuity. Any failure of the project authorities to provide alternatives to these entitlements means a violation of rights. On the other hand, the project authorities usually require outright and timely possession and low costs of development in order to forge ahead with their sectoral development task. This suggests that asymmetry and incommensurability are built into the project's land acquisition from the start. Recognition that there are overlapping and conflicting systems of national law, universal rights, and national and local citizen entitlements that have to be recorded, reconciled and negotiated, may lead to greater clarity and less controversy than those methods that place too much trust in formal policy statements and vague implementation chains. If PAPs and PIAs are both fully aware of the legal rights and national and customary entitlements that are in conflict it ought to be possible, in theory, to design the best compromises available and to 'double-design' the administrative teamwork and public consultations needed to negotiate rehabilitation solutions.

Conclusion

Policy and implementation practices are very vulnerable to the decay of common purpose and to breaks in the many chains linking those making decisions with those taking their effects into their lives. Perhaps the only foolproof mechanism for ensuring a higher level of success is to ensure that a common understanding/vision of aims is maintained; and that successive levels of subordinates are held accountable to it. Clarification of policy frames 'on the hill' is essential to begin the process of standard setting, but ensuring compliance to whatever R&R standards are chosen throughout the whole system, including at field level, is essential. Perhaps compliance could be gained in ways similar to those used to secure compliance with environmental standards in Orissa. For the last decade at least in India, new mining developments have required clearance from the environmental and forest conservation authorities at state level. Orissa has effectively condoned productive mining development with suspected adverse environmental impacts on forest land by ignoring certain strictures of Central Government. Central Government has now given notice that the state will be made to comply by holding the Orissa Cabinet Secretary personally liable to prosecution for any variations from the standards set. The only way for the Cabinet Secretary to remove the liability is to notify the Chief Minister and, by due process, to pass the liability onto the State Cabinet.

If high quality standards in displacement and restitution in DIDR were stated in terms of PAPs' clear rights and entitlements and officials' accountabilities, then perhaps similar mechanisms to those used in the environmental field to ensure compliance could be used to enforce them. The credibility gaps in DIDR policy practice at present are sufficiently daunting that anything less seems unlikely to work.

Notes

1. Alan Rew directed the research and is responsible for this chapter's main conclusions; Eleanor Fisher investigated the east Africa case studies; Balaji Pandey and Alan Rew researched the eastern India case studies.
2. Findings appeared in Rew et al. (2000) – a review prepared for the Economic and Social Research Unit (ESCOR) and the Research Programme on DIDR organised by the Refugees Studies Centre at the University of Oxford. An earlier version of this chapter was given, as Paper 00599, at the 10th World Congress of Rural Sociology, Rio de Janeiro, Brazil, in August 2002.
3. Much useful advice and comment was received at the RSP workshops from Chris de Wet, Elizabeth Colson, Warren Waters, S. Parasuraman, Dolores Koenig and Tony Oliver-Smith. Follow-up fieldwork in the two regions has been funded by the Centre for Development Studies (CDS) and as part of 'Social Development

Research Capacity' work (also funded by the Department for International Development (DfID)) between CDS, Swansea and the Institute for Socio-Economic Development (ISED), Bhubaneswar. Alan Rew and Balaji Pandey gratefully acknowledge discussions on the management of DIDR in eastern India with D. Bandopadhyay, Partha Chatterjee and Satish Agnihotri.

4. The integration of physical resettlement with economic and social rehabilitation planning has been a feature of some of the DIDR experience in China, so that the link can be far more than only a theoretical possibility.

References

Asif, M. 2000. 'Why Displaced Persons Reject Project Resettlement Colonies'. *Economic and Political Weekly*, 10 June.

Bandyopadhyay, D. 1999. 'Industrialisation and Sustainability in the Tribal Belt'. *Mainstream*, pp. 18–21. September.

Borzel, T. 1998. 'Organising Babylon: On the Different Conceptions of Policy Networks'. *Public Administration*, 76: 253–73.

Cernea, M.M. 1988. *Involuntary Resettlement in Development Projects: Policy Guidelines in World Bank-financed Projects*. World Bank Technical Papers, 80. Washington DC: The World Bank.

———— 1993a. 'Anthropological and Sociological Research for Policy Development on Population Resettlement'. In M.M. Cernea and S.E. Guggenheim (eds). *Anthropological Approaches to Resettlement*, pp. 13–38. Boulder CO: Westview Press.

———— 1993b. 'The Crafting of Policy on Population Resettlement'. *Knowledge and Policy: The International Journal of Knowledge Transfer and Utilisation*, 6(3/4): 176–200.

———— 1997a. 'African Involuntary Population Resettlement in a Global Context, Environment Department'. *Social Assessment Series 045*. Washington DC: The World Bank.

———— 1997b. 'The Risks and Reconstruction Model for Resettling Displaced Populations'. *World Development*, 25(10): 1569–88.

———— 1999. 'Development's Painful Social Costs: Introductory Study'. In S. Parasuraman (ed.). *The Development Dilemma: Displacement in India*, pp. 1–31. London: Macmillan.

———— 2000. 'Risks, Safeguards and Reconstruction: A Model for Population Displacement and Resettlement'. In M.M. Cernea and C. McDowell (eds). *Risks and Reconstruction: Experiences of Resettlers and Refugees*, pp. 11–55. Washington DC: The World Bank.

Cernea, M.M. and C. McDowell (eds). 2000. *Risks and Reconstruction: Experiences of Resettlers and Refugees*. Washington DC: The World Bank.

Dwivedi, R. 2002. 'Models and Methods in Development-induced Displacement'. *Development and Change*, 33: 709–32.

Fernandes, W. and V. Paranjpye (eds). 1997. *Rehabilitation Policy and Law in India: A Right to Livelihood*. New Delhi: Indian Social Institute.

Fisher, E. 2002. 'Forced Resettlement, Rural Livelihoods and Wildlife Conservation Along the Ugalla River in Tanzania'. In D. Chatty and M. Colchester (eds). *Conservation and Mobile Indigenous Peoples: Displacement, Forced Settlement, and Sustainable Development*, pp. 119–41. New York, Oxford: Berghahn Books.

Gow, D.D. and E.R. Morss. 1988. 'The Notorious Nine: Critical Problems in Project Implementation'. *Review of African Political Economy*, 16: 1399.

Hill, M. (ed.). 1993. *The Policy Process: A Reader*. London: Harvester-Wheatsheaf.

India, Government of. 1989. *Report of the Commissioner for Scheduled Castes and Scheduled Tribes. 29th Report*. Delhi.

Jain, R.B. 1997. 'Managing Public Policy in India: The Implementation Gap'. *Indian Journal of Public Administration*, 43: 345–61.

Kurian, P.A. 1996. 'A Gender Evaluation of World Bank Policies on Involuntary Displacement: Implications for Environmental Sustainability'. *Asia Pacific Journal on Environment and Development*, 3: 15–28.

Leckie, S. 1994. 'Forced Evictions'. *Environment and Urbanization*, 6: 131–46.

Lipsky, M. 1980. *Street-level Bureaucracy: Dilemmas of the Individual in Public Services*. New York: Russell Sage Foundation.

Mahapatra, L.K. 1999. *Resettlement, Impoverishment and Reconstruction in India: Development for the Deprived*. Delhi: Vikas.

Marsh, E. and C. Kego Laker. 1999. *Land Act Implementation Study (Annex 3: Social Impact Appraisal)*. Final Report for DfID, 6 September.

Mathur, H.M. and D. Marsden (eds). 1998. *Development Projects and Impoverishment Risks: Resettling Project-affected People in India*. New Delhi: Oxford University Press.

Morse, B. and T.R. Berger. 1992. *Sardar Sarovar: The Report of the Independent Review*. Ottawa: Resource Futures International Inc.

Oliver-Smith, A. 1996. 'Fighting for a Place: The Policy Implications of Resistance to Resettlement'. In C. McDowell (ed.). *Understanding Impoverishment: The Consequences of Development-induced Displacement*, pp. 77–97. Providence RI, Oxford: Berghahn Books.

Orissa, Government of. 1994. *Orissa: Resettlement and Rehabilitation of Project Affected Persons Policy*. Government of Orissa: Department of Water Resources.

Oxfam. 1998. 'Safeguarding Standards in Resettlement: Oxfam's Recommendations on the Proposed Revision to the World Bank's Policy on Involuntary Resettlement'. Unpublished policy paper, Oxfam U.K. and Ireland Policy Department.

Parasuraman, S. 1999. *The Development Dilemma: Displacement in India*. London: Macmillan.

Pearce, D. 1999. 'Methodological Issues in the Economic Analysis for Involuntary Resettlement Operations'. In M.M. Cernea (ed.). *The Economics of Involuntary Resettlement: Questions and Challenges*, pp. 50–82. Washington DC: The World Bank.

Pressman, J.I. and A. Wildavsky. 1973. *Implementation*. Berkeley: University of California Press.

Purcell, R. and A. Babumba-Kyeyune. 1999. *Land Act Implementation Study (Annex 2: Land Fund Appraisal)*. Final Report for DfID, 6 September.

Rein, M. and D.A. Schon. 1994. *Frame Reflection: Toward the Resolution of Intractable Policy Controversies*. New York: Basic Books.

Rew, A. 1996. 'Policy Implications of the Involuntary Ownership of Resettlement Negotiations: Examples from Asia of Resettlement Practice'. In C. McDowell (ed.). *Understanding Impoverishment: The Consequences of Development-induced Displacement*, pp. 201–21. Providence RI, Oxford: Berghahn Books.

———— 2003. 'Tapping the Bell at Governance Temple: Project Implementation as Moral Narrative'. In P.Q. Van Ufford and A.K. Giri (eds). *A Moral Critique of Development: In Search of Global Responsibilities*, pp. 118–36. London: Routledge.

Rew, A., E. Fisher and B. Pandey. 2000. *Addressing Policy Constraints and Improving Outcomes in Development-induced Displacement and Resettlement Projects*. Unpublished report, Refugee Studies Centre, University of Oxford.

Roy, A. 1999. *The Cost of Living*. London: Flamingo.

Sengindo, J. 1995. *The Need for Resettlement Policy in Developing Countries: A Case of Uganda*. Mawazo, Uganda: Makerere University Press.

Stewart, J. 1996. 'A Dogma of Our Times: The Separation of Policy-making and Implementation'. *Public Money and Management*, 16(3): 33–40.

Thomas, J.W. and M.S. Grindle. 1990. 'After the Decision: Implementing Policy Reforms in Developing Countries'. *Review of African Political Economy*, 18: 1167–75.

Uganda, Government of. 1995. *Resettlement Policy and Institutional Capacity Building for Resettlement Planning in Uganda*. Report, Office of the Prime Minister.

UNCHR. 1999. *United Nations Centre for Human Rights: Fact Sheet No. 25, Forced Evictions and Human Rights*. http://www.unhchr.ch/html/menu6/2/fs25.htm: United Nations Sub-commission on Prevention of Discrimination and Protection of Minorities.

Villadsen, S. and F. Lubanga (eds). 1996. *Democratic Decentralisation in Uganda: A New Approach to Local Governance*. Kampala: Fountain Publishers.

Weber, M. 1947. *The Theory of Social and Economic Organisation*. Glencoe IL: Free Press.

World Bank. 1980. *Social Issues Associated with Involuntary Resettlement in Bank-financed Projects*. Operational Manual Statement 2.33. Washington DC: The World Bank.

———— 1990. *Involuntary Resettlement*. Operational Directive 4.30. Washington DC: The World Bank.

———— 1994. *Resettlement and Development: The Bankwide Review of Projects Involving Involuntary Resettlement 1986–1993*. Washington DC: The World Bank.

4

International Law and Development-induced Displacement and Resettlement

Michael Barutciski

Introduction

In referring to various legal problems associated with development-induced displacement and resettlement (DIDR), the former Senior Vice-President of the World Bank has noted that the 'scholarly literature on resettlement, to which sociologists and social anthropologists have made the main contributions, has by and large overlooked such legal aspects' (Shihata 1993: 42). A decade later, the comment continues to be relevant. This chapter attempts to contribute to filling this gap by exploring the role of international law in situations of DIDR. International legal norms are analysed in order to clarify the particular protection needs of persons displaced by development projects and to highlight accessible legal remedies.

The chapter begins with an examination of the features that distinguish DIDR from other forms of forced migration. This is followed by a presentation of the international legal norms that are supposed to provide protection to persons affected by DIDR. Given the frequent problems of abuse in development projects, various strategies of remedial action available in terms of international law are also explored. The chapter concludes with a prescriptive analysis that seeks to improve the international involvement in development-induced displacement and to increase the responsibility of borrowers in ensuring respect for human rights.

Legal Distinctions between DIDR and Other Types of Forced Migration

Throughout the twentieth century, states have committed themselves to respect a wide range of legally binding rules concerning persons who flee persecution or conflict situations. Despite these developments, the areas of international law that specifically address the plight of forced migrants do not really provide legally binding rules that guarantee distinct protection for people who have been displaced by development projects. The norms that protect people affected by development projects have to be found in related fields of international law that concern human rights more generally.

International refugee law concerns the plight of foreigners who have fled persecution and who seek protection in a host country. International humanitarian law concerns the protection of populations caught in armed conflicts. Specific norms that have recently been drafted regarding internally displaced persons (IDPs) have not been transformed into legally binding rules and in any case provide only a limited number of provisions directly applicable to persons displaced by development projects.[1]

Indeed, the relevance of the aforementioned areas of international law to DIDR has its limitations. The contribution of international refugee law and the debate on IDPs in terms of understanding DIDR is limited because they deal generally with violent conflict or politically motivated persecution. Political or conflict-related violence is not necessarily a characteristic of DIDR. Yet it would be a mistake to ignore the fact that displacement resulting from development projects can sometimes be related intimately to political tensions or conflicts within states. Given that numerous examples of displacement resulting from development projects occur in areas affected by armed conflict, it is clear that a connection with larger political tensions can be a significant factor in displacement. For example, the large-scale displacement of Ugandans resulting from the European Commission-financed conservation project near the Ugandan-Congolese border (Kibale Forest Reserve and Game Corridor) (Oxfam 1996a) and the expropriations relating to the Chad-Cameroon Oil and Pipeline project co-financed by the World Bank[2] cannot be analysed seriously without considering the ongoing armed conflicts affecting these countries.

Although the IDP guidelines recently proposed by the UN Commission on Human Rights (UNCHR) may not address comprehensively situations of DIDR, they can be an instrument used by international or local actors to attract attention and mobilise public opinion in relation to human rights violations and displacement. Indeed, several of the provisions explicitly mention development projects (paragraph 6(2–3)), while others contain norms that are clearly relevant (paragraph 7(3)).

Yet the relevance of these analogous forms of protection should not be overstated. Refugee protection standards are restricted in nature because they deal with specific problems related to the treatment of foreigners. As a subcategory of immigration law, refugee law addresses the particular needs of endangered foreigners who are trying to survive in host countries where their rights relating to integration are limited. These are not the concerns usually associated with DIDR. The kinds of rights granted to refugees would not make sense for displaced persons who are still in their country of origin and who expect to be compensated for the hardships that they have endured in the name of eminent domain law. The rights that refugees receive include basic socio-economic entitlements that allow them to survive in a foreign country where they do not have citizenship rights. These include, for example, rights related to gainful employment, welfare, identity and travel documents.[3] There is no point in insisting that a government grant typical refugee entitlements such as partial rights to employment or access to certain types of welfare benefits when it is responsible for having internally displaced its own people in the first place. These rights would be redundant if granted to citizens in their own state because they are already supposed to benefit from the highest protection standards accorded by states. The formal reaffirmation of the existence of protection standards will not address the reality of abuse in these cases. Due to the fact that persons displaced by development projects are generally not asylum seekers in foreign countries, they should benefit from the higher standards normally guaranteed to citizens in their own state. Clearly, the internal migration dimension of DIDR makes refugee law an imperfect source of analogy in terms of protection standards.[4]

Although some social scientists may suggest that the reality of displacement is the same whether one is internally or externally displaced, the above analysis helps to understand certain specific features of DIDR. The root causes of the flight and protection needs of refugees and IDPs are not generally the same as those relating to DIDR situations. This is one of the reasons why it is inappropriate to compare the work of the Office of the United Nations High Commissioner for Refugees with that of the World Bank (cf. Pettersson 2002). The latter is supposed to provide financial loans to governments for projects that will supposedly lead to greater economic good despite the possible displacement of populations, while the former is supposed to provide charitable emergency protection and assistance to refugees in countries of asylum. These are fundamentally different mandates.

While conceptual models that emphasise the reconstruction of livelihoods are appropriate for DIDR situations that may involve infringements of human rights law, they are not necessarily appropriate for refugee emergencies that are by definition situations in which the victims' human rights are violated. If development-based displacement is justified as a necessary hardship endured for a supposedly greater economic good, it can be anticipated that the expectations of the displacees will be higher than those of refugees deliberately victimised by war or persecutory policies. It is difficult to draw the parallels between these two distinct problems in the manner suggested by some social scientists[5] and it would be overly ambitious to insist that emergency refugee assistance is intended to restore the livelihoods of victims of persecution to their pre-flight levels.[6] Yet this reconstruction of livelihood would be precisely a reasonable expectation of a person displaced by a development project.

The preceding analysis suggests that a clear distinction should be drawn between the refugee regime and situations of internal displacement, and even more so when the internal displacement is caused by development projects (cf. Leckie 2002). As explained above, refugee protection is essentially about promoting asylum in foreign countries. Action on behalf of IDPs is basically about humanitarian intervention in troubled countries. These two activities are fundamentally distinct from the problems of DIDR. The latter focus on internal state problems relating to situations of forced eviction that occur for an ostensible greater economic good.

The preceding points highlight several features specific to DIDR. Development-induced displaced persons (DIDPs) generally remain in their country of origin and their legal protection should theoretically be guaranteed by their state's government. In terms of the international state system, the government is responsible for ensuring that the rights of people under its jurisdiction are respected. These rights include entitlements under the domestic legal system and international human rights law. The complexities of DIDR result specifically because the government that is responsible for the displacement is also responsible for ensuring the protection of DIDPs.

This clarification of the nature of the problem can help in establishing the appropriate legal protection. Unlike other forms of coerced migration, the protection needs of DIDPs appear to focus on three aspects: planned resettlement, compensation and rehabilitation. The chapter will explore the contribution of international law in relation to these protection needs.

DIDR Protection Norms in International Human Rights Law

A rights-based approach to development is grounded in the acceptance of human rights standards as an important basis of development policy and the recognition that human rights accountability can be used to support development activities. The meaning of the term 'rights' may be varied, so a certain amount of caution is necessary when dealing with this term in a legal sense. For example, some 'rights' are meant to be immediately enforceable binding commitments, whereas others only indicate a desire to achieve certain types of behaviour in the future.

To a large extent, a rights-based approach to development requires effective legal enforcement (ODI 1999). Legal action that is limited to monitoring respect for rights can nevertheless help in contributing to the promotion of a culture of compliance. Related activities of publicity and advocacy also contribute to create conditions that favour the implementation of rights. The overall objective is to encourage a rights-based approach that is founded on participatory processes which allow greater public involvement and which can empower disadvantaged people.

All human beings benefit from the protection found in international human rights law. This area of international law is basically concerned with imposing limitations on state sovereignty in the sense that it requires populations within the jurisdiction of states to be treated in conformity with internationally agreed standards. While DIDPs do not benefit from a specific and comprehensive, legally binding protection regime in international law, they do benefit from well established general human rights standards that apply to all human beings. These guarantees are meant to provide them with basic protection against arbitrary detention,[7] cruel or degrading treatment,[8] torture,[9] forced labour,[10] genocide[11] and violations of the right to liberty and security of the person.[12] Even if state authorities may sometimes legally evict people, the manner in which they carry out evictions has to respect certain fundamental rules to which these states have formally consented.

Given that states have not yet signed legally binding international instruments that provide specific and comprehensive rights to DIDPs, certain, more general, rights found in international treaties have to be invoked in DIDR situations in order to encourage a rights-based approach. The following section examines some of the more promising of these international legal provisions.

General Human Rights Norms

The 1966 International Covenant on Civil and Political Rights (ICCPR) and the 1966 International Covenant on Economic, Social and Cultural Rights (ICESCR)[13] are the two main treaties in international law that deal with general human rights protection. They both contain provisions that directly concern situations of DIDR.

Article 11(1) of the ICESCR provides the following:

> The States Parties to the present Covenant recognize the right of everyone to an adequate standard of living for himself and his family, including adequate food, clothing and housing, and to the continuous improvement of living conditions. The States Parties will take appropriate steps to ensure the realization

of this right, recognizing to this effect the essential importance of international co-operation based on free consent.

Article 12(1) of the ICCPR also stipulates that: 'Everyone lawfully within the territory of a State shall, within that territory, have the right to liberty of movement and freedom to choose his residence'.[14] Article 17(1) of the ICCPR further stipulates that: 'No one shall be subjected to arbitrary or unlawful interference with his privacy, family, home or correspondence, nor to unlawful attacks on his honour and reputation'.

Other guarantees from these two basic human rights treaties concerning the right to family life (ICESCR art. 10) and the right to education (ICESCR art. 13(1)) may also be relevant to DIDR. It is important to note that neither treaty includes a right to property,[15] although it is mentioned in the Universal Declaration of Human Rights.[16] The latter is a UN General Assembly resolution and not a legally binding treaty signed by states. It is also worth noting that few developing states have translated these international norms into domestic legislation or adopted such extensive legal provisions in their national legal systems. South Africa is one of those states and its constitution includes provisions that in many ways exceed the above protection guarantees.[17]

Given that abuses committed by state authorities against DIDPs often result from distinctions based on ethnic origins, the 1965 International Convention on the Elimination of All Forms of Racial Discrimination (CERD)[18] provides protection norms that can be used to prohibit such discriminatory treatment. Article 5 of the CERD stipulates the following.

States Parties undertake to prohibit and to eliminate racial discrimination in all its forms and to guarantee the right of everyone, without distinction as to race, colour, or national or ethnic origin, to equality before the law, notably in the enjoyment of the following rights: ... (d)(i) The right to freedom of movement and residence within the border of the State; ... (v) The right to own property alone as well as in association with others; ... (e) Economic, social and cultural rights, in particular: ... (iii) The right to housing.

DIDPs are often members of groups that have established traditional lifestyles on lands that they have used over long periods. If the groups can be recognised as 'indigenous',[19] then the norms of the International Labour Organisation (ILO) Convention No. 169 (Convention Concerning Indigenous And Tribal Peoples In Independent Countries) provide additional legal protection. Article 14 of the Convention states the following:

(1) The rights of ownership and possession of the peoples concerned over the lands which they traditionally occupy shall be recognised. In addition, measures shall be taken in appropriate cases to safeguard the right of the peoples concerned to use lands not exclusively occupied by them, but to which they

have traditionally had access for their subsistence and traditional activities. Particular attention shall be paid to the situation of nomadic peoples and shifting cultivators in this respect. (2) Governments shall take steps as necessary to identify the lands which the peoples concerned traditionally occupy, and to guarantee effective protection of their rights of ownership and possession.[20]

Most importantly, article 16 of ILO Convention No. 169 includes provisions that relate directly to DIDR and indigenous peoples:

(1) Subject to the following paragraphs of this Article, the peoples concerned shall not be removed from the lands which they occupy. (2) Where the relocation of these peoples is considered necessary as an exceptional measure, such relocation shall take place only with their free and informed consent. Where their consent cannot be obtained, such relocation shall take place only following appropriate procedures established by national laws and regulations, including public inquiries where appropriate, which provide the opportunity for effective representation of the peoples concerned. (3) Whenever possible, these peoples shall have the right to return to their traditional lands, as soon as the grounds for relocation cease to exist. (4) When such return is not possible, as determined by agreement or, in the absence of such agreement, through appropriate procedures, these peoples shall be provided in all possible cases with lands of quality and legal status at least equal to that of the lands previously occupied by them, suitable to provide for their present needs and future development. Where the peoples concerned express a preference for compensation in money or in kind, they shall be so compensated under appropriate guarantees. (5) Persons thus relocated shall be fully compensated for any resulting loss or injury.

It is worth noting that the above provisions regarding indigenous peoples impose duties of consultation rather than obligations for governments to obtain consent prior to enacting certain measures. Furthermore, the provisions do not specify the means or form of participation that is legally required in decision-making. Nonetheless, these provisions can offer a considerable degree of protection and represent the most progressive DIDR-related norms currently found in treaty law. Many states that have not ratified or acceded to the ILO Convention No. 169 continue to be bound by the ILO Convention No. 107 that it replaced. The latter provides comparable protection, although it is not as comprehensive. For example, article 12 of Convention No. 107 declares the following:

(1) The populations concerned shall not be removed without their free consent from their habitual territories except in accordance with national laws and regulations for reasons relating to national security, or in the interest of national economic development or of the health of the said populations. (2) When in such cases removal of these populations is necessary as an exceptional measure, they shall be provided with lands of quality at least equal to that of the

lands previously occupied by them, suitable to provide for their present needs and future development. In cases where chances of alternative employment exist and where the populations concerned prefer to have compensation in money or in kind, they shall be so compensated under appropriate guarantees. (3) Persons thus removed shall be fully compensated for any loss or injury.[21]

The preceding provisions relating to the treatment of indigenous peoples highlight the importance of encouraging a participatory approach to DIDR. The recently signed Convention on Access to Information, Public Participation in Decision-Making and Access to Justice in Environmental Matters[22] is the most far-reaching treaty that involves public participation on a subject related to DIDR. In establishing which members of the public have access to review by courts, the Convention refers to the term 'public concerned' with the following meaning: 'the public affected or likely to be affected by, or having an interest in, the environmental decision-making; for the purpose of this definition, non-governmental organizations promoting environmental protection and meeting any requirements under national law shall be deemed to have an interest' (article 2(5)).

This expansive notion of public participation and democracy in environmental issues reflects evolving models of governance in many societies. The ICCPR's article 25 also contains a provision relating directly to participation:

> Every citizen shall have the right and the opportunity, without any of the distinctions mentioned in article 2 and without unreasonable restrictions: (a) To take part in the conduct of public affairs, directly or through freely chosen representatives; (b) To vote and to be elected at genuine periodic elections which shall be by universal and equal suffrage and shall be held by secret ballot, guaranteeing the free expression of the will of the electors.

However, the leading case relating to this provision does not provide much support for encouraging public participation in decision-making. In *Mikmaq Tribal Society* v. *Canada*, the UN Human Rights Committee remarks that it 'must be beyond dispute that the conduct of public affairs in a democratic State is the task of representatives of the people, elected for that purpose, and public officials appointed in accordance with the law'.[23] The Committee elaborates:

> Although prior consultations, such as public hearings or consultations with the most interested groups, may often be envisaged by law or have evolved as public policy in the conduct of public affairs, article 25(a) cannot be understood as meaning that any directly affected group, large or small, has the unconditional right to choose the modalities of participation in the conduct of public affairs. That, in fact, would be an extrapolation of the right to direct participation by the citizens, far beyond the scope of article 25(a). (*ibid.*)

This interpretation suggests that states have considerable discretion in determining the content of the right to political participation.

Yet participatory measures have been included in development projects precisely to increase their legitimacy. This is particularly important when foreign-aided projects attempt to address the views of local inhabitants that are likely to be adversely affected.[24] Participatory procedures allow generally for greater acceptance of the project and help to enhance the capacities of governance. This is why the Convention on Access to Information, Public Participation in Decision-Making and Access to Justice in Environmental Matters explicitly refers to NGO involvement that may bring attention to issues that would otherwise be ignored by administrative authorities (who are often understaffed and have limited time to address problems affecting local populations). The knowledge, insights and expertise of NGOs working on development projects can be seen as parallel contributions to the decision-making process that supplements governmental actions in securing the interests of the affected populations. In this sense, public participation can be seen as encouraging economic efficiency.

By allowing DIDPs to participate in the various phases of a project, there is a greater probability that their protection needs will be addressed and that the project will be able to involve planned resettlement, along with effective compensation and rehabilitation. It is this type of participation that allowed the Cree Amerindians to contest various aspects of the James Bay Hydroelectric Project in the Canadian province of Quebec. As expressed in the following citation by a lawyer representing the Cree, the role of the courts in this case should not be underestimated:

> The courts heavily influenced the settlement of the claims of the Crees and Inuit of Northern Quebec arising from the James Bay hydroelectric project, and had a marked impact on the treatment of the environment by the builders of the project. There is yet another way in which the courts ultimately played an important part: through the recognition of rights and interests of the native people of Northern Quebec, the governments of Quebec and Canada were incited to address squarely the reorganization of some three-fifths of the province of Quebec through a new legal regime. Without the 15 November 1973 judgment of Mr Justice Albert Malouf of the Superior Court of Quebec, it is highly doubtful that the Crees and Inuit would have obtained the rights and benefits which they were subsequently acknowledged to have under the James Bay and Northern Quebec Agreement ... Had the Inuit and Indians completely failed in court, they would have been subject to the political mercy of the Quebec government led by Mr Bourassa, who in the fall of 1973 had just received an overwhelming mandate from the people of Quebec to proceed with the project. (O'Reilly 1985: 30)

Although the Cree had lost a crucial judgement,[25] the public debate created by the issue meant that the government authorities had to negotiate seriously with the Cree representatives if they wanted to proceed with the project (see Lassailly-Jacob 1983: 51).[26] The result was the signing of the James Bay and Northern Quebec Agreement (signed on 11 November 1975) in which the Cree consented to participate in the project, which ultimately led to minimal displacement of the local population. Within the context of the legal framework in which they participated, the Cree continued to contest aspects of the government's project and even contested certain aspects of the Agreement they had signed. Although these attempts met with limited judicial success,[27] access to effective legal recourse helped to increase pressure on government authorities, who felt obliged to abandon the second phase of their northern hydroelectric project centred around the Grande Baleine river (Mercier and Richot 1997).[28] From the Cree perspective, the legitimacy of the development projects were dependent on their participation and their consent. Whether governments are ready to proceed without the consent of the affected populations, the treatment and processes accorded to the latter will influence heavily the legitimacy of the project. This ethical issue is addressed at the end of the chapter.

The European regional human rights system provides additional norms that are useful in analysing DIDR. Although human rights law within the European Union (EU) is developing rapidly, less attention has been paid to the role of human rights in the external affairs of the EU. It is well established that activities of the European Commission (EC) should be conducted in conformity with basic human rights standards.[29] The European Court of Justice held in *Nold* v. *Commission* that it could not uphold measures incompatible with fundamental rights recognised by the constitutions of EC member states ([1974] ECR 491, 507). As pointed out recently by the European Parliament:

the promotion of human rights, the rule of law and democratic principles is now an integral part of the European Union's development policy (and, in particular, of ACP-EU cooperation, which is the most complete expression of that policy), and an essential priority component thereof.[30]

Although the EC has not adhered to the European Convention for the Protection of Human Rights and Fundamental Freedoms,[31] there are signs indicating a trend towards a fuller human rights competence of the EC in its external affairs. For example, co-operation agreements with third countries now include human rights clauses that can be used to suspend the agreements if human rights are not respected. The Maastricht Treaty, which amended the Treaty of Rome and established the European Union in 1992, provides in its article F(2) of Title I that the Union 'shall respect fundamental rights' found in the European Convention on Human Rights and the common constitutional traditions of member states 'as general principles of Community law'.

The European Development Fund (EDF) is the principal means by which the European Economic Community provides aid, concessionary finance and technical assistance to developing countries. Aid that is granted out of the EDF must be done in accordance with the provisions relating to human rights protection found in the Fourth ACP-EEC Convention (Fourth Lomé Convention).[32] Even if abusive evictions occur outside the scope of a project that is financed by the EDF, the human rights protection found in the Fourth Lomé Convention still applies if the evictions are financed with funds originating from the EDF. For example, the mass evictions of tens of thousands of people from the Kibale Game Corridor in Uganda during the spring of 1992 appear to violate similar provisions found in the Third Lomé Convention, regardless of whether they were explicitly included in the EDF-financed conservation project planning.

The European Parliament has also expressed its concern that agents and contractors of the EC should be aware of the relevant development guidelines and human rights principles. In paragraph 23 of the resolution regarding the establishment of a 'code of conduct for European enterprises operating in developing countries', the Parliament

[c]alls on the Commission to enforce the requirement that all private companies carrying out operations in third countries on behalf of the Union, and financed out of the Commission's budget or the European Development Fund, act in accordance with the Treaty on European Union in respect of fundamental rights, failing which such companies would not be entitled to continue to receive European Union funding, in particular from its instruments for assistance with investment in third countries; calls on the Commission to prepare a report on the extent to which private companies to which it awards contracts have been made aware of these obligations; further recognises that private companies acting as agents of the Commission in the field of development cooperation are already obliged to adhere to OECD standards concerning best aid practice and human rights and sustainable development principles enshrined in the Lomé Convention.[33]

DIDR-specific Guidelines

The most extensive developments in terms of international law and DIDR in recent years have resulted from self-imposed limitations made by certain lending agencies. If international lenders provide funding for development projects, then they are in a position to impose conditions that provide even more protection guarantees than the existing legally binding international instruments signed by states. To the extent that these lenders are accountable to organisations or constituencies concerned about human rights, they can require the recipient government to ensure that specific human rights norms are respected in DIDR situations. Ultimately, these lenders may even make loans dependent on such respect.

The resettlement guidelines drafted recently by a number of international organisations are the best example of this kind of progress. This example of 'soft law' has provided the most hope for improvements in the treatment of DIDPs at the international level. However, to the extent that some of these guidelines have been drafted by banks that provide financial loans within the context of their explicitly nonpolitical mandates,[34] they may lack the strong political mandate that is required to confront governments responsible for mistreating DIDPs.

The World Bank's Operational Policy (OP) 4.12 on Involuntary Resettlement, adopted in December 2001, is perhaps the most progressive international legal document relating specifically to DIDR. Along with Bank Procedure (BP) 4.12,[35] it replaces the Operational Directive 4.30 that constituted a leading protection document for project-affected people ever since its adoption in June 1990.[36]

The World Bank's guidelines as expressed in OP 4.12 require planned resettlement (para. 6), compensation (para. 6(a)(iii)) and rehabilitation (para. 2(c)) when displacement is absolutely necessary for the development project (para. 2(a)). The guidelines go beyond simple compensation in that they require measures that actually restore the living standard of project-affected people (PAPs). The right to rehabilitation is the protection that PAPs who do not benefit fully from compensation can receive in order to become established and economically self-sustaining.[37]

By focusing on the inclusion of a planned resettlement operation, the guidelines deal with displacement situations that can be expected to provide the most guarantees for displaced persons. If governments officially acknowledge that they are displacing some of their constituents, then there is a greater likelihood that the rights of DIDPs will be respected and that this will lead to conditions in which fair compensation is more easily achievable. Likewise, the ability to participate in the decision-making process (OP 4.12 para. 2(b)) and the recognition of compensation eligibility fundamentally changes the 'rights' situation of PAPs.

The importance of specific guarantees relating to compensation and rehabilitation cannot be overstated. Many development projects suffer precisely because local measures do not provide adequate compensation. The High Court of Tanzania's judgement on the Mkomazi Game Reserve Case[38] is an example in which inadequate compensation was awarded even when the judge ruled in favour of the pastoralist plaintiffs by accepting that they had customary land rights over the concerned wildlife conservation area.[39] The reluctance of judges to provide effective remedies is illustrated by the court's decision that an 'order for restoration would be impracticable' because the evictions had taken place years before the judgement.[40] Despite accepting that the pastoralists were treated with particular discrimination and that their evictions were carried out without prior court authorisation, the court simply asked the government to look for alternative land on which to resettle the pastoralists. This is an example of how compensation provisions can be almost irrelevant when they are not backed by genuine rehabilitation measures in practice.

Although '[t]he right of a State to exploit its natural resources and its right to take private property for public purposes, are universally recognized' (Shihata 1988: 63), there are many problems associated with the issue of compensation. Domestic laws that recognise the right of citizens to private property usually provide that no-one can be deprived of his/her property without fair or just compensation (see Escudero 1988: 3). This poses many basic questions regarding the meaning of 'just compensation' or the determination of the legal right to lost assets. Legal provisions relating to compensation are also often problematic in that they treat the displaced person as a willing seller. Since they do not take into account the coercive element that made the acquisition possible, the meaning of compensation is equated with the market value (or notional value in the market) (see, for example, Ramanathan 1996: 1488).

Most importantly, the majority of people displaced by development projects rarely have property rights that would allow compensation because they are in the lowest strata of the community. Rights relating to possession should therefore also be examined. Tenants and those who have not taken appropriate steps to acquire ownership through prescription are among the various types of possessors that need to be recognised. Yet domestic systems rarely provide for such refined and equitable treatment regarding compensation. Particular concern has to be paid to landless DIDPs who may lose their main source of income, even if they do not own property or do not have any rights of possession.

If community property exists instead of individual titles, then the legal aspects still have to be taken into account when addressing issues of identifying the landowners, the landless and the appropriate compensation for lost assets. Further problems regarding compensation as a legal means for addressing the problems inherent in acquisition are apparent when considering individual versus group rights. For example, notions of individual ownership do not address problems caused by displacement of whole communities. Acquisition laws are concerned essentially with individuals whose rights are to be acquired and they do not address the breakdown of communities or mass displacement. Provisions on compensation therefore ignore the damages caused by the fragmentation of communities, the breakdown of support structures and the increased susceptibility to exploitation that accompanies displacement. Elaborate compensation measures such as those proposed by the World Bank's guidelines can begin to address the problem.

The Organisation for Economic Co-operation and Development (OECD) has also produced progressive guidelines (OECD 1991) that focus on providing planned resettlement (para. 7), guarantees concerning compensation/rehabilitation (paras 6b and 7) and participation (para. 4) when displacement of local populations is unavoidable for development projects (para. 6a). The influential thirty member states of the OECD have committed themselves politically to respect these 'soft law' standards.

Attempts at producing nonbinding norms specifically addressing DIDR have also been made by the UNCHR. Indeed, its Sub-Commission on Prevention of Discrimination and Protection of Minorities has requested that an expert seminar be held on the practice of forced evictions 'with a view to developing comprehensive guidelines on forced evictions, including development-based displacement and forced evictions carried out in conjunction with international events'.[41] Although the request itself contains references to potentially distinct legal situations (forced evictions and development-based displacement), the expert seminar has produced a set of relatively comprehensive guidelines on the subject. The document entitled 'The Practice of Forced Evictions: Comprehensive Human Rights Guidelines on Development-based Displacement' (Geneva, 13 June 1997) focuses more on preventing forced evictions[42] and less on the resettlement guarantees that are the focus of the World Bank and OECD guidelines on DIDR. As a result, the document appears quite progressive regarding the issue of forced evictions,[43] while remaining less comprehensive than already existing human rights standards on resettlement issues.

DIDR Legal Action and Remedies at the International Level

The enunciation of protection norms can be an exercise of only limited value if it is not accompanied by an examination of the options available in case of violations. While many of the legally binding standards of international human rights law described above are relatively well developed and well known, the main problem lies in the area of enforcement. Can the rising awareness of human rights standards related to development projects lead to better enforcement of international norms? Is there sufficient political will on the part of various international actors to address seriously the frequent abuses associated with DIDR? This section explores legal strategies available at the international level when protection standards are not respected.

Current international developments suggest that there is an increasing tendency to lift the veil of national sovereignty to confront massive human rights abuses. Many recent examples of dramatic international involvement in domestic issues have been justified ostensibly on the grounds of human rights violations. In this context, the courageous work of NGOs that publicise abuses concerning development projects needs to be highlighted. In order to confront government or business actors who consider that the perceived economic benefits of development projects necessarily outweigh the human consequences of displacement, there is a need to mobilise the increasing number of international actors who have an interest in putting up a challenge.

Violations of human rights in DIDR situations can lead to public outcry and this can lead to political action.[44] For example, EU development-related activities governed by the Fourth Lomé Convention can be suspended by voting procedures in cases of human rights violations committed by third countries (Brandtner and Rosas 1998: 468, 489). Systematic violations of the general human rights outlined above can even be raised during an annual public debate in which governments and NGOs are allowed to identify country-specific situations that they believe require the attention of the UNCHR.[45] Although the Commission can theoretically pressure governments accused of systemic violations and even decide to conduct investigations,[46] the effectiveness of this public procedure has been limited (see, for example, Steiner and Alston 1996: 316). In 1970 the Commission also introduced a confidential procedure for human rights complaints that allows it to consider communications and government replies.[47] With the consent of the concerned government, this procedure can lead to the establishment of an ad hoc committee of investigation. Once again, however, the effectiveness of this procedure has been limited (see Shaw 1997: 227).

As mentioned earlier, one of the most fundamental tensions in DIDR results from the relationship between states and individuals. In order to acknowledge the basic principle of equality and sovereignty of states underlined in the UN Charter, international law generally recognises that states should be allowed to solve their internal problems within the confines of their own legal procedures before international mechanisms can be invoked. The existence of this 'exhaustion of local remedies' rule (Amerasinghe 1974: 3) is particularly important in DIDR situations and in the various attempts to obtain effective legal remedies at the international level. If genuine local remedies exist in practice, then they must be exhausted before international legal procedures can begin.

While international law has traditionally focused on states as the primary subjects, human rights law has gradually contributed to a conceptual evolution so that individual human beings have also become subjects. It is relatively clear that effective legal action related to DIDR at the international level relies on the availability of mechanisms that allow individual complaints. A legal procedure that incorporates the possibility for PAPs to lodge complaints can best protect their interests and create sufficient pressure so that respect for basic norms can be ensured.[48]

Several of the treaties described in the previous section have bodies that are meant to encourage enforcement. The ICCPR establishes a Human Rights Committee that administers or implements the rights found in the Covenant: its Optional Protocol[49] extends the competence of the Committee and allows it to consider individual communications to the Protocol that allege violations of the ICCPR by a state party. The Committee can consider individual complaints after all domestic remedies have been exhausted and then provide the relevant parties with a 'final view'. For example, if an individual alleges that a project involving DIDR has violated his/her right to liberty of movement or subjected him/her to arbitrary interference with his/her family or home, then according to article 4 of the Optional Protocol s/he can initiate a written proceeding and have the Committee examine the concerned state's 'written explanations or statements clarifying the matter'. Although the Committee's effectiveness is clearly handicapped by the fact that its 'views' are not legally binding decisions, it is a general UN human rights forum where violations that are not of a systematic nature can be addressed.

Part II of the International Convention on the Elimination of All Forms of Racial Discrimination also establishes a Committee of Experts that can examine reports and hear interstate complaints. This treaty-based body can hear individual petitions if the concerned state has made a declaration accepting the competence of the Committee to consider such confidential communications. For example, an individual can lodge a complaint if s/he feels discriminated against in relation to his/her right to freedom of movement, right to own property or right to housing. However, the provision came into effect at the end of 1982 (upon the tenth declaration) and less than two dozen states have accepted this individual complaints procedure to date.[50] This legal recourse remains relatively unexplored by actors concerned with DIDR.

Although it is not a treaty-implementing body that is authorised explicitly to consider individual complaints such as the two UN committees mentioned above, the Committee on Economic, Social and Cultural Rights has proven itself to be one of the UN bodies that is most serious in examining DIDR-related issues (UNCHR 1996:27). The Committee began operations in 1987 and it has focused basically on developing the rights found in the ICESCR, as well as holding states accountable through the examination of reports. It does this through deliberations during 'general discussion' days, the drafting of 'general comments' and the scrutiny of regular reports that are submitted by state parties.

Given that the Committee has elaborated extensively on the right to adequate housing found in article 11 of the ICESCR (see General Comment No. 4), creative methods to encourage its influence over other international bodies should be explored. For example, NGOs should be encouraged to present submissions to the Committee so that it informs agencies such as the World Bank about issues arising from the reports and provides them with recommendations in respect of article 22.[51] This has been attempted, for example, by Oxfam (1996b) in a submission concerning the World Bank and EC involvement in the Kibale Forest Reserve and Game Corridor evictions carried out in Uganda in the spring of 1992. The possibility for NGOs to recommend that the Committee seek reports from agencies such as the World Bank concerning the progress made on the right to adequate housing in respect of article 18 should also be explored.[52]

The Committee's ability to pressure governments on DIDR issues should not be underestimated. The type of reports elicited by its guidelines, its particular use of 'general comments' to develop the right to adequate housing and its examination of reports submitted by governments[53] have all contributed to making this body a forceful promoter of rights relating to DIDR. General Comment No. 2 illustrates the Committee's commitment to upholding human rights in DIDR situations:

> international agencies should scrupulously avoid involvement in projects which, for example ... promote or reinforce discrimination against individuals or groups contrary to the provisions of the Covenant, or involve large-scale evictions or displacement of persons without the provision of all appropriate protection and compensation ... Every effort should be made, at each phase of a development project, to ensure that the rights contained in the Covenant are taken duly into account.[54]

An expansion of its role should be explored by local and international actors interested in defending DIDPs. If an optional protocol that provides for a petition procedure is adopted, as proposed by the Committee (UNESC 1996), then the legal possibilities for people affected by development projects will increase significantly.

Violations of the provisions protecting indigenous peoples that are found in ILO Conventions 107 and 169 should be contested under the procedures found in the ILO Constitution. In many ways, the ILO is a unique body concerned with human rights in that it is composed of a tripartite structure involving governments, workers and employers. This allows for a variety of interests to be heard.[55] The regular state reporting that is required on the implementation of the Conventions (ILO Constitution: art. 22) offers an opportunity for a twenty-member Committee of Experts on the Application of Conventions and Recommendations to produce 'observations' and 'general surveys' on state compliance.

The ILO affirms that 'all human beings, irrespective of race, creed, or sex, have the right to pursue both their material well-being and their spiritual development in conditions of freedom and dignity, of economic security and equal opportunity' and that 'all national and international policies and measures, in particular those of an economic and financial character, should be judged in this light and accepted only in so far as they be held to promote and not to hinder the achievement of this fundamental objective'.[56] Local and international actors concerned about abuses committed in DIDR situations should therefore make use of the complaints mechanism found in articles 24–25 of the ILO Constitution. This allows 'industrial associations of employers or workers' to make representations regarding alleged violations of the ILO Conventions, which the Governing Body can follow up with the concerned government (art. 24). Communications and replies concerning the violation can be published if the Governing Body is not satisfied with the government statement (art. 25). This is an example of additional pressure that NGOs can place on authorities who do not respect internationally agreed norms relating to DIDR.

In the European context, damages caused by EC actions can be challenged at the European Court of Justice if it can be demonstrated that the actions are illegal and if a causal link can be established between the damages and the illegal actions. Article 215 (2) of the EC Treaty stipulates that '[i]n the case of non-contractual liability, the Community shall, in accordance with the general principles common to the laws of Member States, make good any damage caused by its institutions or by its servants in the performance of their duties'. Persons who have suffered the damages do not have to be EC nationals.[57] However, there is a limitation period which means that any applicant must begin the legal procedures five years from the time when it is realised that the EC's action was the cause of injury.[58] It is unlikely that the Court's small legal aid budget will be used in DIDR cases, given that these will probably be considered as somewhat speculative. Likewise, it is necessary to note that courts tend to be conservative on the issue of what constitutes liable damage. Some damages identified in the literature on DIDR will probably be irrecoverable because lawyers will consider that they are vague and indefinite.[59] Given that only persons who have actually suffered the damages can bring actions under the EC Treaty, specific applicants have to plead their particular cases and demonstrate the damage they have individually suffered. It is therefore difficult for DIDR-affected communities to be represented by large international NGOs.

The EC Treaty also gives the European Parliament the right to appoint an ombudsman empowered to receive complaints from any citizen of the Union or any natural or legal person residing in a member state concerning 'instances of maladministration in the activities of the Community institutions or Bodies' other than the Court of Justice and the Court of First Instance acting in their judicial role (EC Treaty: art. 195). Considering the extensive provisions that outline the human rights and development standards accepted by the EC, this recourse should be explored by NGOs and concerned parties.

A recent complaint lodged by Oxfam gives reason for prudent optimism concerning the role of the European Ombudsman. The complainant alleges that the Commission and its agents did not respect the human rights provisions found in the Lomé Conventions regarding an EDF-financed conservation project in southern Ethiopia. The Ombudsman did not decide in favour of the complainant because he had 'not received evidence of a nature to prove that involuntary resettlement of local population has taken place, or that the Commission services could have been involved in any such practice'.[60] Although the evidence demonstrating that any displacement had actually occurred was weak in this particular case, it is important to note that the Ombudsman accepted the main thrust of the complainant's argument: 'The Ombudsman therefore concludes that in the preparation and implementation of programmes and projects funded through the EDF, the Commission plays an important role and has to follow a number of obligations' (*ibid.*: para. 1.5). This aspect of the decision suggests that the European Ombudsman will be able to play a positive role in future DIDR situations that fall within its Statute.[61]

In many ways, issues related to the implementation of the World Bank's resettlement guidelines offer the best insight into the contribution of international law on DIDR. While the guidelines may contain progressive requirements for the treatment of PAPs, they contain protection guarantees that are not uniformly respected.[62] Although the World Bank must respect its nonpolitical mandate, an effective internal mechanism that ensures respect for the guidelines can lead to more economically sound projects that can influence indirectly the development of international human rights norms.

The World Bank's Inspection Panel provides such a mechanism. The Panel is an independent forum established by Resolution No. 93–10 of the International Bank for Reconstruction and Development and by the identical Resolution No. 93–6 of the International Development Association, both adopted by the Executive Directors of the respective institutions on 22 September 1993. The Panel's creation was largely motivated by the desire to make the World Bank more accountable and transparent in order to increase public confidence. The controversy surrounding the Sardar Sarovar Dam on the Narmada river in India was undoubtedly an important landmark in this step forward. Other examples of mismanagement also contributed to galvanising the Executive Directors to take concrete action in favour of greater accountability. This arguably contributed to setting new standards of governance for all financial institutions.

The Inspection Panel was therefore established to help ensure that Bank operations adhere to the institution's policies and procedures. Its establishment now allows any group of individuals who consider that they may be harmed by Bank-supported projects to ask the Panel to investigate complaints alleging that the Bank failed to abide by its own policies and procedures. As the first forum in which private parties can seek to hold international organisations directly accountable for their involvement in DIDR, the World Bank's Inspection Panel clearly has considerable influence in the development of international human rights law (Bradlow 1994: 553). It is therefore important to understand the recent and apparent desire on the part of the Executive Directors to limit the activities of the Panel.

The World Bank's Inspection Panel began operating in September 1994. The influence of its work was established by the first request it received in October 1994 concerning an investigation of the Arun III hydroelectric project in Nepal.[63] It is important to note that the Board's authorisation of an investigation relating to the Arun III project immediately led to a Bank mission that proposed design changes before the investigation took place. Consequential changes could still be made to the project because the hearing actually occurred before the borrower signed a loan agreement. The Panel's investigation included site visits and consultations with PAPs that were more extensive than the previous studies conducted by the Bank.[64] The Panel's interpretation of some provisions in the Bank's guidelines also provides the Bank with a jurisprudence that is favourable to PAPs. Indeed, the Panel noted the inadequate nature of the compensation and particularly the lack of forms of compensation other than cash.[65] It also expressed concern regarding the government's ability to rehabilitate the PAPs and the Bank's inadequate project monitoring. A further benefit from the process is that the extensive information gathered should logically be used to enhance the design of any future projects in Nepal.

Following the Panel's investigation, the President of the World Bank announced that it was withdrawing its offer to fund the project. It did this even before the Board could issue a decision on the Panel's investigation. The Bank was clearly embarrassed and it remains concerned that similar investigations could undermine future projects. The Board is arguably now trying to limit the effectiveness of the Panel, while shifting blame to borrowing countries in the context of investigations.

The legal opinion[66] provided by the Bank's General Counsel to the Board concerning the eligibility of requesters was an indication of future trends. The management has used the General Counsel's procedural arguments to challenge requesters and complicate access to the Panel by turning the mechanism into a technical debate over eligibility and jurisdiction. To the extent that the Board was motivated by the desire to create an accessible and independent review of the Bank's actions, it appears to have changed its approach and is now attempting to limit access to the Panel. Even the preliminary studies conducted in situ have been curtailed.[67]

It is worthwhile to note that investigations were not authorised on grounds of eligibility for the two requests[68] that followed the Arun III investigation.[69] Following these requests, investigations began to be refused regularly because 'action plans' had been agreed quickly between the borrower and the Bank.[70] Given the Inspection Panel's lack of oversight authority concerning the remedial plans, the credibility of the overall complaints mechanism is open to challenge. Indeed, the Board's limited attention to the details and implementation of 'action plans' is considered unsatisfactory by some human rights advocates (see, for example, Clark 2002: 220).

The Board's reluctance to undergo the embarrassing Arun III exercise is clear. As pointed out by a former Panel Chairman, the 'first two years demonstrated two things: that the panel might have more effect on projects through indirect pressure than through its formal procedures set out by the executive directors, and that the latter were uncomfortable with the legal approaches set out in the enabling resolutions and therefore frequently opted for alternative approaches' (Bissell 1997: 742).

After almost a decade of operation, twenty-nine requests for inspection have been filed and thirty-three reports have been issued by the Panel. To some observers, the fact that only one of the three Panel members is expected to work full-time may indicate the lack of a genuine commitment on the part of the Executive Directors.[71] If banks are sincerely committed to upholding the norms enunciated in DIDR guidelines and borrowers do not allow the banks to respect their standards, then the banks should logically not be involved in the projects. Likewise, the World Bank's credibility and the legitimacy of its projects are at stake if it does not respond seriously to allegations that people challenging projects have been murdered and subjected to cruel treatment by local officials of the borrowing country.[72] The public image of the Bank can only suffer if it does not live up to the progressive ideals of its founders and instead satisfies itself by shifting the blame to borrowing countries. Maintaining the Bank's positive image is difficult to achieve if it is not held accountable for violations of its own policies.

Ultimately, progress in panel-type legal mechanisms of enforcement will depend on the willingness of development banks to jeopardise projects for the sake of human rights. This in turn will depend on public pressure. While avoiding a more radical position that requires banks actively to promote international human rights law,[73] this perspective acknowledges the indirect role of human rights in the economic decisions made by financial institutions.[74]

It is difficult for lenders to ignore the fact that they can promote good governance and human rights,[75] even though their mandates may relate primarily to the reduction of poverty and not the development of human rights (Shihata 1988: 39).[76] As pointed out by the World Bank's former General Legal Counsel, the 'Bank's advocacy of participatory development is not meant to constitute political interference in the affairs of its borrowing countries; it is a lesson drawn from the experience of development effectiveness, and thus founded on sound economic grounds' (Shihata 1997: 641; see also Handl 1998: 642). For financial institutions, concern about human rights in this context can be understood as an economic consideration that is affected by the general political stability of the borrowing country.[77] As outlined by the African Development Bank Advisory Council, 'while economic growth is necessarily dependent on strictly economic factors[,] ... these factors by themselves are not sufficient[:] ... an effective public administration, a functioning legal framework, efficient regulatory structures, and transparent systems for both financial and legal accountability – in brief, those essential attributes of what is now referred to as good governance – have to be in place'.[78]

Yet modesty in institutional mandates or ambitions has its value. Einhorn (2001) suggests that there is pressure on the World Bank to rationalise its functions and reallocate some of its tasks to other institutions. There are also solid reasons to maintain the nonpolitical character of the World Bank and to protect this global financial institution from political interference.[79] Negotiations conducted by the World Bank are complicated if potential borrowers fear political interference in their internal affairs.[80] As a financial institution functions on the basis of loans to borrowing countries, the World Bank has legitimate reasons for worrying that governments will stop borrowing for controversial projects in order to avoid high standards of accountability. The ethical dilemma is relatively clear. The Bank can maintain high standards and consequently run the risk that clients will turn to less scrupulous elements in the private sector or to bilateral creditors for financing problematic projects. Alternatively, the Bank can lower its standards and ensure that its participation prevents risky projects from avoiding any international scrutiny.

In this context, the increasing role of the private sector in DIDR projects needs to be emphasised. In 1999, the member of the World Bank group that promotes sustainable private sector investment in developing countries, the International Finance Corporation (IFC), created a Compliance Advisor/Ombudsman. Operational guidelines for this body were adopted in April 2000, which set forth how the office carries out its different functions, including the ombudsman role that relates to complaints by persons affected by IFC projects.[81] This independent post, which reports to the President of the World Bank Group, has received thirteen complaints during its first three years of operations: two were rejected, one was successfully mediated, one was investigated and recommendations made, one was taken up by local authorities, two are presently involved in multiparty mediation, two are pending instructions from complainants, three are under investigation and one is closed as incapable of being further pursued.[82]

A particularly encouraging step has been taken by ten private financial institutions that adopted the Equator Principles on 4 June 2003 at the headquarters of the IFC. Less than a year later, twenty-five financial institutions from Europe, North America, Japan and Australia had committed themselves to respecting these Principles, thereby taking a leadership role on global environmental and social issues (Servastopulo and Holder 2004). According to the Equator Principles, the participating financial institutions will only provide loans for projects if the borrower completes an environmental assessment that addresses forced resettlement and the participation of affected parties in design, review and implementation (paras 3(k) and (n)).

A number of governments have also adopted the (revised) OECD Guidelines for Multinational Entreprises. These Guidelines (adopted 27 June 2000) provide recommendations addressed to multinational enterprises operating in or from adhering countries[83] and represent standards for responsible business conduct in a variety of areas involving human rights and the environment. According to the Guidelines, multinational enterprises should 'respect the human rights of those affected by their activities consistent with the host government's international obligations and commitments' (para. II (2)). Any person or organisation may approach the government institutions responsible for furthering implementation of the Guidelines (known as 'National Contact Points').

As much as the preceding observations concerning DIDR relate to positive steps forward, there is a basic problem concerning the type of actors that have actually adopted enforcement mechanisms. These are essentially financial institutions with nonpolitical mandates, which seriously limit the extent to which they can make loans dependent on respect for human rights. This fundamental dilemma remains even if institutions like the IFC and the private sector accept guidelines and panel-based complaint mechanisms.

Governments and their development departments or agencies making bilateral loans are better placed than banks to link assistance to human rights considerations. This is particularly the case when these departments or agencies also have mandates that emphasise the promotion of good governance and the realisation of human rights.

The 1997 White Paper on International Development presented by the British Secretary of State for International Development claims that the U.K.'s Department for International Development (DfID) will '[g]ive particular attention to human rights, transparent and accountable government and core labour standards, building on the Government's ethical approach to international relations'.[84] If this commitment is to be translated into genuine action, then a special effort should be made so that the OECD guidelines are respected when British development aid is granted for projects which may involve displacement. The guidelines stipulate that '[d]onor countries should not support projects that cause population displacement unless they contain acceptable resettlement plans protecting the rights of affected groups' (para. 6(a)) and that '[t]he implementation of the resettlement plan is to be effectively supervised' (para. 6(g)). In order to lead the field and set a positive example of transparency and public participation, the DfID should also avoid involvement in projects that would not satisfy national standards and public expectations in the U.K.

In its resolution encouraging a 'code of conduct for European enterprises operating in developing countries', the European Parliament notes that

> in the present context of globalisation of trade flows and communications as well as of increased vigilance of NGOs and consumer associations, it seems to be increasingly in the interests of multinational undertakings to adopt and implement voluntary codes of conduct if they want to avoid negative publicity campaigns, sometimes leading to boycotts, public relation costs and consumer complaints.[85]

The Parliament needs to act upon its recommendation that there be 'coordinated action within the OECD, the ILO and other international fora to promote the establishment of a truly independent and impartial monitoring mechanism which is internationally accepted' (*ibid.* para. 15).

Clearly, donor governments engaging in bilateral loans are in a better position to make such loans conditional on respect for human rights. Encouraging lending governments to accept individual complaints mechanisms similar to the inspection panel adopted by the World Bank would represent a considerable step forward in the protection of DIDPs. It is unfortunate that EC law[86] currently appears to offer more potential at this level than the DfID's bilateral programmes. If progress is made regarding the establishment of international adjudication in situations of DIDR, then it would contribute to creating a dynamic where even the private sector would acknowledge its interest in funding only development projects that meet basic human rights norms.

Conclusion

As suggested by the analysis of the preceding sections, DIDR remains a relatively undeveloped area of international law. Yet this chapter also indicates that some legal tools are currently available in the struggle to protect the rights of DIDPs. Until legally binding international instruments that deal specifically and comprehensively with development-induced displacement are signed by states, concerned parties have to pursue their difficult work by making full use of the various human rights norms and existing mechanisms that can provide protection.

Despite the existence of a variety of international norms, it is evident that the main problems relate to enforcement. NGOs can play a valuable role by exploring innovative methods which increase pressure on governments so that they respect these norms. The various UN committees described in the chapter offer such possibilities and help to illustrate the importance of establishing individual complaint mechanisms for PAPs. The World Bank's Inspection Panel is an example of a useful complaint mechanism for DIDPs that highlights how approval for development projects can ultimately depend on respect for human rights.

Yet making this connection between good economics and human rights promotion is done most effectively in the context of bilateral loans, where lending governments can explicitly invoke political considerations, unlike international financial institutions. Important steps in this direction have been taken recently by the EU in order to increase human rights account-ability in its external relations. The examples of the European Parliament's Ombudsman and the European Court of Justice can serve to encourage complaints regarding EU-funded projects that result in abusive treatment of PAPs, as was the case in the Ugandan conservation project discussed in this chapter.

In some ways these progressive developments in EU policies underline the lack of political courage on the part of member states that have not established complaint mechanisms concerning the international activities of their own development agencies. Public scrutiny is most effective when transparency and accountability form integral parts of development proj-ects and allow PAPs to challenge the authorities with legal procedures. As illustrated by the case of the James Bay hydroelectric project, access to legal procedures raises public scrutiny and encourages authorities to obtain the consent of the PAPs. A shift towards the encouragement of con-sensual participation is one of the important contributions of a human rights-based approach to DIDR.

In extreme cases involving abusive development initiatives that cater largely to business interests, self-determination as envisioned in human rights treaties allows a community to invoke protection against coercive removals if there is a threat to the existence of the group. In terms of legal-ity, the implicit logic of international human rights norms suggests that the authorities have to offer sufficient compensation so that those required to resettle do so voluntarily.

The problem with this perspective is that it allows PAPs to demand compensation that is beyond the amount needed to avoid being worse off as a result of the project (Penz 2002: 5). The result is that the development project can become financially unfeasible or that the benefits to other dis-advantaged groups within the larger society are divested. After all, con-siderations of egalitarianism suggest that the benefits of the development project should actually be shared by the PAPs as well as by other disad-vantaged groups.

In this context, a need to restrict the right to veto development projects can be justifiable. When such public-interest considerations are sufficient-ly important, the emphasis on negotiations and consent can be comple-mented by adjudication relating to appropriate compensation. In other words, an ethically compelling response to the potential problem described above can involve an arbitration mechanism that follows when a deal is not achieved with the DIDPs. Ultimately, the legitimacy of a DIDR project that does not involve free and informed consent will reflect the fairness of a state's judicial bodies. The president of the Inter-American Development Bank from 1988 to 2002 acknowledges indirectly this fundamental point in his defence of the institution's venture into new fields involving the modernisation of the state and its judicial structures:

> There has been a consensus for some time now among the Bank's member countries and within the Bank that an effective legal system is an essential component of a legitimate and orderly democratic political system and a well-functioning market economy. There is a growing demand among the citizenry of the Bank's borrowing member countries for fairness, transparency and access to justice; impatience with the denial of justice as a result of delays in court systems and miscarriages of justice in the judicial process. (Iglesias 2002: 22)

Although foreign development actors generally have an obligation to abide by the domestic legislation of the host state, they also 'normally have a mandate to assist only ethically justifiable development' (Penz 2002: 5). Yet the political influence of ethical responsibilities is not always translated into concrete legal obligations. International law can play a positive role by providing examples of fair adjudication mechanisms and by subjecting international actors to legal criteria similar to those they would expect in their own countries. The following ethical position is useful in encouraging this type of human rights-related accountability.

> [T]here is such a thing as moral progress, and ... this progress is indeed in the direction of greater human solidarity. But that solidarity is not thought of as recognition of a core self, the human essence, in all human beings. Rather, it is thought of as the ability to see more and more traditional differences (of tribe, religion, race, customs, and the like) as unimportant when compared with similarities with respect to pain and humiliation – the ability to think of people wildly different from ourselves as included in the range of 'us'. (Rorty 1989: 192)

It is in this sense that the goals of international development projects cannot be dissociated from the progress which comes with greater human solidarity. The persuasiveness of international law relies on its ability to tap into this moral legitimacy.

Notes

1. In response to a request of the UN Commission on Human Rights (UNCHR) to develop a framework for the protection and assistance of the internally dis-

placed, the Representative of the Secretary-General on Internally Displaced Persons has prepared the 'Guiding Principles on Internal Displacement' which were submitted to the UNCHR at its fifty-fourth session. See UN document E/CN.4/1998/53/Add.2.

2. ExxonMobil is the project's principal shareholder.

3. See articles 17–24 and 27–28 of the 1951 Geneva Convention relating to the Status of Refugees, *United Nations Treaties Series* vol. 189, p. 137.

4. This analysis considers refugee protection as an activity that is more specific than the general aid identified in Stavropoulou (1994a).

5. See Voutira and Harrell-Bond (2000). They argue that current refugee policy has more to learn from DIDR related policy concerning entitlements than was the case in the past.

6. In relation to refugee relief programmes, it has been suggested that '[t]hese interventions are never sufficient to allow for the restoration of livelihoods' (Voutira and Harrell-Bond 2000: 57).

7. Article 9 of the International Covenant on Civil and Political Rights (ICCPR). UN General Assembly resolution 2200 A(XXI) of 16 December 1966.

8. Article 7 of the ICCPR.

9. See Convention against Torture and Other Cruel, Inhuman or Degrading Treatment or Punishment, signed on 10 December 1984.

10. Article 8(3) of the ICCPR.

11. See Convention on the Prevention and Punishment of the Crime of Genocide, signed on 9 December 1948. Plater (1988: 143) states: 'such claims of genocide, however, represent an extremely drastic avenue for integrating human costs into development planning. A genocide argument is not likely to promote careful adjustment of interests, but rather invites inflexible polarization'.

12. See article 9 of the ICCPR.

13. UN General Assembly resolution 2200 A(XXI) of 16 December 1966.

14. However, this right may be qualified according to Article 12(3): 'The above-mentioned rights shall not be subject to any restrictions except those which are provided by law, are necessary to protect national security, public order (*ordre public*), public health or morals or the rights and freedoms of others, and are consistent with the other rights recognized in the present Covenant'.

15. 'Its omission is due to the inability of governments to agree on a formulation governing social takings and the compensation therefore' (Steiner and Alston 1996: 263).

16. Article 17 states: '(1) Everyone has the right to own property alone as well as in association with others. (2) No one shall be arbitrarily deprived of his property'. UN General Assembly resolution 217 A(III), adopted on 10 December 1948.

17. See sections 25–26, Constitution of the Republic of South Africa, 1996, adopted on 10 December 1996, entry into force on 4 February 1997. See also Smith (1997).

18. Adopted by the UN General Assembly resolution 2106 A (XX) on 21 December 1965.

19. For a legal discussion of this term, see Steiner and Alston (1996: 1006).

20. This provision contains additional protection to that found in article 11 of ILO Convention No. 107.

21. Article 6 of Convention No. 107 is also relevant in this context.

22. Signed in Aarhus (Denmark) on 25 June 1998. The signatories include 35 member states of the UN Economic Commission for Europe and the EC. UN Document ECE/CEP/43(1998). For a commentary, see Ebbesson (1998).

23. Communication 205 (1986). Official Records of the Human Rights Committee 1991/92 (11), UN Document CCPR/11/Add.1.

24. According to the World Commission on Dams (WCD), the recognition of rights and the assessment of risks form the basis for the identification and inclusion of adversely affected stakeholders in joint negotiations on mitigation, resettlement and decision-making. See generally WCD (2000).

25. The decision rendered by Judge Malouf of the Superior Court of Quebec on 15 November 1973, which was supportive of Cree claims, was reversed by a decision from the Court of Appeal on 21 November 1974.

26. See also O'Reilly (1985: 35): 'If the government wished to respect the schedule, it could no longer afford to take the chance that it would be the courts that would decide whether the project proceeded or not'.

27. See, for example, *Attorney General of Quebec* v. *Eastmain Band*, Federal Court of Appeal, A-1071–91, 20 November 1992, pp. 7–8.

28. A more recent agreement has been achieved; (as reported on Radio Canada, *Québec et les Cris s'entendent pour developer la Baie James*, 23 October 2001).

29. See, for example, Case 4/73, *Nold II* [1974] E.C.R. 507, §13.

30. ACP/EU: Democracy, rule of law and human rights, A4–0411/98 (15 January 1999), Resolution on the Commission Communication entitled 'Democratisation, the Rule of Law, Respect for Human Rights and Good Governance: The Challenges of the Partnership between the European Union and the ACP States' (COM(98)0146 – C4–0390/98).

31. Signed in Rome on 4 November 1950.

32. See articles 4, 5, 10 and 13, Fourth ACP-EEC Convention signed in Lomé on 15 December 1989, Official Journal L 229, 17/08/1991 p. 0003–0280.

33. Resolution on EU Standards for European Enterprises Operating in Developing Countries: Towards a European Code of Conduct, A4–0508/98.

34. See, for example, article IV, section 10 of the International Bank for Reconstruction and Development's Articles of Agreement: 'The Bank and its officers shall not interfere in the political affairs of any member; nor shall they be influenced in their decisions by the political character of member or members concerned'.

35. OP and BP 4.12 apply to all projects for which a Project Concept Review takes place on or after 1 January 2002.

36. The reformatting of the guidelines has been criticised for shielding or 'panel-proofing' the Bank in the context of the Inspection Panel procedures described below.

37. For a discussion on rehabilitation, see Shihata (1993: 44–48).

38. Civil Case Number 34 (1994). For a detailed commentary on this case, see Juma (1999).

39. The lawsuit was filed in the name of individual pastoralists who claim to have suffered harm because the law relating to representative suits remains unclear. The judge determined that the consolidated case was not a representative suit and consequently proceeded to determine the customary land rights of only the plaintiffs who actually testified.

40. This determination does not appear to have been based on any presented evidence. Courts can often avoid dealing with the violent abuses during the evictions by separating these actions from the land issues and considering the former as torts for which there is a short period of limitation for legal action. For example, Tanzania's Law of Limitation Act (Act Number 10, 1971) prescribes a three-year limitation for tort actions.

41. See UN Sub-Commission on Prevention of Discrimination and Protection of Minorities, resolution 1996/27.

42. Paragraph 4 of the guidelines reads: 'Forced evictions constitute *prima facie* violations of a wide range of internationally recognized human rights'. Paragraph 14 reads: 'States should adopt legislative measures prohibiting any evictions without a court order'.

43. Perhaps the document even goes too far in this respect by invoking a 'right to remain' that is not generally accepted in international law. Indeed, a general prohibition on displacement does not exist in treaty law. For an attempt at outlawing displacement, see Stavropoulou (1994b: 869). See also UNCHR (1996: 32): 'While no human rights treaty states an explicit "right not to evicted", the intimate links between this ideal, the right to housing and other human rights are clear'.

44. 'If the political actor deems political and legal considerations to be dominant over international commitments, there is no effective constraint except the burden of world opinion – that of member states and the international legal profession' (Plater 1988: 152).

45. The UN Economic and Social Council resolution 1235(XLII) adopted in 1967 authorises the Commission on Human Rights to develop its public debate function relating to specific situations.

46. ECOSOC resolution 1235(XLII), paragraph 3.

47. ECOSOC resolution 1503 (XLVIII), adopted in 1970.

48. According to the WCD (2000), it is the responsibility of states and developers to ensure accountability through legal means such as contracts and through accessible legal recourses at a national and international level.

49. UN General Assembly, 16 December 1966 (Date of entry into force: 23 March 1976). This is a distinct legal instrument that requires separate ratification or accession.

50. Algeria, Costa Rica, Ecuador, Peru, Senegal and Uruguay are among the states that have made the declaration.

51. Article 22: 'The Economic and Social Council may bring to the attention of other organs of the United Nations, their subsidiary organs and specialized agencies concerned with furnishing technical assistance any matters arising out of the reports referred to in this part of the present Covenant which may assist such bodies in deciding, each within its field of competence, on the advisability of international measures likely to contribute to the effective progressive implementation of the present Covenant'.

52. Article 18 of the ICESCR: 'Pursuant to its responsibilities under the Charter of the United Nations in the field of human rights and fundamental freedoms, the Economic and Social Council may make arrangements with the specialized agencies in respect of their reporting to it on the progress made in achieving the observance of the provisions of the present Covenant falling within the scope of their

activities. These reports may include particulars of decisions and recommendations on such implementation adopted by their competent organs'.

53. See, for example, *Concluding Observations on the Report of the Dominican Republic*, UN Document E/C.12/1994/15.

54. General Comment No. 2 (1990) of the Committee on Economic, Social and Cultural Rights on international technical assistance measures (art. 22 of the Covenant), paragraphs 6–8.

55. Delegations from each member state include two government representatives, one representative of workers and one representative of employers. The Governing Body is composed of twenty-eight government representatives, fourteen representatives from workers' organisations and fourteen representatives from employers' organisations. See Articles 1–13 of the ILO Constitution.

56. Declaration Concerning the Aims and Purposes of the International Labour Organization, adopted on 10 May 1944 in Philadelphia.

57. See *Adams v. Commission*, Case 145/83, [1985] E.C.R. 3539, which involves a Maltese national, and Case T-185/94 *Geotronics* [1995] E.C.R. II-2759, which involves a Swedish national.

58. Article 43 of the Statute of the Court. See *Adams*, Case 145/83, [1983] E.C.R. 3539.

59. See, for example, Case 26/74 *Roquette* [1976] E.C.R. 677.

60. Decision of the European Ombudsman on complaint 530/98/JMA against the European Commission, 26 October 2000, paragraph 3.2.

61. Adopted on 9 March 1994. Official Journal L 113, 4.5.1994, p. 15.

62. In the field of human rights, it is not sufficient to note the progressive nature of the official policies adopted as done in Shihata (1988: 63). The lessons from the World Bank indicate that the issuance of guidelines is not sufficient to ensure that human rights will be respected. Implementation is a distinct problem that needs to be specifically addressed.

63. For a general account of this case, see Bradlow (1996).

64. *The Inspection Panel Investigation Report: Nepal: III Proposed Hydroelectric Project and Restructuring of IDA Credit-2029–NEP*, 21 June 1995.

65. '[T]he only compensation identified so far was cash – no land, no jobs, and no training'. *The Inspection Panel Investigation Report*, p. 9.

66. *Role of the Inspection Panel in the Preliminary Assessment of Whether to Recommend Inspection: A Memorandum of the Senior Vice-President and General Counsel*, The World Bank, 3 January 1995.

67. *Conclusions of the Board's Second Review of the Inspection Panel*, 20 April 1999, paragraph 7.

68. Ethiopia: *Compensation for Expropriation of Foreign Assets in Ethiopia*, May 1995; Tanzania: *Emergency Power IV Project* (IDA Credit 2489–TA), June 1995.

69. The Executive Directors of the World Bank eventually had to clarify the eligibility issue addressed in the resolution establishing the Inspection Panel: 'It is understood that the "affected party" which the Resolution describes as "a community of persons such as an organization, association, society or other grouping of individuals" includes any two or more persons who share some common interests or concerns'. *Clarifications to the Resolution*, 17 October 1996.

70. Examples include: Brazil: *Rondonia Natural Resources Management Project* (PLANAFLORO) (IBRD Loan 3444–BR, 1992), June 1995; Bangladesh: *Jamuna*

Bridge Project (IDA Credit 2569–BD), August 1996; Argentina and Paraguay: *Yacyretá Hydroelectric Project,* October 1996; Brazil: *Itaparica Resettlement and Irrigation Project* (IBRD Loan 2883–1 BR), March 1997; India: *NTPC Power Generation Project in Singrauli* (IBRD Loan 3632–IN), May 1997.

71. See paragraph 9 of IBRD resolution No. 93–10 and IDA Resolution No. 93–6.

72. See the examples involving India, Chad and China cited in Clark (2002: 210–11).

73. See, for example, Paul (1998: 69): 'The duty to protect and promote rights must now be seen as a mandatory obligation imposed by law'.

74. 'Human rights may ... become a relevant issue but the degree of respect paid by a government to human rights cannot by itself be considered an appropriate basis for the Bank's decision to make loans to that government or for the voting of its Executive Directors' (Shihata 1988:47).

75. As suggested earlier in the chapter, participation by PAPs is key to reinforcing human rights. See Nanda (1998: 32).

76. This position is directly contested by the view that basic personal freedoms are the means and ends of development: see Sen (1999: 10).

77. 'Human rights violations may in specific cases also have broader implications related to the country's stability and prospective creditworthiness or to its ability to carry out Bank-financed projects, or to the Bank's ability to supervise them, which obviously are factors that the Bank must take into account to the extent they prove relevant in the circumstances of a specific case' (Shihata 1988: 66).

78. African Development Bank Advisory Council, *Recommendations: The Democratization Process in Africa, Governance and the Role of the African Development Bank* 10–11 (Report No. 1, January 1994).

79. For a positive view of such interference, see Plater (1988: 146): 'A critical motivation for the World Bank's policy shift ... appears to have been a practical threat of statutory pressure on Bank appropriations and a subsequent barrage of pressures from donor nations, orchestrated by the coalition of environmental NGOs'. For another view sympathetic to human rights interventionism, see Horta (2002: 229–30).

80. 'The Bank's dialogue with borrowing governments would obviously be greatly undermined if these governments were to doubt the Bank's objectivity or to see its conditionality as simply a reflection of certain political interests or views' (Shihata 1988: 48).

81. The Guidelines were revised following the publication of an external review and response by the IFC. See generally *Beyond Compliance? An External Review Team Report on the Compliance Advisor/Ombudsman of IFC and MIGA* (Multilateral Investment Guarantee Agency), June 2003, and *Response by the Office of the Compliance Advisor/Ombudsman to the External Review,* July 2003.

82. Annual Report 2002–2003 (September 2003).

83. These include the thirty OECD states, as well as Argentina, Brazil, Chile, Estonia, Israel, Latvia, Lithuania and Slovenia.

84. See *White Paper: Eliminating World Poverty: A Challenge for the 21st Century,* White Paper on International Development, Presented to Parliament by the Secretary of State for International Development by Command of Her Majesty, November 1997.

85. Resolution A4–0508/98 on EU standards for European enterprises operating in developing countries: Towards a European Code of Conduct, paragraph 8.

86. Code of conduct for European enterprises operating in developing countries, A4–0508/98, Resolution on EU standards for European Enterprises Operating in Developing Countries: Towards a European Code of Conduct: 'The European Parliament, (D) bearing in mind that there is increasing consensus amongst business and industry, trade unions, NGOs and governments, both from developing countries and from the industrialised world, to improve business practices through voluntary codes of conduct, (E) whereas in this connection a process of review is currently under way in the OECD, in consultation with representatives of companies, labour and other components of civil society, to strengthen the guiding principles set out by the Organisation for multinational companies'.

References

Amerasinghe, C.F. 1974. 'The Rule of Exhaustion of Local Remedies and the International Protection of Human Rights'. *Indian Yearbook of International Affairs*, 17.

Bissell, R.E. 1997. 'Recent Practice of the Inspection Panel of the World Bank'. *American Journal of International Law*, 91: 741–44.

Bradlow, D.D. 1994. 'International Organisations and Private Complaints: The Case of the World Bank Inspection Panel'. *Virginia Journal of International Law*, 34.

_____ 1996. 'A Test Case for the World Bank'. *American University Journal of International Law and Policy*, 11: 247–94.

Brandtner, B. and A. Rosas. 1998. 'Human Rights and the External Relations of the European Community: An Analysis of Doctrine and Practice'. *European Journal of International Law*, 9: 468–90.

Clark, D.L. 2002. 'The World Bank and Human Rights: The Need for Greater Accountability'. *Harvard Human Rights Journal*, 15: 205–26.

Ebbesson, J. 1998. 'The Notion of Public Participation in International Environmental Law'. *Yearbook of International Environmental Law*, 51: 51–97.

Einhorn, J. 2001. 'The World Bank's Mission Creep'. *Foreign Affairs*, 80(5): 22–35.

Escudero, C.R. 1988. *Involuntary Resettlement in Bank-assisted Projects: An Introduction to Legal Issues*. Washington DC: The World Bank.

Handl, G. 1998. 'The Legal Mandate of Multilateral Development Banks as Agents for Change toward Sustainable Development'. *American Journal of International Law*, 92: 642–65.

Horta, K. 2002. 'Rhetoric and Reality: Human Rights and the World Bank'. *Harvard Human Rights Journal*, 15: 227–43.

Iglesias, E.V. 2002. 'The Bank Prepared for the Long Haul'. *Latin Lawyer*, April/May: 22–23.

Juma, I.H. 1994. 'Wildlife Conservation Versus Customary Land-use: Lessons Drawn from Mkomazi Game Reserve Case'. Paper presented at Centre for Political Studies, University of Michigan.

Lassailly-Jacob, V. 1983. 'Un développement contesté: Amérindiens et écologistes face aux aménagements hydro-électriques dans la province de Québec'. *Hommes et Terres du Nord,* 2: 44–55.

Leckie, S. 2002. 'Towards a Right to Security of Place'. *Forced Migration Review,* 12 (January): 20–21.

Mercier, G. and G. Richot. 1997. 'La Baie James: Les dessous d'une rencontre que la bureaucratie n'avait pas prévue'. *Les Cahiers de Géographie du Québec,* 41(113): 137–69.

Nanda, V.P. 1998. 'Human Rights and Environmental Considerations in the Lending Policies of International Development Agencies – An Introduction'. *Denver Journal of International Law and Policy,* 17: 29–37.

OECD. 1991. *Guidelines for Aid Agencies on Involuntary Displacement and Resettlement in Development Projects.* OCDE/GD (91) 201.

O'Reilly, J. 1985. 'The Role of the Courts in the Evolution of the James Bay Hydroelectric Project'. In S. Vincent and G. Bowers (eds). *James Bay and Northern Quebec: Ten Years After.* Montreal: Recherches amérindiennes au Québec.

Overseas Development Institute (ODI). 1999. *What Can We Do With a Rights-based Approach to Development?.* Briefing Paper, September. London: ODI.

Oxfam (U.K./I Policy Department). 1996a. *A Profile of European Aid: Natural Forest Management and Conservation Project – Uganda.* Oxford: Oxfam.

———— 1996b. *The Advisability of International Measures Adopted by the European Commission and the World Bank which Facilitated Evictions from the Kibale Forest and Game Corridor in Uganda in March/April 1992: Submission to the Committee on Economic, Social and Cultural Rights in Respect of Article 22 of the International Covenant on Economic, Social and Cultural Rights.* 12 April. Oxford: Oxfam.

Paul, J.C.N. 1998. 'International Development Agencies, Human Rights and Humane Development Projects'. *Denver Journal of International Law and Policy,* 17: 67–120.

Penz, P. 2002. 'Development, Displacement and Ethics'. *Forced Migration Review,* 12 (January): 4–5.

Pettersson, B. 2002. 'Development-induced Displacement: Internal Affair or International Human Rights Issue?'. *Forced Migration Review,* 12 (January): 16–19.

Plater, Z.J.B. 1988. 'Damming the Third World: Multilateral Development Banks, Environmental Diseconomies, and International Reform Pressures on the Lending Process'. *Denver Journal of International Law and Policy,* 17: 121–53.

Ramanathan, U. 1996. 'Displacement and the Law'. *Economic and Political Weekly,* 15 June: 1486–91.

Rorty, R. 1989. *Contingency, Irony, and Solidarity.* Cambridge: Cambridge University Press.

Sen, A. 1999. *Development as Freedom.* New York: Alfred A. Knopf.

Servastopulo, D. and V. Holder. 2004. 'Greening of Financial Sector Gathering Speed'. *Financial Times,* 4 June.

Shaw, M.N. 1997. *International Law* (4th edn). Cambridge: Cambridge University Press.

Shihata, I.F.I. 1988. 'The World Bank and Human Rights: An Analysis of the Legal Issues and the Record of Achievements'. *Denver Journal of International Law and Policy*, 17: 39–66.

———— 1993. 'Legal Aspects of Involuntary Population Resettlement'. In M.M. Cernea and S.E. Guggenheim (eds). *Anthropological Approaches to Resettlement: Policy, Practice, and Theory*, pp. 39–54. Boulder CO: Westview Press.

———— 1997. 'Democracy and Development'. *International and Comparative Law Quarterly*, 46: 635–43.

Smith, H. 1997. *Forced Evictions and Development-based Displacement*. Expert Seminar on the Practice of Forced Evictions, Geneva, 11–13 June. 21 May 1997 UN Document HR/SEM.1/FE/1997/WP.1

Stavropoulou, M. 1994a. 'Indigenous Peoples Displaced from Their Environment: Is there Adequate Protection?'. *Colorado Journal of International Environmental Law*, 5: 105–25.

———— 1994b. 'The Right Not to be Displaced'. *American University Journal of International Law and Policy*, 9: 689–749.

Steiner, H.J. and P. Alston. 1996. *International Human Rights in Context*. Oxford: Clarendon Press.

UN Centre for Human Rights (UNCHR). 1996. *Fact Sheet No. 25: Forced Evictions and Human Rights*. Geneva: UNCHR.

UN Economic and Social Council (UNESC). 1996. *Draft Optional Protocol to the International Covenant on Economic, Social and Cultural Rights*. UN document E/CN.4/1997/105. 18 December.

Voutira, E. and B. Harrell-Bond. 2000. '"Successful" Refugee Settlement: Are Past Experiences Relevant?'. In M.M. Cernea and C. McDowell (eds). *Risks and Reconstruction: Experiences of Resettlers and Refugees*, pp. 56–76. Washington DC: The World Bank.

World Commission on Dams (WCD). 2000. *Dams and Development: A New Framework for Decision-making*. London, Sterling VA: Earthscan.

5

Enhancing Local Development in Development-induced Displacement and Resettlement Projects

Dolores Koenig

Introduction

It has long been clear that those displaced or resettled by development projects have not usually benefited from the process. Instead, they have more often been impoverished, losing economic, social, and cultural resources. National governments typically have justified development-induced displacement and resettlement (DIDR) by invoking goals of national growth and development, and the belief that the greater good justifies some loss. In response, some have questioned whether projects that involve large-scale DIDR ever offer just development, while others have argued that impoverishment can be mitigated or avoided by careful planning that includes development initiatives for the affected.

This chapter addresses the latter argument. For at least thirty years, those studying the effects of resettlement have looked for ways to improve future initiatives (Chambers 1969, Scudder 1981, Hansen and Oliver-Smith 1982, Cernea 2000). Knowledge about avoiding impoverishment has also been codified in guidelines. Here the World Bank led the way, promulgating an initial policy in 1980. Versions of its guidelines were later adopted by the OECD, other international organisations and some countries (Rew et al. 2000). Although guidelines have been instrumental in improving outcomes, displacement and resettlement continue to be problematic.

If we have learned so much about DIDR, why, indeed, is resettlement still so impoverishing? This chapter suggests two major reasons. First, development initiatives for the displaced have not sufficiently recognised the complexity of the socio-economic systems they are trying to re-establish. Second, and more importantly, resettlement planning and implementation have paid insufficient attention to the political aspects of DIDR.

Using published sources, grey literature and my own first-hand experience of resettlement at Manantali (Mali),[1] this chapter considers the existing approaches to resettlement and their achievements and suggests that problems persist because existing approaches overlook the distribution of societal power and ignore crucial conflicts of interest among different stakeholders. Although these approaches suggest 'doing resettlement as development', they have not defined development to take into account the distribution of power. The chapter then discusses some areas where lack of attention to complexity and power have led to unresolved problems. It offers suggestions to improve theory, policy and practice so that resettlement may lead to greater equity and growth. It looks at the implications of including power issues and understanding the larger political-economic environment that frames DIDR. A final section offers some suggestions for implementing a new kind of DIDR.

The Achievements of Existing Approaches

Planners soon discovered that simply moving people out of areas planned for infrastructure projects created problems for those relocated. Many early projects planned to make economic resources available to resettled people, and employed social scientists to look after their welfare. These included the Tennessee Valley Authority in the U.S. (Satterfield 1937), Mexico's Papaloapan Dam (1949–1952) (Partridge et al. 1982) and India's Hirakud Dam in 1956 (Baboo 1996). Planning was complemented by laws and policies. In 1970, the United States Congress passed the Uniform Relocation Act, which required that every displaced family be housed in a comparable dwelling and a comparable or more desirable location (Rubinstein 1988). Orissa state (India) created a policy in 1973 to benefit those displaced by the Rengali dam; this was later extended and improved (Pandey 1998).

Despite planning and the participation of social scientists in attempts to improve resettlement, results remained problematic. Moreover, unanticipated problems often arose. These included economic suffering, loss of resources, and social stress; those already poor were most vulnerable to impoverishment by DIDR. Early work also pointed to the particular problems of urban resettlement. Many people were relocated far from city centres, rupturing social networks and making it difficult for them to find jobs (Perlman 1982). DIDR also affected people not actually displaced. In dam projects, those who found their livelihoods compromised by changing river flows were far more numerous than those physically displaced.

To address these problems, social scientists developed synthetic understandings based on multiple prior experiences. Drawing on both forced and voluntary resettlement, Chambers (1969) proposed a three-stage model of the resettlement process. Building on this, and also taking both voluntary and forced cases into account, Scudder (1981) and Scudder and Colson (1982) elaborated a four-stage model, to which Scudder (1993) later added a fifth stage. This model emphasised the following resettlement phases: (1) initial planning; (2) site preparation, recruitment and settler selection; (3) transition and the initial years of adaptation; (4) potential development, when settlers formed communities and invested in economic activities; and (5) handing over and incorporation, involving the integration of settlers into effective political units. Some of this early work looked at the commonalities of DIDR and other forms of population displacement; one of the first edited volumes on resettlement brought together information on refugees, those suffering from natural disasters, and DIDR relocatees (Hansen and Oliver-Smith 1982). Others argued for a focus on the unique issues facing those displaced by DIDR. From a policy perspective, the most influential approach has been Cernea's (2000) risks-and-reconstruction model which seeks to diagnose and predict the major problems of forced resettlement and to offer suggestions for problem resolution and further research.

Cernea's work was particularly influential because he also played a central role in crafting the World Bank's resettlement guidelines. The first policy was created in 1980; it was reformulated in 1986 and again in 1990. The most recent policy, Operational Policy/Bank Procedure 4.12, was put into effect in December 2001 (World Bank 2001a). Since their inception some twenty years ago, these guidelines have become the standard used to judge the adequacy of resettlement initiatives (Gray 1996, Feeney 1998, Rew et al. 2000).

Cernea's model focuses on the socio-economic aspects of DIDR and only minimally discusses its political aspects. The model links eight primary risks in three separate ways. First, as causes of impoverishment, the risks influence one another. For example, health problems caused by resettlement can exacerbate economic problems. Second, the risks and the actions to address them are linked; if landlessness is a problem, this can be addressed by providing land. Third, mitigating the different risks can work synergistically to reconstitute more sustainable future livelihoods (Cernea 2000). The eight risks are grouped into three categories: economic, sociocultural and social welfare risks.

Economic risks relate to the loss of resources necessary to earn a viable living and reproduce the next generation. Three economic resources are included: land, common property and jobs. Land for production is most crucial when people have land-based production systems. Loss of common property is important where people (notably the poor) depend to a significant extent upon a commons or open-access resource. Joblessness will confront those who lose employment. Commutes may become too long or firms may fold; the self-employed may lose raw materials or clientele. People often face multiple economic risks. The poor especially use productive resources to make ends meet. Resettlement initiatives need to consider complex combinations of resource loss and replacement.

Replacement of economic resources should focus on replacing assets, not just incomes. A displaced farmer loses not only the income from a crop, but the asset (land) that permits future production. Compensation for asset loss needs to be at replacement cost, not market value (Cernea 1996a). Since loss of productive capacity is a major cause of impoverishment, the reconstitution of productive resources has been at the heart of livelihood reconstitution strategies. However, reconstituting productive resources does not directly lead to meaningful lives.

Since human beings also depend on social and cultural systems, socio-cultural risks exist. When displacement weakens or dismantles social networks and life-support mechanisms, local authority systems collapse and groups lose their capacity for self-management (Downing 1996). This can cause social disarticulation, the dispersion and fragmentation of existing communities and loss of reciprocity networks, all of which increase powerlessness, dependence and vulnerability (Cernea 2000). Social disarticulation is especially common when existing social groups cannot resettle together, but may also occur when existing groups lose their ability to act effectively.

Marginalisation is an individualised process that occurs when families or individuals experience downward mobility. Resettlement may bring a loss of control over physical space and put people in new environments where existing knowledge and skills are less useful (Downing 1996, Oliver-Smith 1996). Economic marginality can lead to social or psychological marginality (Cernea 2000). Entire ethnic groups may lose status if they become incorporated at the bottom of national stratification systems. Both social disarticulation and marginalisation can be mitigated by resettlement strategies that emphasise the reconstruction of communities and social networks and deliberately pursue strategies of social cohesion (Cernea 2000). Building education and skills that allow people to use new resources can also combat marginalisation (Mahapatra 1999a).

The final three risks are social welfare risks: homelessness and lack of shelter, food insecurity and increased morbidity and mortality. Although they require the mobilisation of significant resources over a relatively short time, these humanitarian issues can be dealt with using existing approaches similar to those used in the aftermath of natural disasters. Homelessness can be dealt with by housing construction or provision of construction materials. Food insecurity can be dealt with through food-aid programmes. Physical morbidity can be addressed by vaccination and disease prevention programs and the assignment of medical and mental-health personnel. Many resettlement programmes have met the challenges of short-term homelessness, food insecurity and increased morbidity and mortality successfully. However, because these risks are highly visible and relatively easy to mitigate, many resettlement projects stop after addressing them and do not deal with other risks. If food insecurity, homelessness and increased morbidity and mortality continue over the long term, it is usually because other risks have not been effectively addressed.[2]

Accumulated knowledge, better theoretical models and the propagation of guidelines have created an environment where at least some DIDR is done with the goal of avoiding impoverishment and reconstituting the livelihoods of the displaced. The World Bank review of resettlement projects showed that projects following the guidelines performed better than those that overlooked them (Rew 1996: 205). Among the areas that have shown considerable improvement are: avoiding displacement, social welfare issues, land replacement, sociocultural reconstruction and an appreciation of the complexities of compensation. There has also been improved consultation.

Some have begun to look for alternative technical choices that avoid or lessen displacement. The Danxian-Wanxian railway (China) was laid out to minimise acquisition of cultivated and fertile land (NRCR 1999, Appendix 1: 16). In Uganda, public consultation with local communities led to changes for canal sites in a hydropower project (WCD 2000: 109). This strategy could be used more often, however. Alternative possibilities need to be discussed before activities begin, for example, through legal frameworks that allow the potentially affected to comment on initial plans (Appa and Patel 1996).

There has also been an improvement in dealing with the social welfare risks of DIDR. Homelessness has been addressed in a wide variety of ways. Consultation with affected urban populations has begun earlier (Mejía 1999: 165). Construction of individual housing is often complemented by social infrastructure, such as schools, health clinics and administrative offices, giving many displaced people better access to social services and bringing broad benefits (WCD 2000). The short-term risk of food insecurity has been addressed by national and international organisations such as the World Food Programme. Standard food-aid can be supplemented by food-for-work or feeding programmes for the particularly vulnerable.

Land replacement has also seen improvement. There is general agreement that land-for-land replacement is the most appropriate way to reconstitute land assets in rural, agriculturally based resettlement, where there is often insufficient land for sale, speculation, price inflation and a lack of monetarised land markets.[3] If land replacement is not possible, compensation needs to be based on replacement cost rather than market value. Even though Indian law requires market-value compensation, some projects have moved towards replacement value and Orissa's 1994 Water Resources Policy makes land-for-land the preference (Pandey 1998: 20).[4]

Understanding the complexities of agricultural land ownership has led to general acceptance of the idea that long-term users without title (e.g. those with customary tenure, 'squatters' or 'encroachers') ought to get replacement land. Recognition of extended families has given nonhousehold heads rights as well (Pandey 1998).

The importance of maintaining functional units of social organisation is reflected in strategies that move people as groups. Chinese policies have focused on restoring and preserving social units (Eriksen 1999), and at Manantali (Mali), entire villages were reconstructed. While moving as units does help preserve social cohesion, there are trade-offs. In urban resettlement, keeping social groups together may require that they move some distance from the central city, with negative economic repercussions. There is also a trade-off between individual choice and moving as units. Lower caste and younger people who wish to take advantage of new opportunities sometimes prefer new social networks.

Where monetary compensation is appropriate, implementation is nonetheless complex and involves a host of practical problems. Projects have begun to address some of these, for example, calculating land values without an active land market. In China, a multiple of the value of crops produced has been used (Meikle and Walker 1998). Recognising that lump-sum payments can cause problems, some Indian projects have implemented schemes for payouts over time (Pandey 1998).

Despite these achievements, forced resettlement continues to impoverish people. This is in part because of the nature of DIDR; it takes away economic, social and cultural resources at the same time. People find it very difficult to plan on their own for this eventuality. Information is often not available, since implementing organisations fear resistance if people know about the impending move. Even when information is available, people often find it difficult to believe that they will actually have to move.

Forced resettlement is also impoverishing because it takes away political power, most dramatically the power to make a decision about where and how to live. Those affected most are usually those who already have the fewest economic and political resources. Those with more political resources are often more able to resist displacement, and when wealthier people are displaced, they are more likely to be able to negotiate adequate compensation. At the same time, DIDR creates possibilities for some to increase their power and access to resources. At the national level, powerful groups may pursue strategies that allow them to increase control over the resettlement process and resettling groups.

Within displaced communities, DIDR also influences the distribution of power. Some groups of displaced people may not want to reconstruct units and types of social cohesion that disfavoured them, for example lower castes in India (Mahapatra 1999a) or politically inferior villages in Mali. Divergent interests between men and women, and youth and elders, are also common. Youth, especially young men, may see opportunities for new jobs and favour resettlement. Internal divisions among relocatees facilitate implicit or explicit divide-and-conquer strategies of the powerful and affect the ability of the displaced to determine and act on group interests. Local leaders who cannot maintain control often lose credibility (Scudder and Colson 1982), and power struggles may arise when DIDR provides an élite with the opportunity to realise political goals. DIDR strategies to reconstitute cohesive social units and to avoid marginalisation are likely to work better if they recognise and address this diversity of interests.

In sum, resettlement programmes have not worked as well as they could have because they have focused on the economic aspects of resettlement, while neglecting the political. To be sure, political aspects have not been ignored entirely. Cernea (2000: 30) has specifically noted that social disarticulation can worsen powerlessness, dependency, and vulnerability. Scudder and Colson's (1982) last stage of resettlement, i.e. handing over and incorporation, addressed the relationship of the new community to larger political-economic structures, and Scudder's (1993, 1996) work has increasingly made reference to political constraints. The approach to DIDR used by McGill University anthropologists did focus on issues of local autonomy and aboriginal rights, but their work has not been significantly used outside of Canada. When anthropologists from McGill University were asked to study the social impacts of the James Bay hydroelectric development, they insisted on a partnership between themselves and the Cree, which provided a framework for the Cree to organise and reconstitute their livelihoods (Salisbury 1986). This approach, while foregrounding the political, paid insufficient attention to the economic, and the Cree faced serious problems as they lost resources later on (Scudder 1996).

These experiences suggest that DIDR needs to take an approach that integrates social, economic and political aspects of resettlement. Although anthropological models have discussed the sociocultural and economic aspects in some depth, questions about the distribution of power, its impact on resource allocation and the implications for the poor have been less central, despite their importance to other development debates. Thus, some of the issues linked to DIDR might be better addressed in the context of more general debates about economic and social development. Although DIDR does have unique characteristics, it also has commonalities with other development concerns. Strategies to re-establish livelihoods and viable sociocultural systems can draw upon general develop-ment theory and practice. Stressing the unique characteristics of DIDR has made issues related to resettlement more visible, but has limited the abil-ity of mitigation efforts to draw upon other development knowledge.

Development within DIDR

Despite the fact that DIDR means *development*-induced displacement and resettlement, and despite the notion that programmes for the displaced should be carried out as *development* programmes, there is little discussion in the DIDR literature about what the criteria for development might be. The World Commission on Dams (WCD 2000) did raise the issue of defin-ing development. It looked for guidance to the 1986 UN Right to Development, which saw development as 'a comprehensive process aimed at the constant improvement of the well-being of the entire popu-lation' (WCD 2000: viii). The commissioners considered that development included five basic objectives: equity in resource allocation and benefits; sustainability of the world's resource base; openness and participation in decision making; efficiency in management; and accountability to present and future generations (WCD 2000: ix). In most of the other DIDR litera-ture, definitions of development are implicit rather than explicit.

For example, the concern to decrease impoverishment and target development to the least well off can be linked to strategies to decrease poverty and increase equity of benefits across society. The DIDR literature foregrounds the contradiction between increasing 'national' welfare and the consequent poverty when the welfare of the displaced is 'sacrificed' to this end. Other contemporary concerns such as environmental sustain-ability, human and social development, equitable distribution of national political power, and protection of basic human rights are also present in the literature. Human and social development have been integrated through the emphasis on reversing social disintegration and marginalisa-tion, decreasing morbidity and mortality, and the value of education. Issues around environmental sustainability have also been important, and environmentalists have allied with resettlers to protest against large infrastructure projects (Oliver-Smith 2001). Human rights issues have been raised by NGOs, analysts and international organisations (Oxfam 1996a, 1996b, Robinson 2003).

In contrast, explicit concerns about power are much less well repre-sented in the DIDR literature, despite the fact that even the World Bank now considers empowerment to be a major goal of development and a major strategy to combat poverty. The World Bank (2001b: 33) has defined empowerment to include 'making state institutions more accountable and responsive to poor people, strengthening the participation of poor people in political processes and local decision-making, and removing the social barriers that result from distinctions of gender, ethnicity, race, and social status'. Empowerment thus includes the ability of individuals and local groups to make choices about their own lives and to participate in directing their societies. The growth of interest in decentralisation and the role of civil society is also linked to the concern for empowerment.

Improvements to DIDR would be more likely with greater integration of the political aspects of resettlement. At present, political perspectives have been present only at the margins of the DIDR literature (Gibson 1993), although they have informed the arguments of some of those people who are against it (Patkar 2000). Involuntary resettlement, by its very nature, disrupts the ability of locals to control the reproduction of their own institutions (Asch 1982) – a key aspect of development. Yet political differences exist, not only between the displaced and those more powerful, but also among different groups of the displaced. Resettlement programmes need to take into account the divergent interests of those affected by DIDR, as well as the conflicts they may generate. The different groups affected by DIDR need to develop the capacity to negotiate with one another to resolve conflicts.

Contemporary development debates about the appropriate role for the state and, in particular, its activities in planning, should inform the approach to power within DIDR. The political left and right have both critiqued the state. While the Left has focused on the inequity of state actions that favour the powerful, the Right has discussed the state's economic inefficiency and inferiority to the market (Rapley 1996). Other political scientists have nevertheless argued that states will work in the interests of multiple constituencies if pressured to do so. This means that the empowerment of local groups is essential for development; by organising and increasing their capacity to pressure the state, they can constrain it to act more in their interest. Building the capacity of local groups to become pressure groups is thus an important part of avoiding long-term impoverishment for DIDR.

Some DIDR analysts have considered national integration problematic because formerly isolated groups have often been integrated at the bottom of national class systems. States do appear to emphasise cultural homogeneity and have shown difficulties in integrating groups that remain culturally distinct (Gibson 1993, Paine 1994). Yet DIDR projects inevitably link people more tightly to national systems. Effective resistance and pressure may, however, create new relationships and forms of integration that give local groups more power (Oliver-Smith 1996). For example, Italian-American women who fought urban renewal in 1960s Chicago paved the way for the entry of women into community leadership roles (Squires et al. 1987). Moreover, many of those resettled are already integrated, especially in urban areas. For them, DIDR disrupts integration into markets and national social service systems that bring some benefits (Perlman 1982, Mahapatra 1999b). Impoverishment involves being cut off from those systems. DIDR needs to consider explicit ways to improve the forms and kinds of integration necessary to avoid impoverishment.

Contemporary development analysts have also criticised planning, especially state planning (Escobar 1995). This is linked to a criticism of the state: a state that does not act in the public interest cannot be expected to plan equitably. A second criticism of planning is that it relies on experts, specialists assumed to have more knowledge than other people involved. Yet the knowledge of experts is always limited (Escobar 1995, Lohmann 1998). Resettlement plans may pay little attention to the daily lives of affected people, or boiler-plate plans may undergo ad hoc modification to meet local conditions, leading to inconsistent implementation (Meikle and Walker 1998). Critique of planning has been largely absent within DIDR, perhaps because resettlement plans have been seen as an essential strategy to avoid disastrous resettlement. Yet the critique of planning suggests that it ought to be done differently, not that it be done away with altogether. For DIDR, planning needs to be done in a more democratic, more inclusive way that takes into account unequal power distribution.

An operational definition of development for DIDR should include:

- increasing the availability and utility of economic resources;
- environmental sustainability, with equitable access across generations;
- respect for basic human rights;
- increasing equity between affected groups and other national groups, as well as among the different groups within affected populations;
- increasing local autonomy and control; and
- improving people's ability to influence national institutions.

This definition of development includes considerations about the distribution of power as well as of economic resources. Groups who have been 'sacrificed for' other people's development projects enter the process as relatively powerless and are further impoverished because they lack the economic, social, cultural or political capital to make their claims to resources and rights heard effectively. DIDR projects need to consider the existing distribution of power and to integrate empowerment as a goal alongside economic, social and social welfare improvement.[5]

Unaddressed Risks

While some aspects of DIDR have shown significant improvement, there is still a substantial likelihood of impoverishment among resettled people.

This is linked to the complexity of existing socio-economic systems and the unequal power distributions within resettling populations. The critique of planning suggests that the complexity of existing systems cannot be reproduced because planners simply cannot take all relevant factors into account. Conflicts of interest among those affected by DIDR cannot be addressed unless a model for resettlement directly takes political concerns into account.

Complexity

Naturally occurring social systems are always complex. In order to create workable plans for action, planners inevitably simplify to some extent. The argument here is that DIDR planners have made inappropriate or too many simplifying assumptions. This section looks at three indicative areas: rural land tenure, urban resettlement and general economic diversity.

Even in rural areas where projects have begun land-for-land replacement, the emphasis has been on individual farms as opposed to other kinds of land use. Projects have often been reluctant to allot land as other than individual property, as, for example, in giving replacement land to groups, even though many alternatives to individual ownership already exist (e.g. Indian reservations in the United States, agricultural villages in China (Meikle and Walker 1998) or limited liability corporations in many places). Moreover, community lands used for purposes other than agriculture, for example, hunting, herding or bush resources, have rarely been taken into account (Lassailly-Jacob 1996). Those with customary tenure and long-term 'squatters' have often been treated worse, even though many policies claim to treat them the same as people with full legal rights. In part, this is because it is often difficult to discriminate between long-term residents and free-riders who enter the area to get rights to new land, a problem that does appear worse where people depend on collectively owned resources (Pearce 1999). Standard-sized lots are often given, with the size of landholdings only rarely being tailored to the labour or capital endowments of households (Eriksen 1999: 113). Simplification of tenure can decrease the average size of landholdings after resettlement. In India, middle-income farm households often decline in status to smallholders; shopkeepers and craftspeople lose income as their major clientele becomes poorer (Pandey 1998).

Urban projects suffer in part because the knowledge gained from dam-related, rural resettlement is not always transferable to them. For example, urban populations are often used to moving; they are rarely bound by tradition since their survival often depends upon being able to see and take advantage of new resources quickly (Bartolomé 1993). Yet, voluntary and forced moves are not the same, and urbanites do risk impoverishment from DIDR. High population densities mean that even when small areas are affected, the number of people displaced may be large. The desire to relocate people close to jobs is often bedevilled by high urban land costs. Because it is often difficult to find suitable land for rehousing the displaced close to their old homes, many are moved far from social networks and markets. They may face new financial burdens, such as electricity and water bills and increased transport costs. If social ties are ruptured, people may have to pay for services that previously were free, for example, child care or security. There may be insufficient education or health facilities (Perlman 1982, Bartolomé 1993, Mejía 1999). Land in more central locations may be available only in small parcels, breaking the resettled population into smaller units and compromising social cohesion. There may be trade-offs between reconstituting economic and social systems.

The greatest problem facing urban resettlement is that most projects continue to be conceived of as housing projects and consider the reconstitution of jobs as unproblematic. It has often been naively assumed that people will simply keep existing jobs, even though the economic context changes (Meikle and Walker 1998, Mejía 1999). The reliance of the poor on an informal economy that depends on the surrounding environment has not been sufficiently taken into account (Perlman 1982). Because of the links between jobs and residences, site selection is crucial in restoring employment, income and social networks (Mejía 1999).

Job-based reconstruction is more complex than land-based reconstruction. A major issue is which enterprises will provide the jobs. Potential employers vary in scale, level of technical modernisation and ownership, all of which affect hiring policies. Some Indian states and China used to include jobs from large-scale industries in rehabilitation strategies, yet the move to more market-driven economies has made this option less palatable. Projects have therefore turned to micro-enterprises in production or trade to create jobs, which has a certain logic, since many of the jobs held by the displaced before resettlement were of this type (Perlman 1982, Mejía 2000). Yet, building successful micro-enterprises requires substantial planning, including an analysis of the existing regional economy, the goods and services it needs and the kinds of changes likely to occur post-DIDR. It needs a good understanding of the resources needed for particular micro-enterprises and good market analyses – which are not always undertaken. Moreover, a DIDR strategy that depends heavily on micro-enterprises is subject to the same hazards faced by micro-enterprises in non-DIDR contexts. Small-scale entrepreneurs cannot always take advantage of economies of scale and are subject to economic fluctuations. Employment benefits such as pensions and health insurance are often limited. In contrast to the two extremes (large enterprises at one end and micro-enterprises at the other), consideration of the actual or potential role of the middle (small- and medium-scale business) is almost absent from the DIDR literature. Whatever the job strategy taken, training programmes are needed to increase the capacities of local people to qualify for better-paid jobs.

These examples illustrate a larger problem: lack of attention to the diversity of ways in which people in any area earn their living. Viable social systems usually include people with a variety of occupations. Even if most rural residents are farmers, there are artisans, traders and other specialised service providers (e.g. health or religious practitioners), who are often ignored in DIDR programmes. At the same time, many households and individuals earn from multiple activities. In much of the world, rural residents who define themselves primarily as 'farmers' cannot live by farming alone (Lassailly-Jacob 1996). The urban poor also undertake multiple activities to make ends meet. Yet resettlement projects rarely reconstitute more than a single major resource.

The variety as well as the quantity of post-DIDR resources needs to be increased. In addition to recognising the diverse livelihoods present before resettlement, it may be useful to conceptualise the resettlement zone as a site for regional development, with linkages between specialists within it, as well as with organisations and individuals outside. Scudder (1981: 360–68) has suggested planning for the resettlement region as a whole, including both hosts and relocatees, with possibilities for small business, industry, tourism and/or mining. Planning for heterogeneous rather than homogeneous production systems may offer greater opportunities for future development, reconstituting livelihoods in a more viable fashion. Planners need to look at the diverse ways in which the zone is likely to grow, and look for ways to integrate relocatees into those diverse possibilities.

A final aspect of complexity is that the range of those affected is often minimised by planners and implementers. While hosts are sometimes considered, the rest of the adversely affected – but not displaced – people are rarely included in projects. Sometimes at a great distance from the project site and spread over wide areas, they are often less likely to mount effective resistance. Yet the non-displaced can be affected in many ways. Downstream fisherfolk may find their livelihoods disrupted (Appa and Patel 1996). So too may those who have used downstream water for agriculture (Salem-Murdock et al. 1994). Construction may cause long-term air and water pollution (Oxfam 1996b); those living close to mines and industrial colonies may face lower water tables, lack of potable water, and mineral dust (Pandey 1998). Local merchants or artisans may lose raw materials, supplies, labour or clientele. All who use resources in areas affected by DIDR face potentially negative impacts (de Wet 2001: 4639–40). Since DIDR disrupts regional economic systems, it interferes with the livelihoods of many different groups, affecting far more people than those immediately and directly displaced.

Power and Conflicts of Interest

DIDR projects catalyse conflicts of interest among the many groups affected. Conflicts between authorities and affected groups have been taken into account in existing approaches. At the same time, the conflicts between those displaced and others affected but not displaced, such as hosts, have not been adequately addressed. Moreover, the range and impacts of conflicts of interest among the displaced themselves have not been sufficiently recognised.

The divergent interests between national authorities and the displaced can be illustrated by the approach to common property. One reason that common property is not sufficiently reconstituted appears to be that many governments are uneasy about those who use either common property or open-access resources.[6] Boundaries are not always clearly demarcated and there is no single owner to approach for taxes or compensation. These resources are often used by people whom central governments find problematic, for example, pastoralists, fisherfolk or ethnic minorities. Although some uses of commons have been recognised (see Cernea 1996b), other categories of common-property land use are almost absent from the literature, such as resettled pastoralists. The scant literature suggests that their needs are rarely taken into account (Scudder 1982, Marx 1988, Salem-Murdock 1989, Aberle 1993, Chatty and Colchester 2002).

Common-property users may have conflicts of interest with other groups as well as with government authorities. In many places, new constituencies have pressured governments for access to these resources (Charest 1982, Waldram 1988, Paine 1994). At other times there have been conflicts among constituencies. For example, Saami reindeer pastoralists and Norwegian conservationists allied against hydroelectric development in the early 1980s, but after the publication of the Brundtland Commission report at the end of that decade, conservationists drew away from the pastoralists and closer to the government. Conservationists tended to see the tundra as wilderness; they argued that Saami could claim a special relationship to nature and a distinctive ethnic status only if they used 'traditional' techniques (Paine 1994). They criticised Saami use of technology such as landing-craft ferries, field telephones, all-terrain vehicles and snowmobiles. In some projects in India, people proposed declassifying forests to provide land for farmers, but this led to conflicts with environmentalists.

Because resettlement thinking has not yet taken into account the social science critiques of expert planning, it has downplayed the conflicts of interest between the state and its representatives vis-à-vis the displaced. The underlying belief is that resettlement authorities can plan fair and equitable projects; yet the different perspectives of government and people suggest that this is problematic. In any event, this takes into account only public sector initiatives. The conflicts of interest around private developers have been analysed even less, given that many major resettlement initiatives were and still are state funded or executed. However, private-sector projects are carried out, sometimes in partnership with governments, and, as criticisms of state planning have grown, many countries have moved towards more private-sector projects.

Even where authorities show concern for displaced people, they often exhibit paternalistic attitudes. For example, those displaced have been criticised for spending money meant for construction on consumption, for spending compensation on living expenses, to clear debts and to carry out marriages and other religious ceremonies (Thangaraj 1996, Pandey 1998). Others have wondered whether displaced people have made appropriate choices, for example, with regard to the choice of resettlement sites (Konaté 1993).

There are also conflicting interests between those physically displaced and other people affected by the project, who include the hosts among whom they settle, other affected residents, and immigrants (Scudder 1996). Even if they agree to accept displaced groups, the interests of hosts may conflict with those of resettlers due to competition over natural resources, common property and social services (Koenig and Diarra 1998a, Pandey 1998). To the hosts, displaced people might seem prosperous because of the cash compensation or new infrastructure they have received (Pandey 1998: 90), while the displaced often realise that this cash cannot replace lost assets – which hosts still have intact.

Most neglected is the internal political life of displaced groups and the potential conflicts of interest among them. Even when groups seem relatively homogeneous to outsiders, affected individuals may have different needs and interests; individuals may use DIDR to advance specific agendas (Oliver-Smith 1996). One important difference concerns those with the most vested in the old system and those who can get access to new resources post-DIDR. In patriarchal and gerontocratic social systems, older men can lose the most from resettlement. In contrast, women and younger men may be able to take advantage of new opportunities (Koenig and Diarra 1998a). If heterogeneity of interests is not recognised, people may have limited ability to organise effectively to respond to resettlement.

Three major axes of social differentiation are gender, age and class. Of these, gender has been most discussed (Koenig 1995, Colson 1999, Indra 1999). Just as in other development arenas, women in DIDR have usually received fewer benefits than men. The tendency to ignore diverse productive resources has had particularly negative impacts on women. Women may also suffer more from the social changes of DIDR. Participating in DIDR programmes has often been difficult for women, as their obligations in both domestic and productive work give them less free time. Yet, women have also been more open to new opportunities since they do not have the same interest in maintaining existing patriarchal traditions (Spring 1982, Salem-Murdock 1989, Koenig and Diarra 1998a). There has been some movement towards respecting entitlements for women, but this needs to be expanded.

Age also affects responses to resettlement, since younger and older people often have different interests. While the elderly are often most affected by placelessness, the young may greet resettlement as a chance to escape the control of elders. Young people are often well positioned to take advantage of the opportunities from DIDR projects. Taking up new opportunities may also offer them ways to address social inequities beyond their own village (Mahapatra 1999b). Sometimes, young people adapt with such ease that this leads to negative changes for other family members, such as dependency on the part of elders or splits within households (Thangaraj 1996, Pandey 1998).

Divergent class interests have not been well studied. Class differences can give élites more resources, privileged access to different resources or easier access to power. Even though many élite neighbourhoods and individuals are able to avoid DIDR, many displaced communities do contain people with more power and influence and greater links to national systems. These people appear to adjust to resettlement with greater ease. Often more integrated into commercial economies, they are usually better served by strictly monetary compensation schemes. Scudder and Colson (1982) noted that both the rich and self-relocated had a better chance to exert control over their new social and physical environment. Local élites often were able to manipulate project benefits to their advantage because they had better political access and resources. They were more likely to follow entrepreneurial strategies and to use project spin-offs and scheme benefits (de Wet 2001).

Yet, existing élites can also be compromised by resettlement. If they become too closely identified with DIDR administration, they can lose position and status. If they resist too strongly, they show their weakness. At the Papaloapan dam (Mexico), a new élite, using resources brought by resettlement, rapidly replaced traditional leaders (Partridge et al. 1982). As isolated areas are integrated into national systems, stratification can change quickly, leaving the displaced at the bottom (Charest 1982, Wali 1993, Pandey 1998). They may even fall behind other locals who used to be their peers (Mahapatra 1999b).

We need a greater understanding of the workings of local class systems and of how local élites can be encouraged to work in the interest of the local community and not uniquely for their own ends. Insofar as resettlement activities encourage élites to see themselves as integral members of the community, they are likely to increase the ability of the community to put pressure on its government. Strategies for change that encourage the cohesion of entire resettled communities, across classes, might offer more opportunities for reconstituting livelihoods than those that concentrate on more vulnerable segments. While local élites and lower classes do not have the same interests, they may have common interests vis-à-vis other groups on the national scene, particularly in the context of DIDR. Resettlement strategies need to encourage groups to recognise and address internal differentiation.

Gender, age and class are not the only lines that divide resettlers. In many cases, different ethnic groups may be differently affected, as shown by case studies from Panama (Wali 1989), Canada (Waldram 1980), and India (Pandey 1998). In urban areas, neighbourhoods may be differentially affected. In metropolitan Manila, neighbourhood groups worked with different NGOs and negotiated varying compensation (Meikle and Walker 1998). Those undertaking DIDR ought to understand the conflicts of interest and political issues within resettled groups, as well as those between the resettled and the obviously more powerful.

Measures to Enhance Development

Improving the lives of those affected by DIDR requires an explicit consideration of development issues, as well as an appreciation of the complexity and of the political aspects of existing social systems. This calls for an approach to DIDR that moves towards a more interactive approach to DIDR planning.

To a certain extent, technical changes can address the complexity of existing systems. Better data are needed for better planning, for example, baseline information on more aspects of the economy and environment. Baseline surveys should include the size and composition of the affected population and analysis of existing levels and sources of household and individual incomes. Efforts should be made to analyse family and individual income from all sources (Eriksen 1999). Many projects have used unreliable social and economic information from secondary sources (Eriksen 1999, Mejía 1999). DIDR initiatives need to collect contemporaneous data and avoid estimates; on-the-ground, in-depth data gathering techniques should be emphasised.

When resettlement occurs in a new area, in-depth knowledge of the receiving environment is needed. Personnel need to know what enterprises to promote, the time required to establish new enterprises, and the levels of potential income and risks involved in establishing them (Eriksen 1999). Better data are needed on potential sources of economic recovery, including greater understanding of the regional economy and existing economic development policies and initiatives (Cernea 1999). Projects would benefit from innovative ideas about income generation and better analysis of their income-earning potential. For example, adding value to existing local products can provide economic opportunities (Asch 1982, Feeney 1998). For the economic groundwork to be done well, more time will be required for forward planning and more resources for local studies.

To achieve this, economists need to be more involved (Cernea 1999). Environmental economics provides a model for including full social costs, e.g. psychological damage and loss of non-priced environmental and cultural assets, social cohesion and market access (Cernea 1999, Pearce 1999). It is essential to go beyond conventional cost-benefit analysis, which does not take into account distribution of benefits. Risk analysis should be broadened to recognise risks to all project actors and their distribution (Cernea 1999: 16). Economic sustainability, including intergenerational equity, needs to be foregrounded so that stocks of capital assets do not decrease. Consideration of assets must include the stock of skills and knowledge (human capital), physical and social capital and environmental assets (Hayes 1999, Pearce 1999).

However, technical approaches are insufficient, because they do not take into account the political aspects of DIDR. De Wet (2001: 4639) has raised the question of whether the inherent complexity of DIDR may create problems not readily amenable to operational and rational planning, predisposing projects to failure. Resettlement programmes that involve many actors in different activities must be undertaken in a timely fashion and in a particular sequence. Nonetheless, a formal, linear view of policy, from formulation to implementation, obscures an understanding of DIDR complexities (Rew et al. 2000).

The first aspect of a more political approach is to understand better the existing political-economic context in which DIDR is carried out. First, national development strategies and administrative structures with concerns other than DIDR may influence it. Second, national stratification systems distribute resources unevenly and give some groups more voice in decisions about the future. For example, developing countries often have distorted energy and water pricing policies that encourage large infrastructure projects (Pearce 1999). On the other hand, some policies may favour displaced groups. The Cree (Canada) were able to be more effective because a new prime minister (Trudeau) worked to create a just society with participatory democracy (Salisbury 1986: 32). International contexts also count. Indian social scientists arguing for better treatment for displaced tribal peoples referred to ILO conventions adopted by the Indian Government (Mahapatra 1999a). International agreements have provided support for asserting the rights of the displaced (Barutciski 2000, Robinson 2003).

Governments also carry out other development initiatives in resettlement zones. Urban resettlement often becomes intertwined with public housing programmes (Mejía 1999: 154). At Manantali (Mali), DIDR outcomes were affected by the simultaneous implementation of structural adjustment (Koenig and Diarra 1998b). In Indian resettlement colonies, resettler access to existing social welfare and credit programmes was enhanced when they became recognised administrative villages (Mahapatra 1999a: 99, 121). Many Asian, African and Latin American countries have existing schemes for area development, rural and urban housing and agricultural intensification, among others.

Resettlement agencies should attempt to understand how existing development initiatives may impact on resettlement possibilities. In some cases, existing programmes may interfere with resettlement strategies, as when the Manantali (Mali) resettlement project planned to use agricultural extension services being phased out by structural adjustment initiatives (Koenig and Diarra 1998b). In other cases, however, co-operation with existing programmes and organisations may offer real synergies for restoring livelihoods. Involving existing agencies without co-opting them may help attenuate the resentment of other, often inadequately funded, organisations that work alongside better-funded DIDR projects. Analysis of the administrative capabilities of different organisations ought to consider explicitly the potential problems of co-ordination (Rew 1996). Resettled areas also need to be officially incorporated into national administrative structures to increase their ability to participate in political affairs. These structures also provide a forum for hosts and resettlers to work together. Scudder and Colson's (1982) concepts of incorporation and integration offer a useful way to conceptualise such issues. The resettlement zone is part of a regional political-economic system that needs to be understood better to anticipate problems and to create meaningful job generation programmes.

Yet in all cases, simply by being forced, DIDR stresses the relatively powerless position of those affected. When people foresee few benefits to displacement, they search for ways either to stop it or to create benefits. People have often turned to organised resistance when they have not had political and legal arenas in which to defend, bargain for and promote their interests, or where policy and legal vacuums have offered few alternatives to political struggle (Cernea 1996a: 28, 29). Some resistance movements have aimed to stop the development activity requiring resettlement; at other times, people have used resistance to obtain better outcomes (Oliver-Smith 1996). Resistance may also serve as a protest against a government not considered to be working in the public interest; a poorly designed project may induce a rejection of the nation's right to define local agendas (Oliver-Smith 1996: 89). People resist resettlement because they recognise the potential for impoverishment.

Therefore, the second aspect of recognising the complexity of DIDR development is moving towards the democratisation of resettlement planning. The emphasis on policies and planning has given many resettlement initiatives a top-down character. Rew, Fisher and Pandey (2000) showed that, even if policies are exemplary, good implementation will not necessarily follow. The critique of planning suggests that, even with the best intentions, planners cannot foresee every eventuality. They usually lack sufficient knowledge about local conditions; they cannot anticipate all the consequences of particular implementation choices; and they cannot foresee independent policy and political changes at the national level. As noted above, the state needs to be pressured to work in the interests of all its citizens.

Yet other aspects of current DIDR initiatives lead one to question whether this will work. In public resettlement projects, the state is both the initiator of resettlement and the source of laws and regulations, leading to potential problems in securing the rights of resettled people (de Wet 2001: 4640–41). Lenders do not always follow their own policy guidelines (Oxfam 1996a). Even if laws can be used to pressure resettlement institutions, they may be contradictory, leading to arbitrariness in implementation (Hansungule et al. 1998). At the administrative level, many DIDR implementation institutions are weak; they lack policy mandates, organisational capacity and professional social-engineering skills. The multifaceted, highly emotional and politicised nature of resettlement requires flexibility and high commitment, yet administrators may become especially risk-averse in light of the high public scrutiny given to DIDR. It is easy to lose sight of the many possible responses and trade-offs and hard to coordinate the many and varied administrative demands and procedural links between organisations (Rew 1996: 211). In addition, some administrative agencies lack legitimacy because of a history of rent-seeking or corruption (Pandey 1998).

In this context, some have suggested that resettlement activities should be decentralised and independent, since local officials generally have better knowledge of and are often more sympathetic to those displaced (Eriksen 1999: 107). In principle, decentralisation should be more efficient because local decision makers know more about local conditions, allowing them to match resources and needs more precisely. Decision makers who live locally need to be exposed to more scrutiny and under greater pressure for accountability. There should also be more opportunities for local participation. But empirical data suggest that devolving control will not necessarily improve accountability or efficiency. Local governments do not necessarily give greater priority to human development and local élites may seize power. Lack of strong control from above may also create more opportunities for abuse or rent-seeking. In any case, central governments are often reluctant to devolve the funds or decision-making power to permit truly effective local control. Many local governments suffer from insufficient budgets, weak planning and control systems and lack of administrative competence (Feeney 1998, Meikle and Walker 1998).

Despite these problems, improving DIDR requires greater democratisation of planning. This means more than consultation or participation; the term 'democratisation' makes its political nature clear. Top-down planning alone cannot successfully protect the interests of the people below, in this case the displaced. At best, it is limited in its perspectives; at worst, it is mired in corruption and administrative inefficiency. Planners will work consistently in the local interest only if locals keep consistent pressure on them to do so. Depending on the sociocultural and political context, pressure may be polite and nuanced or raucous and confrontational. But if affected people believe they can have a positive impact on the actions of government administrators, private-sector actors and political operatives, they will work to create projects that improve their lives. Moreover, administrators will have more incentives to act in the interests of displaced people. This would not be a simple process, but would take time, effort, commitment and money. It offers the potential to lead to better post-DIDR experiences and to reduce impoverishment.

Practical Approaches to Improved DIDR

Actions needed to democratise DIDR include: increased commitment to democratisation and participation, greater transparency in planning, capacity building among local and administrative organisations, creating coalitions and increasing choice.

Greater Participation

Participation has been enthusiastically endorsed by many governments, financial institutions and bilateral donors, who have, however, shown different levels of practical commitment (Feeney 1998). Effective participation means influencing decisions, not simply involvement in implementation; it is an essential component of political life (Feeney 1998). Practically, participation helps increase the responsiveness and accountability of development initiatives. It needs to go beyond 'consultation'. Strategies to democratise DIDR will be most effective when they build on a growing understanding of democratisation in a larger sense and the many contemporary experiments in decentralisation, deconcentration and empowerment.

Some agencies have feared that participation will lead to cost over-runs and delays (Meikle and Walker 1998, Mejía 1999). DIDR planners have also expressed concern that sharing information and consulting affected people will create unrealistic expectations and attract free-riders. Participation does require effort and commitment from donors, governments and NGOs, and it often requires more time and funds at the beginning of a project to secure the involvement of all affected parties and to work out major disagreements (Bagadion and Korten 1991). It also needs good initial planning, training to increase local capacity, extra efforts to obtain the input of the especially vulnerable, clear procedures, open lines of communication and time to explore alternatives (Feeney 1998). The extra time and effort involved should be considered one more reason to avoid unjustified DIDR.

Experience shows that up-front effort is not wasted. Genuine participation helps to secure local consensus and reduces conflicts, negative social impacts, and delays later on in the process. It builds trust and collaboration, and communities gain a sense of ownership. Despite agency concerns, building community support in this way may actually inhibit free-riders, since the community, as well as project personnel, gain an interest in keeping them out. Moreover, addressing conflicts of interest in a public forum can avoid the bad decisions of a closed process and the almost inevitable resistance that follows. The presence of all potential stakeholders leads to broader ownership of the implementation process. Public accountability is more likely to lead to competence, caution and humility among officials than if they work without public pressure (Shas 1995).

Participation cannot simply mean involving locals in actions, the lines of which have already been dictated by higher levels. The process brings the potential for abuse if the more knowledgeable or more organised can dominate it. 'Placing different stakeholders on centre stage as if they are on a level playing field belies a situation in which power relations are extremely unequal, particularly for local people' (Rew et al. 2000: 37). Yet a commitment to participation can change the relationship between locals and other groups, as shown by the experiences of the Cree in Quebec, who restructured the relationship between themselves and larger societal institutions, taking over local administration and service delivery (Feit 1982, Salisbury 1986).

Democratic planning cannot happen on its own; it needs to be facilitated by positive actions and an interactive (learning-process) approach to planning that recognises the time and unpredictability inherent in changing behaviour and institutions. Adaptation and change midstream should be anticipated. This approach can work only if national authorities and project funders will devolve the necessary control (de Wet 2001). Because the approach is open-ended and requires more negotiation, project costs are not necessarily clear at the beginning, which concerns funders. Yet projects already change course in midstream and adapt policies in an ad hoc way (e.g. Meikle and Walker 1998, Mejía 1999). Moreover, many DIDR projects already face increased and unanticipated costs; Mejía (1999: 170, 171) noted that actual costs were often 300 to 400 percent higher than initial estimates in conventionally designed Latin American urban projects.

The incremental changes of interactive planning occur, but without explicit learning.

Top-down planning usually assumes, falsely, no significant changes in sociocultural, political-economic or physical context during the project. A plan created without the participation of local residents devalues their local knowledge. It is better to recognise the contingent nature of social change and envision a framework for action, which will be adapted as circumstances change. Given the complexity of DIDR, unanticipated consequences are the rule. An interactive approach seems the only way to address systematically unanticipated consequences, to integrate those who suffer negative impacts along the way and to include unanticipated solutions.

Transparency

One of the first conditions of democratic participation is that all interested parties have access to the knowledge necessary to make inferences about potential consequences. The fact that many government agencies decide in secret often forces people to participate by opposition and resistance rather than by bargaining and cooperation (Cernea 1996a: 29). The first step in increasing access to knowledge is transparency (Sen 1999). This includes informing people in time about resettlement, legal entitlements and eligibility, due process and grievance mechanisms (Cernea 1996a: 30). It also includes openness about budgets and public expenditures and mechanisms for conflict resolution, arbitration and redress that apply to all interested parties (Feeney 1998). Knowledge needs to be disseminated throughout the resettlement project and not just at the beginning. The media can be used to convey relevant information on progress and to maintain momentum (Feeney 1998: 138). ·

Under pressure from stakeholders, there has been progress towards transparency. The WCD (2000: 176–8) noted that information disclosure has increased steadily since the 1950s and that transparency linked with public participation has led to improved outcomes. Both donors and national governments have pursued strategies to increase transparency (Cernea 1996a, Feeney 1998). Agencies began to show greater openness in decision making in response to disastrous resettlement initiatives and concerted resistance to DIDR. Many in the power sector appear to have realised the high economic, social and political costs of corrective actions (Serra 1993).

Building Capacity

Knowledge by itself is insufficient to create effective participation. People need skills to participate effectively in a process whose outcomes result from negotiation. Participatory approaches require efforts to build capacity at all levels, including NGOs (increasingly involved in DIDR) and private-sector organisations.

Administrative organisations must understand their particular strengths and weaknesses, those linked to structural constraints as well as contingent features linked to such aspects as the capabilities and personalities of individual personnel. Local administrators also need the ability to collect necessary information, including details of existing and potential options and areas of cleavage or conflict. Local administration needs enhanced management skills such as administrative planning, conflict resolution and facilitation in encouraging residents to voice their needs (Rew 1996).

Displaced people need training to build their organisational skills so that they can participate more equitably in negotiations. It is rare that existing organisations can simply be transferred to the DIDR situation, yet capacity building should begin with them. Feeney's (1998: 50) discussion of Brazilian development initiatives illustrates the problems related to creating new associations rather than working with existing organisations.

NGOs, which have taken on a growing role in development and DIDR, may also need to enhance skills. Many are committed to participatory approaches, yet there is often a gap between ideology and practice (Feeney 1998: 27). A small, overstretched NGO community may not be able to carry out the multiple roles demanded of it, which have come to include planning, implementation and monitoring. Small NGOS working in remote areas and with limited experience of democratic process need basic technical training (Feeney 1998). Given the existing conflicts of interest, capacity building should include skills in negotiation and conflict resolution.

Small or isolated populations may find it difficult to create effective organisations. They can often enhance effectiveness by building coalitions with others and developing local umbrella organisations that include multiple local groups, as did the Cree of Quebec (Scudder 1996). Yet, building this capacity took time and experience; leaders had to learn to negotiate with fellow politicians and cope with the administration (Salisbury 1986). Local coalitions have been able to resist more effectively the divide-and-conquer strategies often used by agencies, such as persuading a few communities to sign agreements so that it becomes more difficult for others to refuse (Waldram 1988).

Capacity building takes commitment, up-front money, time and appropriate personnel. Some DIDR agencies may not want to fund local organisations that will pressure them to modify existing plans. In this context, international organisations must foreground the importance of development as a process of increasing local autonomy and political effectiveness. They also need to emphasise the practical aspects of enhanced local organisation: greater efficiency, local ownership, potential for local management, and sustainability. Many DIDR agencies will not change of their own volition, but will do so under pressure from other interested parties.

Coalition Building

Even when the capacities of their own organisations are enhanced, often displaced people still have less power to put forward their agendas. They may need to form coalitions with other groups to increase their ability to pressure more powerful groups and organisations. Forging relationships with international organisations has allowed local groups to gain visibility and clout (Gray 1996). In the case of DIDR, alliances have been primarily with environmental and human rights groups (Oliver-Smith 1996).

Locals can also create coalitions with neighbours and co-ethnics who have left the local area and have complementary knowledge and/or social relationships. More cosmopolitan co-ethnics have social links to the protestors but more experience with government bureaucracies. Groups may also create coalitions with other individuals or groups who work in their zone, such as social scientists, churches and missionaries, unions or NGOs (Salisbury 1986, Serra 1993, Patel 1995, Das et al. 1996).

Project administrators at any level may become allies. In World Bank funded projects, Gray (1996: 117) found that opposition from an influential sector inside the Bank was a condition for effective resistance. At Manantali (Mali), displaced villagers allied with key government personnel (Koenig 1997). In Canadian projects, individuals in local administrative positions sometimes played important roles (Waldram 1988). The work of McGill University anthropologists with the Cree was facilitated by anthropologists working for Indian and Native Affairs and the Privy Council office (Salisbury 1986).

Looking beyond international alliances is important because the agendas of large outside organisations sometimes threaten to overtake those of the displaced groups. Local organisations within Narmada were split about which problem to prioritise: the immediate resettlement or the larger issue of dam-based development. International organisations seemed more interested in the latter (Koenig and Diarra 2000). Coalitions between environmentalists and local-resource users may face problems when the locals want to continue hunting, fishing or nomadic pastoralism (McCutcheon 1991, Paine 1994). Coalitions among national actors help keep the focus on local concerns.

Social scientists have been divided on the appropriate role for outsiders. Pandey (1998) looked to NGOs to initiate collective thinking and action at the community level. In contrast, Mahapatra stressed the importance of people's own organisations. These grassroot organisations 'exemplify participation in goal sharing for community benefit … [since they are] *of, for,* and *by* the people' (Mahapatra 2000: 133, emphasis in original). In many cases, outsiders can offer important complementary pressure on agencies that do not want to change how they do business; they also can help build local capacity. On the other hand, the long-term goal of development implies moving towards more reliance on local people's own organisations and building their capacity to decide their own affairs.

In any case, conflicts of interest need to be addressed. Since resettled groups are internally differentiated, community reconstruction and the creation of effective pressure groups depend upon creating cohesion among people with disparate needs and interests. A practical strategy may be to start by promoting small homogeneous self-help groups (Feeney 1998: 70). Successful cases need to move beyond small groups to three other levels: intracommunity organisation, links among different communities, and organisations that join hosts and those displaced (Mahapatra 1999a). Creating cohesion is easier when old structures are transplanted, but it also needs to be done where there are no previous linkages between residents or between them and hosts. In these cases, tensions, mistrust and estrangement may result from different ethnic traditions or resource competition, exacerbating the difficulties (Lassailly-Jacob 1996, Mahapatra 1999b), but also making the creation of effective social solidarity and interdependence more important for long-term development.

Increasing Choice

The goal of democratising planning and implementation is to increase choice and autonomy; development should expand the freedoms that people enjoy (Sen 1999: 3) and reinforce their sense of control over their lives (de Wet 2001: 4638). Options also offer a response to the diverse needs and interests of affected populations. Yet, all choices are liable to unanticipated consequences, both positive and negative. People will have to consider trade-offs between optimal economic and sociocultural benefits. If they have the freedom to choose, they are likely to cope better with the adverse impacts they will undoubtedly encounter. Sometimes people will choose greater control over more tangible benefits (e.g. Thangaraj 1996).

Existing DIDR projects have not offered a wide range of choices. Eriksen (1999) found that DIDR projects in rural areas generally offered a single option, a contrast to voluntary resettlement where most projects evaluated two or more packages. Projects should consider a wide range of compensation and resettlement options keyed to specific needs; rural programmes should include non-farming activities (Eriksen 1999). Participation criteria should be developed so that people can be guided to options with a greater likelihood of success. One option should be a safety net for people with compromised prospects for rebuilding livelihoods, for example, retirement homes for elderly people with little social support (NRCR 1999, Appendix 2: 25).

Projects also need to reconsider how to facilitate options that encourage more affluent people to stay in resettlement areas and use their skills for the benefit of their communities. The issue of what new stratification systems might or should look like in resettled communities has not been sufficiently addressed. Although moving towards more equitable social systems is an integral part of development, it is nonetheless unrealistic to expect resettled communities to be egalitarian when few if any of the surrounding communities are (see Scudder 1981).

Projects should borrow and adopt appropriate ideas from other projects or countries. For example, Indian social scientists have argued for adopting certain Chinese strategies (Mahapatra 1999a). Chinese collective land ownership might also be a model for areas trying to change informal customary tenure to something more formalised, for example, in West Africa. It is risky simply to borrow institutions and insert them into a different sociocultural context, but they can be used to help think through new alternatives and options.

At its best, interactive planning can integrate new possibilities even in midstream. New human, financial or environmental resources can be capitalised upon as they appear. New small- or medium-scale enterprises that wish to locate themselves in the resettlement zone might be offered incentives if they train and hire displaced people. Options should allow people to mix different activities to create economic strategies using individual and family capacities and knowledge. An interactive approach that allows people to adapt projects to their needs is likely to improve overall success by building on the sense of ownership of affected persons. The participation of those displaced, organised by themselves and allied with others to bring pressure upon implementing agencies, is necessary for successful DIDR. Negotiated and democratic project strategies will undoubtedly lead to less predictable outcomes for DIDR and associated development projects. It is nonetheless needed to move towards real development.

Conclusion: Extra Resources are Needed

An interactive, democratic approach to DIDR will cost more, at least over the short term; it will require new kinds of personnel, as well as supplementary research to address issues raised by such an approach.

Resettlement projects oriented towards development are expensive. The enhancements recommended in this chapter are likely to render DIDR more expensive through more and better technical assistance, longer development initiatives and more training. Nevertheless, there do seem to be pay-offs. The World Bank review showed DIDR projects with high financial allocations to be free of major difficulties, while virtually all projects with low financing faced serious problems (Cernea 1999). Enhancing DIDR through greater democratisation means greater costs at the beginning, but the possibility of fewer costs over time as people take ownership. Greater democratisation should decrease grievances due to lack of participation, which can lead to delays and higher costs. Reconstituting lives promptly should also mean a shorter transition, reducing losses and lowering long-term costs.

Should these increased costs be carried up front by the national government in the case of public projects or by the private investor in the case of private ones? Should international donors be expected to pick up costs that cannot be met locally? It would seem reasonable to look for ways to supplement funding from other sources. Benefit sharing, where people gain directly from revenues generated by the DIDR initiative requiring displacement, offers some promise. A percentage of sales revenues in the energy sector has been allocated to resettlers and the local administration in China, Colombia and the Philippines (Van Wicklin 1999). Those who benefit directly from DIDR can be required to pay for resettlement and development through charges on output, for example, higher electricity or irrigation fees (Pearce 1999). These revenues come post-project, but they can be used to repay loans used for resettlement activities. Foundations can also be established to benefit relocatees (Feeney 1998).

If DIDR development programmes want to increase local autonomy, they might allocate local communities the rights to levy taxes or procure rents and royalties, linking national decentralisation initiatives to DIDR. In China, local units with human and financial resources have undertaken resettlement activities in line with national guidelines but adapted to local circumstances (Meikle and Walker 1998). Where decentralised institutions already exist, for example, on American Indian reservations, experience shows that locals may earn from their resources (Aberle 1993). To be sure, decentralisation programmes need local governments with sufficient administrative capacity and resources.

Some of the financial problems confronting DIDR may be addressed by a more participatory, interactive approach. Real participation and control over resettlement so that people can adapt benefits to individual needs may make people willing to bear some time and money costs. Although this should not become an excuse for outside organisations to lower financial commitments, autonomy and control can substitute for some economic benefits.

Models of DIDR that draw on general development theory as well as on resettlement experiences suggest that the variety of personnel involved in DIDR needs to be broadened. Most of the DIDR projects studied by Eriksen (1999) had primary implementing agencies with mandates oriented almost exclusively to infrastructure installation. In recent years, the involvement of social scientists specialising in resettlement has grown. Yet DIDR projects need a still broader base of personnel. DIDR should be based on knowledge of a wide range of approaches to achieving economically, socially and environmentally sustainable development.

Resettlement implementation teams should include not only specialised Resettlement Officers (Rew et al. 2000), but also experienced rural or urban development specialists. The question of personnel needs to be complemented by consideration of the optimal organisational structure. Commonly more than one agency is involved, although the relationships between the agencies and the mix between conventional public adminis-tration and specialised resettlement agencies can vary widely (Rew 1996). The involvement of NGOs is growing and private-sector agencies may also be involved. The particular mix appropriate for a given DIDR initia-tive will depend on the sociocultural, administrative and political context.

Although the existing literature is substantial, more research is still needed on the issues raised in this chapter. Three are particularly impor-tant: first, the question of how to create jobs for the displaced, including the role of small- and medium-sized private-sector firms in job recon-struction; second, the question of how to reconstitute complex economic and social systems, especially in urban areas; third, the need to under-stand better the conflicts of interest and lines of differentiation among resettled populations. Of special concern is finding ways to encourage local élites to work in the interests of their communities. These issues have economic and social components that require a solid understanding of local and national politics and policies. Two more issues complement the arguments of this chapter. First, comparative analysis of displacement and resettlement in developed and developing countries might broaden our understanding of alternative approaches. Second, given the growing importance of private-sector development, it would be useful to under-stand better the particular characteristics of private-sector DIDR, includ-ing the use of legal instruments and the courts to negotiate relationships between private developers and displaced people.

Notes

This chapter is based on a report funded by DfID and prepared for ESCOR R7644 and the Research Programme on Development-induced Displacement and Resettlement organised by the Refugee Studies Centre, University of Oxford (Koenig 2001). I would like to thank all who provided comments on earlier ver-sions of this paper. The opinions expressed herein are solely mine; they should not be attributed to the funder or the Refugee Studies Centre, University of Oxford.

1. I was a member of the design team for this project (USAID 1984), served as senior social science advisor during implementation, participated in an end-of-project evaluation (Diarra et al. 1994) and carried out research on later effects (Diarra et al. 1995, Koenig and Diarra 1998a, 1998b).

2. DIDR can, however, introduce new health problems; for example, malaria and schistosomiasis in river-basin areas, or risks from pollution in mines or facto-ries. See Ault (1989).

3. Although scholars almost universally favour land-for-land, the displaced themselves do not necessarily do so. In India, a study of twenty-nine projects found that 80 percent chose cash compensation over resettlement colonies (Pandey 1998: 117). In one Ugandan project, many farmers preferred cash because they owned other plots of land or earned income from other sources (Rew et al. 2000).

4. Indian social scientists have worked hard to get national law to recognise the principal of replacement value (Mahapatra 1999a: 154–59).

5. A related question is whether the initiatives that induce displacement are themselves 'development', since it is questionable whether some of them improve even national welfare. This includes activities such as politically mandated mass relocation (Brain 1976, Cohen and Isaksson 1987, de Wet 1993) and the sedentarisation of pastoralists (Merryman 1982). Some have also suggested that projects may have covert anti-development purposes (Oliver-Smith 1996, Scudder 1996), although data on these purposes is rarely available directly. Discussion of this is beyond the scope of this chapter.

6. Common property exists when groups can grant use rights to some and restrict or exclude others. Open-access resources allow use to anyone who can get to the resource; this may lead to resource competition (Berkes and Farvar 1989). Centralising governments have often turned locally managed common property into open-access resources, politicising the reconstitution of common property resources.

References

Aberle, D. 1993. 'The Navajo-Hopi Land Dispute and Navajo Relocation'. In M.M. Cernea and S.E. Guggenheim (eds). *Anthropological Approaches to Resettlement: Policy, Practice, and Theory*, pp. 153–200. Boulder CO: Westview Press.

Appa, G. and G. Patel. 1996. 'Unrecognised, Unnecessary and Unjust Displacement: Case Studies from Gujarat, India'. In C. McDowell (ed.). *Understanding Impoverishment: The Consequences of Development-induced Displacement*, pp. 139–50. Providence RI, Oxford: Berghahn Books.

Asch, M. 1982. 'Dene Self-determination and the Study of Hunter-gatherers in the Modern World'. In E. Leacock and R. Lee (eds). *Politics and History in Band Societies*, pp. 347–71. Cambridge: Cambridge University Press.

Ault, S. 1989. 'The Health Effects of Involuntary Resettlement'. Paper prepared for the Task Force on Involuntary Resettlement, American Anthropological Association.

Baboo, B. 1996. 'State Policies and People's Response: Lessons from Hirakud Dam'. In A.B. Ota and A. Agnihotri (eds). *Involuntary Displacement in Dam Projects*, pp. 203–30. New Delhi: Prachi Prakshan.

Bagadion, B. and F. Korten. 1991. 'Developing Irrigators' Organizations: A Learning Process Approach'. In M.M. Cernea (ed.). *Putting People First: Sociological Variables in Rural Development*, pp. 73–112, (2nd edn). New York: Oxford University Press for the World Bank.

Bartolomé, L. 1993. 'The Yacyretá Experience with Urban Resettlement: Some Lessons and Insights'. In M.M. Cernea and S.E. Guggenheim (eds).

Anthropological Approaches to Resettlement: Policy, Practice, and Theory, pp. 109–32. Boulder CO: Westview Press.

Barutciski, M. 2000. *Addressing Legal Constraints and Improving Outcomes in Development-induced Resettlement Projects*. Final report to DfID. Oxford: Refugee Studies Centre, University of Oxford.

Berkes, F and M.T. Farvar. 1989. 'Introduction and Overview'. In F. Berkes (ed.). *Common Property Resources: Ecology and Community-based Sustainable Development*, pp. 1–17. London: Belhaven.

Brain, J. 1976. 'Less than Second Class: Women on Rural Settlement Schemes in Tanzania'. In N. Hafkin and E. Bay (eds). *Women in Africa*, pp. 265–82. Stanford: Stanford University Press.

Cernea, M.M. 1996a. 'Understanding and Preventing Impoverishment from Displacement: Reflections on the State of Knowledge'. In C. McDowell (ed.). *Understanding Impoverishment: The Consequences of Development-induced Displacement*, pp. 13–32. New York, Oxford: Berghahn Books.

————— 1996b. 'Eight Main Risks: Impoverishment and Social Justice in Resettlement'. Washington DC: The World Bank, Environment Department.

————— 1999. 'Why Economic Analysis is Essential to Resettlement: A Sociologist's View'. In M.M. Cernea (ed.). *The Economics of Involuntary Resettlement: Questions and Challenges*, pp. 5–49. Washington DC: The World Bank.

————— 2000. 'Risks, Safeguards and Reconstruction: A Model for Population Displacement and Resettlement'. In M.M. Cernea and C. McDowell (eds). *Risks and Reconstruction: Experiences of Resettlers and Refugees*, pp. 11–55. Washington DC: The World Bank.

Chambers, R. 1969. *Settlement Schemes in Tropical Africa*. London: Routledge and Kegan Paul.

Charest, P. 1982. 'Hydroelectric Dam Construction and the Foraging Activities of Eastern Quebec Montagnais'. In E. Leacock and R. Lee (eds). *Politics and History in Band Societies*, pp. 413–26. Cambridge: Cambridge University Press.

Chatty, D. and M. Colchester (eds). 2002. *Conservation and Mobile Indigenous Peoples: Displacement, Forced Settlement, and Sustainable Development*. New York, Oxford: Berghahn Books.

Cohen, J. and N. Isaksson. 1987. 'Villagisation in Ethiopia's Arsi Region'. *Journal of Modern African Studies*, 25: 435–64.

Colson, E. 1999. 'Gendering those Uprooted by "Development"'. In D. Indra (ed.). *Engendering Forced Migration: Theory and Practice*, pp. 23–39. New York, Oxford: Berghahn Books.

Das, A., V. Das and B. Das. 1996. 'Involuntary Displacement in Upper Indravati Hydro-electric Project'. In A.B. Ota and A. Agnihotri (eds). *Involuntary Displacement in Dam Projects*, pp. 126–49. New Delhi: Prachi Prakshan.

de Wet, C. 1993. 'A Spatial Analysis of Involuntary Community Relocation: A South African Case Study'. In M.M. Cernea and S.E. Guggenheim (eds). *Anthropological Approaches to Resettlement: Policy, Practice, and Theory*, pp. 321–50. Boulder CO: Westview Press.

————— 2001. 'Economic Development and Population Displacement: Can Everybody Win?'. *Economic and Political Weekly (Mumbai)*. 36(50): 4637–46.

Diarra, T., D. Koenig, Y.F. Koné and F. Maiga. 1994. *Final Evaluation: Manantali Resettlement Project (625–0955)*. Bamako: Institut des Sciences Humaines.

_____ 1995. *Réinstallation et développement dans la zone du barrage de Manantali.* Bamako: Institut des Sciences Humaines.

Downing, T. 1996. 'Mitigating Social Impoverishment when People are Involuntarily Displaced'. In C. McDowell (ed.). *Understanding Impoverishment: The Consequences of Development-induced Displacement*, pp. 33–48. New York, Oxford: Berghahn Books.

Eriksen, J.H. 1999. 'Comparing the Economic Planning for Voluntary and Involuntary Resettlement'. In M.M. Cernea (ed.). *The Economics of Involuntary Resettlement: Questions and Challenges*, pp. 83–146. Washington DC: The World Bank.

Escobar, A. 1995. *Encountering Development: The Making and Unmaking of the Third World.* Princeton NJ: Princeton University Press.

Feeney, P. 1998. *Accountable Aid: Local Participation in Major Projects.* Oxford: Oxfam Publications.

Feit, H. 1982. 'The Future of Hunters within Nation-States: Anthropology and the James Bay Cree'. In E. Leacock and R. Lee (eds). *Politics and History in Band Societies*, pp. 373–411. Cambridge: Cambridge University Press.

Gibson, D. 1993. 'Involuntary Resettlement and Institutional Disjuncture'. Paper presented at the annual meeting of the American Anthropological Association, Washington DC, 17–21 November.

Gray, A. 1996. 'Indigenous Resistance to Involuntary Relocation'. In C. McDowell (ed.). *Understanding Impoverishment: The Consequences of Development-induced Displacement*, pp. 99–122. New York, Oxford: Berghahn Books.

Hansen, A. and A. Oliver-Smith (eds). 1982. *Involuntary Migration and Resettlement: The Problems and Responses of Dislocated People.* Boulder CO: Westview Press.

Hansungule, M., P. Feeney and R. Palmer. 1998. *Report on Land Tenure Insecurity on the Zambian Copperbelt.* Oxford: Oxfam GB in Zambia.

Hayes, J. 1999. 'Participatory Development: Mitigating against Impoverishment in Involuntary Resettlement'. M.Sc. Dissertation, Department of Social Policy and Administration, London School of Economics and Political Science, London University.

Indra, D. (ed.). 1999. *Engendering Forced Migration: Theory and Practice.* New York, Oxford: Berghahn Books.

Koenig, D. 1995. 'Women and Resettlement'. *The Women and International Development Annual*, 4: 21–49.

_____ 1997. 'Competition among Malian Élites in the Manantali Resettlement Project: The Impacts on Local Development'. *Urban Anthropology and Studies of Cultural Systems and World Economic Development*, 26(3/4): 369–411.

_____ 2001. *Toward Local Development and Mitigating Impoverishment in Development-induced Displacement and Resettlement.* Final report to DfID. Oxford: Refugee Studies Centre, University of Oxford.

Koenig, D. and T. Diarra. 1998a. 'Les enjeux de la politique locale dans la réinstallation: Stratégies foncières des populations réinstallées et hôtes dans la zone du barrage de Manantali'. *Autrepart: Cahiers des Sciences Humaines* (new series), 5: 29–44.

_____ 1998b. 'The Environmental Effects of Policy Change in the West African Savanna: Resettlement, Structural Adjustment and Conservation in Western Mali'. *Journal of Political Ecology*, 5: 23–52.

_____ 2000. 'The Effects of Resettlement on Access to Common Property Resources'. In M.M. Cernea and C. McDowell (eds). *Risks and Reconstruction: Experiences of Resettlers and Refugees*, pp. 332–62. Washington DC: The World Bank.

Konaté, Y. 1993. 'Resettlement in Manantali, Mali: A View from Inside'. Paper presented at the annual meeting of the American Anthropological Association, Washington DC, 17–21 November.

Lassailly-Jacob, V. 1996. 'Land-based Strategies in Dam-related Resettlement Programmes in Africa'. In C. McDowell (ed.). *Understanding Impoverishment: The Consequences of Development-induced Displacement*, pp. 187–99. New York, Oxford: Berghahn Books.

Lohmann, L. 1998. 'Missing the Point of Development Talk: Reflections for Activists'. Corner House Briefing Paper No. 9. Sturminster Newton U.K.: The Corner House.

Mahapatra, L.K. 1999a. *Resettlement, Impoverishment and Reconstruction in India: Development for the Deprived.* New Delhi: Vikas Publishing.

_____ 1999b. 'Testing the Risks and Reconstruction Model on India's Resettlement Experiences'. In M.M. Cernea (ed.). *The Economics of Involuntary Resettlement: Questions and Challenges*, pp. 189–230. Washington DC: The World Bank.

_____ 2000. 'Resettlement with Participation: The Indian Experience'. *The Eastern Anthropologist*, 53(1/2): 121–40.

Marx, E. 1988. 'Advocacy in a Bedouin Resettlement Program'. Paper presented at the meeting of the International Congress of Anthropological and Ethnological Sciences, Zagreb, July.

McCutcheon, S. 1991. *Electric Rivers: The Story of the James Bay Project.* Montreal, New York: Black Rose Books.

Meikle, S. and J. Walker. 1998. *Resettlement Policy and Practice in China and the Philippines.* Escor Research Scheme Number R6802. London: Development Planning Unit, University College.

Mejía, M.C. 1999. 'Economic Dimensions of Urban Resettlement: Experiences from Latin America'. In M.M. Cernea (ed.). *The Economics of Involuntary Resettlement: Questions and Challenges*, pp. 147–88. Washington DC: The World Bank.

_____ 2000. 'Economic Recovery after Involuntary Resettlement: The Case of Brickmakers Displaced by the Yacyretá Hydroelectric Project'. In M.M. Cernea and C. McDowell (eds). *Risks and Reconstruction: Experiences of Resettlers and Refugees*, pp. 144–64. Washington DC: The World Bank.

Merryman, J. 1982. 'Pastoral Nomad Settlement in Response to Drought: The Case of Kenya Somali'. In A. Hansen and A. Oliver-Smith (eds). *Involuntary Migration and Resettlement: The Problems and Responses of Dislocated People*, pp. 105–19. Boulder CO: Westview Press.

NRCR (National Research Centre of Resettlement, Hohai University). 1999. 'China Resettlement Policy and Practice'. Report to Asian Development Bank, Regional Technical Assistance Project (No. 5781). Prepared for Foreign Capital Project Management Centre of the State Council Office for Poverty Alleviation, Nanjing.

Oliver-Smith, A. 1996. 'Fighting for a Place: The Policy Implications of Resistance to Development-induced Resettlement'. In C. McDowell (ed.). *Understanding Impoverishment: The Consequences of Development-induced Displacement,* pp. 77–97. Providence RI, Oxford: Berghahn Books.

_____ 2001. *Displacement, Resistance and the Critique of Development: From the Grass Roots to the Global.* Final report to DfID. Oxford: Refugee Studies Centre, University of Oxford.

Oxfam. 1996a. *A Profile of European Aid: Natural Forest Management and Conservation Project, Uganda.* Oxford: Oxfam U.K./I Policy Department.

_____ 1996b. *A Profile of European Aid II: Northern Corridor Transport Project, Adverse Social and Environmental Impacts Caused by the Rehabilitation of the Westlands – St. Austins and Kabete-Limuru Roads, Kenya.* Oxford: Oxfam U.K./I Policy Department.

Paine, R. 1994. *Herds of the Tundra: A Portrait of Saami Reindeer Pastoralism.* Washington DC: Smithsonian Institution Press.

Pandey, B. 1998. *Depriving the Underprivileged for Development.* Bhubaneswar: Institute for Socio-economic Development.

Partridge, W., A. Brown and J. Nugent. 1982. 'The Papaloapan Dam and Resettlement Project: Human Ecology and Health Impact'. In A. Hansen and A. Oliver-Smith (eds). *Involuntary Migration and Resettlement: The Problems and Responses of Dislocated People,* pp. 245–66. Boulder CO: Westview Press.

Patel, A. 1995. 'What Do the Narmada Valley Tribals Want?'. In W. Fisher (ed.). *Toward Sustainable Development? Struggling over India's Narmada River,* pp. 179–200. Armonk NY: M.E. Sharpe.

Patkar, M. 2000. 'A Comment'. In World Commission on Dams. *Dams and Development: A New Framework for Decision-making,* pp. 321–22. London, Sterling VA: Earthscan.

Pearce, D.W. 1999. 'Methodological Issues in the Economic Analysis for Involuntary Resettlement Operations'. In M.M. Cernea (ed.). *The Economics of Involuntary Resettlement: Questions and Challenges,* pp. 50–82. Washington DC: The World Bank.

Perlman, J.E. 1982. 'Favela Removal: The Eradication of a Lifestyle'. In A. Hansen and A. Oliver-Smith (eds). *Involuntary Migration and Resettlement: The Problems and Responses of Dislocated People,* pp. 225–43. Boulder CO: Westview Press.

Rapley, J. 1996. *Understanding Development: Theory and Practice in the Third World.* Boulder CO, London: Lynne Rienner.

Rew, A. 1996. 'Policy Implications of the Involuntary Ownership of Resettlement Negotiations: Examples from Asia of Resettlement Practice'. In C. McDowell (ed.). *Understanding Impoverishment: The Consequences of Development-induced Displacement,* pp. 201–21. New York, Oxford: Berghahn Books.

Rew, A., E. Fisher and B. Pandey. 2000. *Addressing Policy Constraints and Improving Outcomes in Development-induced Displacement and Resettlement Projects.* Final report to DfID. Oxford: Refugee Studies Centre, University of Oxford.

Robinson, W.C. 2003. 'Risks and Rights: The Causes, Consequences and Challenges of Development-induced Displacement'. Occasional Paper. Washington DC: The Brookings Institution-SAIS on Internal Displacement.

Rubinstein, J.M. 1988. 'Relocation of Families for Public Improvement Projects: Lessons from Baltimore'. *Journal of the American Planning Association*, 54: 185–96.

Salem-Murdock, M. 1989. *Arabs and Nubians in New Halfa: A Study of Settlement and Irrigation*. Salt Lake City: University of Utah Press.

Salem-Murdock, M., M. Niasse, J. Magistro, C. Nuttall, M. Horowitz and O. Kane. 1994. *Les barrages de la controverse: Le cas de la vallée du fleuve sénégal*. Paris: Harmattan.

Salisbury, R. 1986. *A Homeland for the Cree: Regional Development in James Bay 1971–1981*. Kingston, Montreal: McGill-Queen's University Press.

Satterfield, M.H. 1937. 'The Removal of Families from Tennessee Valley Authority Reservoir Areas'. *Social Forces*, 16: 258–61.

Scudder, T. 1981. *The Development Potential of New Lands Settlement in the Tropics and Subtropics: A Global State of the Art Evaluation with Specific Emphasis on Policy Implications*. Binghamton NY: Institute for Development Anthropology.

——— 1982. *No Place to Go: Effects of Compulsory Relocation on Navajos*. Philadelphia: Institute for the Study of Human Issues.

——— 1993. 'Development-induced Relocation and Refugee Studies: 37 Years of Change and Continuity among Zambia's Gwembe Tonga'. *Journal of Refugee Studies*, 6(2): 123–52.

——— 1996. 'Development-induced Impoverishment, Resistance and River-basin Development'. In C. McDowell (ed.). *Understanding Impoverishment: The Consequences of Development-induced Displacement*, pp. 49–74. New York, Oxford: Berghahn Books.

Scudder, T. and E. Colson. 1982. 'From Welfare to Development: A Conceptual Framework for the Analysis of Dislocated People'. In A. Hansen and A. Oliver-Smith (eds). *Involuntary Migration and Resettlement: The Problems and Responses of Dislocated People*, pp. 267–87. Boulder CO: Westview Press.

Sen, A. 1999. *Development as Freedom*. New York: Knopf.

Serra, M.T.F. 1993. 'Resettlement Planning in the Brazilian Power Sector: Recent Changes in Approach'. In M.M. Cernea and S.E. Guggenheim (eds). *Anthropological Approaches to Resettlement: Policy, Practice, and Theory*, pp. 63–85. Boulder CO: Westview Press.

Shas, A. 1995. 'A Technical Overview of the Flawed Sardar Sarovar Project and a Proposal for a Sustainable Alternative'. In W. Fisher (ed.). *Toward Sustainable Development? Struggling over India's Narmada River*, pp. 319–67. Armonk NY: M.E. Sharpe.

Spring, A. 1982. 'Women and Men as Refugees: Differential Assimilation of Angolan Refugees in Zambia'. In A. Hansen and A. Oliver-Smith (eds). *Involuntary Migration and Resettlement: The Problems and Responses of Dislocated People*, pp. 37–47. Boulder CO: Westview Press.

Squires, G., L. Bennett, K. McCourt and P. Nyden. 1987. *Chicago: Race, Class, and the Response to Urban Decline*. Philadelphia: Temple University Press.

Thangaraj, S. 1996. '"Impoverishment Risks" Analysis: A Methodological Tool for Participatory Resettlement Planning'. In C. McDowell (ed.). *Understanding Impoverishment: The Consequences of Development-induced Displacement*, pp. 223–32. New York, Oxford: Berghahn Books.

USAID (United States Agency for International Development). 1984. *Project Paper: Mali, Manantali Resettlement*. Washington DC: USAID.

Van Wicklin III, W. 1999. 'Sharing Project Benefits to Improve Resettlers' Livelihoods'. In M.M. Cernea (ed.). *The Economics of Involuntary Resettlement: Questions and Challenges*, pp. 231–56. Washington DC: The World Bank.

Waldram, J. 1980. 'Relocation and Political Change in a Manitoba Native Community'. *Canadian Journal of Anthropology*, 1: 173–78.

———— 1988. *As Long as the Rivers Run: Hydroelectric Development and Native Communities in Western Canada*. Winnipeg: University of Manitoba Press.

Wali, A. 1989. *Kilowatts and Crisis: Hydroelectric Power and Social Dislocation in Eastern Panama*. Boulder CO: Westview Press.

———— 1993. 'The Transformation of a Frontier: State and Regional Relationships in Panama, 1979–1990'. *Human Organization*, 52: 115–29.

World Bank. 2001a. '*Operational Policies 4.12: Involuntary Resettlement*' and '*Bank Procedures 4.12: Involuntary Resettlement*'. Washington DC: The World Bank.

———— 2001b. *World Development Report 2000/2001: Attacking Poverty*. New York: Oxford University Press for the World Bank.

World Commission on Dams (WCD). 2000. *Dams and Development: A New Framework for Decision-making*. London, Sterling VA: Earthscan.

6

Displacement, Resistance and the Critique of Development: From the Grass Roots to the Global

Anthony Oliver-Smith

Introduction: Resistance to Development-induced Displacement and Resettlement

Challenging the currently dominant neoliberal policies, voices articulating alternative approaches to development have appeared in the many regions of the world that have been forced to confront a wide variety of losses, costs and calamities brought about by development projects of many kinds. One of the voices increasingly heard today is that of people displaced and resettled by development projects. Uprooting and displacement have been among the central experiences of modernity. Development-induced displacement and resettlement (DIDR) is, in many ways, a clear expression of the ambitious engineering projects of a state with a monopoly on the management of force. Conversely, to be resettled is one of the most acute expressions of powerlessness because it constitutes a loss of control over one's physical space. Indigenous peoples, the poor and other marginalised groups are increasingly choosing to resist DIDR in the hope that this will prove more effective in protecting their long-term interests than co-operation (Fisher 1999).

Uprooted people, and the social movements and organisations that have taken up their cause, are now at the forefront of an emerging transnational civil society (e.g. Fox and Brown 1998), which focuses on a broad spectrum of issues such as trade, democratisation, human rights, indigenous peoples, gender, security and the environment – often in opposition to the state and private capital (Khagram 1999). Development projects have increasingly become the contexts in which these interests and issues are contested and played out through different models of development by local and nonlocal individuals and groups. Uprooted and resettled people have been joined by allies at national and international levels from communities of activists around the world, involving an extremely wide range of peoples, organisations, levels, contexts and relationships that call for greater democratisation and more participation of local populations in the decisions and projects affecting them.

This chapter seeks to explore the ways in which rights, claims and visions of the development process that are expressed in the complex and multidimensional forms of resistance to DIDR, become not only a means to refuse relocation or claim compensation or better conditions, but also help to initiate and become part of a multilevel, multisectoral effort to critique and reconceptualise the development process.

Development, as it has been generally and broadly conceived and applied, is the process through which the productive forces of economies and supporting infrastructures are improved through public and private investment. This can generally be subsumed into the two large-scale transformative trajectories of increased integration into the state and the market. Such processes do not occur without considerable cultural and social discontinuity and quite often conflict (Moore 1966, Wolf 1982). The discussion surrounding these necessary transformations has included a questioning that probes the democratic character of certain forms of development. Democratic regimes are said to be subject to pressures to allocate resources for consumption needs at the expense of investment for growth and development. The process of DIDR, when undertaken despite the opposition of affected peoples, or when accomplished without participation and benefits for affected peoples, calls into question the entire relationship between this form of development and democracy. Furthermore, the capacity of people to protest, resist and influence DIDR policy may constitute an important test of the democratic character of a particular regime.

Until quite recently, infrastructural and productive development have been considered to produce benefits that far outweigh any costs that such processes might entail. In many ways, any costs occasioned by infrastructural and productive development have been externalised, to be absorbed either by the environment or by the general population. DIDR resistance and other alternative forms of development discourse question the fundamental social, cultural and economic assumptions of development, and purport to offer alternative conceptualisations that produce benefits and reduce costs at specific local levels.

Since the end of the Second World War, there has been a relatively continuous spread and institutionalisation of global norms and principles of various types – regulatory, constitutive, practical and evaluative (Khagram 1999: 23). Three domains in particular: human rights; the environment; and the rights of indigenous peoples – all directly related to

DIDR – have seen particularly extensive growth and diffusion to many nations around the world (Khagram 1999: 25). The enormous challenges and problems faced by indigenous peoples around the world have given rise to literally thousands of national and international organisations, particularly in the post-Second World War period of decolonisation (Gray 1996: 113). Consequently, it is in this broader context of an emerging transnational civil society addressing development from the perspective of human rights, the environment and the rights of indigenous peoples that the people and organisations resisting DIDR act.

Resettlement studies have focused largely on dams in particular because of their widespread social and environmental impacts as well as their powerful expression of the Western, technologically driven form of development The most detailed analyses of resistance movements focus on those confronting dam-related DIDR in India and Southeast Asia (Fisher 1995, McCully 1996, Parasuraman 1999) and in Latin America (Bartolomé and Barabas 1990, McCully 1996, Rothman and Oliver 1999). Other forms of DIDR (conservation, tourism development, urban renewal, mining, transportation, pipelines, etc.) and resistance to them have received less attention, although urban renewal in the developed world has been closely examined since the 1950s (Gans 1962, Fried 1963, Smith, N. 1996). Recently, conservation driven resettlement has received considerable attention (Brechin et al. 2003), but more analysis of resistance is still needed (Acselrad and Da Silva 2000). Privately funded DIDR development projects are increasing and the resistance movements that confront them face new and different challenges. The significance of such research will thus only increase in the coming decade.

Disclosure of movement formation, leadership and strategising carries with it the potential of compromising specific individuals, as well as of providing information useful in co-opting, pre-empting or disarming DIDR resistance movements. The danger of such disclosures should always be framed in the context of the importance of disseminating the important information and perspectives necessary for the improvement of development policy and practice that DIDR resistance movements seek to achieve. Resistance brings into high relief the serious defects and shortcomings in policy frameworks, legal options, assessment and evaluation methodologies, and lack of expertise in implementation that plague much of the development effort. However, the question of how we can explain movements without compromising them remains difficult and should be at the forefront of research concerns.

The perception that many of the most vulnerable are forced to share an unfair burden of the costs of development, and that this constitutes a violation of basic human and environmental rights, is the core substance of resistance. In that sense, this chapter, rather than being a simple inventory of causes, forms and contexts of DIDR resistance, aims to address the cultural politics of resettlement policy and practice as constructed by its various participants. It is not accepted as given that development that displaces people is both necessary and inevitable. The chapter does, however, assert the fundamentally political nature of decisions to undertake such projects as result in displacement and resettlement. In addressing the politics of DIDR and resistance to it, the chapter itself cannot be seen as separate from the discourse that has emerged surrounding the core issues.

The Problematics and Politics of DIDR Resistance

As a citizen of the nation one has the right to development through its institutions, and one's rights include participation in the decision-making processes that impact one's life and community. At a fundamental level, DIDR resistance is a discourse about rights. DIDR pits the rights of the state (and, increasingly, of private capital) to develop against the rights of specific peoples targeted for resettlement. Although the rhetoric that accompanies large-scale development projects frequently makes references to national purpose and proposes benefits for a general public, those who must suffer the costs that these projects entail tend to be quite specific communities. It is fundamentally the failure of the state and, increasingly, the private sector to undertake these projects in an ethical and competent fashion that produces conditions that generate major forms of resistance. Human rights groups have challenged the idea that development policy decisions arrived at through techno-managerial forms of cost-benefit analysis should set priorities, rather than other standards of judgment such as distributive justice, the right to adequate livelihood or the right to human dignity (Colchester 1999: 13). The distinction between development defined in terms of economic growth as opposed to development defined in terms of the expansion of social, economic and political rights and power to broader sectors of the population lies at the core of DIDR resistance.

The increasing involvement of private capital shifts the goal of projects from improving social and economic conditions to enhancing the reproduction of capital in the form of profit, which is also considered to enhance the well-being of the society. Generally, people displaced by private development are considered to be voluntary migrants, having accepted a sum of money in exchange for their land. Market transactions have the effect of disguising the difference between voluntary migration and forced displacement. Many factors may influence such a decision to accept payment or other forms of compensation for land, some of which, in both public and privately driven displacement, amount to various forms of coercion. Resistance movements call into question the voluntary nature of much of this 'voluntary' displacement.

Resistance involves a continuum of forms, ranging from passive foot-dragging, nonappearance at official sites and times, inability to understand instructions and other 'weapons of the weak' so ably described by Scott (1985), to protest meetings, civil disobedience, outright rebellion and warfare. The lack of overt resistance does not indicate that displacement is voluntary. By the same token, there are instances in which active resistance does not always indicate a primary agenda of reluctance to relocate. In these instances, resistance becomes a tool of negotiation to increase the levels of compensation.

DIDR Resistance: Diversity, Complexity and Dynamism

A significant percentage of those who face removal, whatever the cause, frequently come from the most disadvantaged and marginalised sectors of society, ranging from tribal groups to peasants to inhabitants of regional towns and large cities. The communities that face displacement are themselves internally diverse, often along class, ethnic and religious lines. Resistance to resettlement is, however, not limited to people whose lives are directly affected by projects. Local, regional, national and international non-governmental organisations (NGOs) and social movements with a wide variety of missions and agendas have joined and assisted in the struggle of peoples around the world to resist DIDR.

The responses and motivations for acceptance or resistance are complex and diverse, ranging from purely material considerations to the most deeply felt ideological beliefs and concerns (Oliver-Smith 1996). Equally as diverse, protests and resistance to resettlement by development projects and practices have taken many forms and expressions. Such actions take place in villages and towns, at project sites, in state and national capitals, at the offices of multilateral institutions and international organisations, in cyberspace and at conferences and seminars in schools and universities around the world. Resistance to DIDR also produces a complex array of purposes and initiatives blending environmental, social, cultural and economic concerns that may focus on resisting specific issues or general models of development.

Resistance to DIDR is also extremely dynamic, both changing with conditions itself and also influencing those individuals, groups and institutions with which it intersects. DIDR resistance may provoke changes in resettlement policy and practice, and ultimately a reframing of fundamental questions in development. Communities and organisations in resistance evolve in response to national governments and multilateral agencies and, in turn, oblige such bodies to evolve themselves.

Organisational Forms in DIDR Resistance

Resistance to DIDR in its most contemporary forms must be seen as taking place in an era in which an extraordinary growth of organised social action of a wide variety of identities and forms has occurred. This expansion of activism has in part been a response by people to needs or challenges not met or presented by government and has unquestionably been facilitated by greater access to both transport and communications technology. Resistance to resettlement in its contemporary forms is one aspect of an increasing grass-roots activism in collaboration with nonlocal allies around the world. Generally these connections across levels of the social scale enable local resistance groups to access assistance in the form of financial resources, media campaigns, political pressure or other forms of aid. One of the key challenges facing these interconnected organisations is articulating a coherent and consistent set of interests across such diverse constituencies.

Resistance to development-induced resettlement in most cases takes place in the form of organised collective action of people in communities and/or in groups, both locally and extra-locally. Such organised activities are manifested in four major forms, which have played important roles in the various forms of expression that resistance to resettlement has taken. These forms are: social movements; NGOs; grass-roots organisations (GROs); and transnational networks.

Social movements have become a particularly important form of collective action for people to engage in to promote or resist change, as these movements act in pursuit of common interests or values to which such people strongly adhere (McAdam et al. 1988). The political goals of social movements are expressed as claims to rights or to the extension and exercise of rights. This language of rights provides the means to organise the elements of social struggle and has found broad application, providing a form of 'master frame' for social mobilisation (Foweraker 2001: 4). Since, in the modern era, the power to grant or withhold rights is vested primarily in the state, social movements make demands on the state.

Non-governmental organisations (NGOs), which are not generally social movements, but may become allies or parts of social movements, have become an integral feature of contemporary development policy and practice. NGOs take on different roles in resettlement work. Some NGOs work for the entity promoting the development project in the planning of resettlement communities. Others work to improve the conditions of those communities that have accepted resettlement, or have already been resettled, such as Arch Vahini in the context of the Sardar Sarovar dam project in India (Dwivedi 1998: 150). Yet others, such as the International Rivers Network, work to assist those communities that have chosen to resist resettlement, providing information, media assistance, organisational capacity, networking and financial resources (Williams 1997). The expansion of the number of NGOs working in DIDR resistance is largely among those devoted to environmental and human rights issues.

Grass-roots organisations (GROs) are membership organisations dedicated to the improvement of their own communities, and often have deep social and cultural roots, evolving from traditional local organisations. In the last three decades, tens of thousands of such groups across the world have emerged in response to worsening social conditions (Fisher 1996: 60). The increasing availability of outside support from national and international NGOs and social movements has also supported the growth of local organisations. The spread of computers has made it possible for local organisations to communicate what they have learned with each other throughout nations and across borders and oceans. Thus, DIDR-affected people around the world can now share knowledge gained in land and resource disputes with provincial and national governments over the Internet and on their websites. In some cases, such as the MAB (Dam Victims Movement) in Brazil, these networks coalesce and form NGOs, national social movements (McDonald 1993, Rothman and Oliver 1999) or transnational networks.

Transnational networks, the most recent DIDR resistance organisational form to emerge, are composed of dynamic, multiple, reticulated transnational linkages. The term 'reticulated' is key here. Facilitated by the rapid expansion of information technology, networks include individuals, NGOs, GROs and social movements, and often blur the distinctions between the subnational, international and transnational (Kumar 1996: 42). Networks are most easily formed on the Internet and when they cluster around political issues; politics, in effect, acquires a new theatre (Kumar 1996).

Two different kinds of activists stand out in their participation in networks. First, networks draw upon a community of scholars and experts who employ the scientific and technical knowledge base to broaden the existing discourse on particular problems. Second, networks depend on grass-roots activists, often members of social movements, NGOs or GROs, who usually take more challenging stands on issues and confront powerholders more directly (Kumar 1996: 32). These two groups definitely overlap, with members from each taking on the roles and functions of the other.

A Political-ecological Approach to DIDR Resistance

In the sense that DIDR resistance involves conflicts over complex relationships, involving sets of rights and risks that people have within a physical environment, this analysis falls under the rubric of political ecology. Political ecology largely focuses on the conflicts that emerge over rights to access, ownership and disposition of resources and environments, for which different social groups, often characterised by widely differing sociocultural identities and economic adaptational forms, contend. In DIDR resistance, although the stakes may be expressed in economic, social and/or cultural terms, the fundamental issue is the political contestation over rights to a place or the resources of a place.

Within the framework of political ecology, the core concepts of vulnerability and risk offer a means to identify and analyse the participants, scales and action levels, as well as the strategies and goal structures of DIDR resistance. Vulnerability and risk refer to the relationships among people, the environment and the sociopolitical structures that frame the conditions in which people live. The concept of vulnerability thus integrates political, economic and environmental forces, in terms of both biophysical and socially constructed risk. This understanding of vulnerability has enabled researchers to conceptualise how social systems generate the conditions that place different kinds of people, often differentiated along axes of class, race, ethnicity, gender or age, at different levels of risk (Giddens 1990, Beck 1992, 1995). Among these conditions, development policy and practice must be considered as generating and distributing risk and vulnerability differentially.

People facing DIDR suffer from uncertainty, and a lack of appropriate information seriously hampers their ability to assess conditions and act. Recently, Dwivedi has asserted that uncertainty and a lack of predictability heighten the perception of risk because, without adequate information, no calculations of losses and benefits are possible (1999: 47). Most mandated resettlement projects deprive people of control and generally do not provide accurate information with which people can reassert satisfactory control over and understanding of the resettlement process. The often extremely negative concrete impacts of resettlement projects on affected peoples compound the disorientation generated by the loss of control and understanding as motivations for resistance. Resistance is a reassertion of both a logic and a sense of control (Oliver-Smith 1996).

Mediating institutions, such as NGOs, also frame and may politicise uncertainties and risks and may be pivotal in the way people construct risk as well. Dwivedi asserts that when people feel that the risks associated with displacement and resettlement exceed cultural norms of what is acceptable, or when compensation is deemed inadequate, resistance will be forthcoming. Dwivedi's approach permits a disaggregation of populations facing DIDR according to the differential risks they perceive and their likelihood of resisting on the basis of those perceptions. The approach also disaggregates risk into project performance risks in terms of costs and benefits, financial risks in terms of adequate funds for implementation, environmental risks, such as reservoir-induced seismicity, insect plagues or waterborne diseases, and distributional risks in which benefits, for example, are captured by the rich (Dwivedi 1999: 45).

The World Commission on Dams (WCD) links risk with the concept of rights in advocating that an 'approach based on "recognition of rights" and "assessment of risks" (particularly rights at risk)' be elaborated to guide future planning and decision-making on dams (2000: 206). In terms of risk analysis, the contribution of the WCD global review lies in distinguishing between risk takers and risk bearers, or the voluntary and involuntary assumption of risk. By combining the consideration of rights and risks, the inadequacies and simplifications of traditional cost-benefit analysis can be avoided and better planning and decision-making can result, based on the complexity of the considerations involved and the values that societies place on different options (WCD 2000: 206). The importance of a rights and risks approach to DIDR is that it allows for the inclusion not just of material concerns, but also of the issues relating to the symbolic and affective domains. As such, it provides not only an approach to improving planning and decision-making for dam projects, but also the template for an approach to understanding and analysing resistance to DIDR in general. Little (1999) has suggested that such a template can be activated by at least one of three methodological and strategic orientations.

An *advocacy anthropology approach* is characterised by an activist stance that privileges a particular group's perspective over competing or contesting positions. Little (1999) suggests that one limitation of an advocacy approach is that only one point of view of the many that may be present in resettlement issues is presented. Conversely, it can equally be argued that advocacy anthropology often articulates a view that otherwise might not be heard, thus promoting dialogue and negotiation.

Stakeholder analysis employs methods of conciliation, negotiation and mediation for reducing levels of conflict and managing disputes. Such efforts at establishing truly effective methods for crosscultural negotiation in DIDR could play meaningful roles in enhancing the capacity of local peoples to represent their interests effectively. On the other hand, stakeholder analysis frequently assumes that all actors have equal or symmetrical stakes in the conflict. Moreover, stakeholder approaches also assume that all participants in a dispute hold and have the abilities to employ the rights of citizenship within the larger political space of the nation. Assumptions of this sort are far from warranted, especially in the case of ethnic minorities or indigenous peoples (Little 1999).

Political ecology ethnography, by focusing on environmental conflicts, generates a social scientific approach that incorporates multiple perspectives and that has the potential, not only to explore the political dimensions of these conflicts, but also to bring new participants into the political frame of action and to initiate new approaches to viewing power relationships across multiple social and natural scales (Little 1999: 4).

Importantly, this approach has the potential to create concepts that may be adopted by the new participants in order to question established public policy and to generate new alternatives for action. Most essentially, it is able to reveal the basic claims to resources and territory that are made by participant social actors, and to analyse the forms by which such claims are promoted and defended within broader political spheres, such that the competing discourses of cultural and political legitimacy are displayed (Little 1999: 5). Although Little (1999) presents these strategies as mutually separate and exclusive, all three approaches can be implemented according to context without necessary contradiction. Advocacy anthropology is appropriate for work at the level of the community to be resettled. Researchers adopting an advocacy stance fulfil a necessary function in assisting communities in their efforts to deal with the crisis facing them and in articulating their views in nonlocal contexts. Enlightened stakeholder analysis can reveal the differentials in value positions that are being negotiated among very disparate participants. Stakeholder analysis that is culturally sensitive can frame the issues in ways that help to balance those situations where there are significant differences in culture, negotiating experience, and bargaining power (as one historian put it, one party has 'a continent to exchange and the other, glass beads'). A political ecology ethnography of resistance helps to place resistance in the context of global conversations about development. The political ecological perspective reveals the commonalities that local resistance movements share with similar struggles elsewhere, contributing to the emergence of new forms of discourse in the shaping of alternative approaches to development that are less destructive to environments and human rights.

Who Resists? The Social Dimensions of DIDR Resistance

Identifying resistors basically involves specifying the interests and identities of those affected peoples who feel that their rights have been infringed upon and who feel that they are being forced to suffer unacceptable risks. Responses will also vary over time as the project and the struggle against it evolve, each in response to the other. Responses also vary because not everyone in a community, much less a region, will be affected in the same way at the same time by either resettlement or the environmental alterations that the project will enact.

A variety of factors has proven to be significant in the development of DIDR resistance movements, including the social identity of individuals and the identity and organisation of groups within the impacted population. Further, political variables, economic factors and cultural issues may influence who participates in resistance movements. Neither rural communities nor urban neighbourhoods are ever entirely homogeneous. Thus, the degree of internal diversity, patterns of conflict and consensus, and social, racial, ethnic and class factors in an affected population will all play an important role in the development of, and the participation of local people in, DIDR resistance movements. Within even small communities, some will resist while others may simply acquiesce and still others will willingly accept resettlement. Such differences in response to both resettlement and resistance may have longer-term implications for the social organisation of a community threatened or affected by DIDR.

Internal differentiation, a multifaceted relationship to the immediate environment and the state, the availability of local and nonlocal allies and the quality of the resettlement process itself are crucial factors in assessing why people resist DIDR (Oliver-Smith 1991, 1994). Dwivedi contends that those who resist usually come from the sectors of the affected populations who perceive that they are placed at greatest risk by the prospect of displacement, the resettlement plan and/or its implementation. He asserts that risks are perceived differentially by men, women, the young, the elderly, rich farmers, landless labourers, indigenous peoples, peasants, outcast groups and other minorities (Dwivedi 1997, 1998, 1999). Resettlement projects evolve over time in interaction with mediating action groups and policy adjustments, both of which have the potential of changing both the perception of risk and the decision-making frameworks of people facing and/or resisting resettlement. The resistance dynamic thus emerges as a 'trialectic' among: the people to be resettled; action group intervention; and policy and project authorities.

The need to organise for resistance will exert a new form of pressure on the internal workings of a community. The organisation of a resistance movement may sharpen both internal and external pre-existing conflicts. Patterns of internal differentiation may inhibit the formation of necessary levels of solidarity and co-operation for effective resistance. Governments and project authorities may attempt to exploit or even create internal divisions within communities to reduce their capacity to organise and negotiate (Parasuraman 1999: 244). In some cases, the threat of resettlement creates a culture of solidarity far more intense than that which had existed prior to the project (Rapp 2000). Resistance requires the intensification of relationships with traditional allies, as well as the development of new relationships with others, often completely foreign to the local context (Magee 1989).

Particular groups may find their interests furthered by certain features of a resettlement project, while other groups will see themselves as suffering great disadvantage. Differential costs and benefits from resettlement projects may vary according to land and labour factor markets, social differentiation, or other local features, predisposing some groups to favour resettlement and others to oppose it. Communities threatened with resettlement cannot be assumed to be homogeneous. In resistance movements all players have specific agendas that they attempt to further.

Much resistance must be seen as a result of the exclusion of affected communities from participation in the planning and decision-making processes of DIDR. The goal of participation is consistent with the emphasis on the recognition and restoration of the rights of affected peoples. Participation is a particularly thorny issue in many cases because, if authentic participation is achieved, it tends to violate many, if not all, of the traditional forms of power relations and social interaction in most societies. Those affected tend to be members of subaltern groups who are generally not considered by élites to have the social and cultural tools necessary for executive, or even advisory, forms of decision-making, planning and execution that pertain to development projects (Parasuraman 1999).

Most resettlement programmes become extremely large bureaucratic and technical organisations operating with specific models of development and progress. Project goals customarily emphasise meeting practical (i.e. material) rather than strategic needs, instrumentality rather than empowerment (Cleaver 1999: 598). The goals of development/resettlement programmes generally emphasise the creation of formalised community organisations that interface well with national bureaucratic structures. Such programmes aim in many ways to remake the community along lines that are compatible with the larger system (Cleaver 1999: 602).

A persistent tension arises from the degree to which grass-roots opinions are consulted and their participation factored into decisions taken at higher levels in the struggle. The articulation and participation of all the diverse interests of extremely heterogeneous populations, in a way that is still coherent with all the organisational agendas regarding approaches to development, is a major challenge for NGOs assisting communities facing DIDR.

One of the principal points of contention in DIDR resistance involves the categories, established by project planners, of people to be included as recipients of resettlement assistance. These categories bring with them bundles of rights that are attached to material and social benefits or costs (Rapp 2000). Consequently, many struggles are undertaken by local groups and their NGO allies to resist exclusion by category from resettlement benefits or compensation – struggles which have also been the source of internal disputes and conflicts. For example, the category of formally titled landholder becomes particularly thorny when indigenous groups hold traditional use rights of land, but no formally recognised titles.

The cultural significance of indigenous identity has also been heightened for both holders and nonholders of that identity by development projects. Kinship categories and distance, often crucial in determining indigenous identity, have also proved to be important in determining entitlement and distribution of resettlement benefits (Dwivedi 1998). The lack of recognition of larger regional environmental impacts of projects has also led to the exclusion of people whose access to resources essential for livelihood is seriously affected by projects, e.g. populations living downstream from dams. A great deal of protest and resistance is organised around the failure to include the downstream populations structurally displaced by dam-induced environmental damage (Magee 1989, Dwivedi 1999).

When a community decides to resist a DIDR project, that decision engages it with a process which, even if successful, entails significant changes for that community, both internally and externally. The threat of resettlement constitutes a crisis of enormous proportions for many communities. Crises are periods of time when customary practices of daily life are suspended and new possibilities of action, alliances and values are created (Fantasia 1988: 14).

Protest and resistance may encompass critiques of project implementation, state development programmes and strategies, and the general global political economy of development. This diversity of idioms and meanings is seen as essential for resistance movements to articulate support at different levels and in different contexts. While consistently based on a foundational concept of the defense of human and civil rights, individuals and groups resisting DIDR construct a number of fundamental themes from which they develop a wide variety of discourses, images, symbols and representations for the various allies and opponents they encounter at various levels. Depending on the characteristics of the project, the social and environmental context in which it is located and the risks and losses that affected people will be or are suffering, some themes may be emphasised over others. The major themes through which the various discourses are developed include: environment, economics, culture, project risks, governance and administration, approaches to development, and justice and human rights.

Environmental Upheaval and Resistance

Resistance is a rejection of an attempt by certain interests to transform an environment in some way that requires the displacement of people. As such, environmentally related conflict is at the centre of grass-roots and NGO resistance to DIDR. Both the state and private interests, in undertaking large-scale infrastructure development and conservation projects, base their decisions on culturally particular constructions of the environment.

For most of the twentieth century, nature and society were seen as distinct, in opposition to one another. This ideological construction focuses on the domination and control of nature by society. Now, as then, certain people get relegated into the 'nature' category as the need arises, and frequently become the objects of development strategies and projects.

Indeed, a frequent subtext of development projects is the acculturation of such people to majority-held culture by obligatory participation, whether through forced displacement and resettlement or through some other activity. In effect, the goal of such projects is often to 'socialise' these 'natural' people and bring them into the national fold.

In the West, nature has been constructed as a fund of resources which human beings have not only a right to tap into, but also a right to alter and otherwise dominate in any way they deem fit. The enlightenment ideals of human emancipation and self-realisation (read 'development') have been closely linked to the idea of the control and use of nature (Harvey 1996: 121–22). The 'plasticity myth', as Murphy has termed it, is based on the idea that the relationship between humans and their environments can be reconstructed at will by the application of human reason (Murphy 1994).

Confronting these images and accompanying norms for action towards nature are innumerable alternative constructions of nature held by the enormous variety of peoples around the world. Many local cultures do not accept the dichotomy between nature and society that has undergirded Western economic positions regarding nature, but rather posit a continuity between the biophysical, human and supernatural worlds, that is established through ritual and symbol and is embedded in social relations. In general, local models of nature are complexes of meanings – usages that cannot be rendered intelligible through modern constructions nor understood without some reference to local culture and place (Escobar 2001: 151).

Perhaps no other instance so epitomises the subjugation of disorderly nature to human rationality as the 'taming' of rivers by channelling and dam construction. The environmental consequences of large dam construction have been the focus of intense campaigns of opposition by environmental groups for several decades. The environmental destruction created by dams has deep spiritual repercussions for many peoples whose religions are based on the close relationship between the natural and supernatural worlds. Although the anti-dam movement essentially began as an environmental movement, it quickly found common cause with human rights activists who quite correctly realised that all the negative environmental impacts were experienced first, and most directly, by local people.

In 1980 the International Union for the Conservation of Nature published the World Conservation Strategy, challenging the national park model and advocating the incorporation of local people into the conservation process. The World Bank followed this initiative with a programme called Integrated Conservation and Development Projects (ICDP), intended to integrate local people into projects to enable them to benefit economically. However, more recently, dissatisfaction with the outcomes of such projects has generated a more exclusionary strain within the conservation movement, recently dubbed the 'protectionist paradigm' (Brechin et al. 2003). It calls for a radical transformation of nature, namely the removal of all human inhabitants from environments deemed endangered (Oates 1999, Terborgh 1999). This strategy entails the forced removal of people from their homelands, producing another variety of environmental refugee (Albert 1992, Geisler and Da Sousa 2001). Barring outright displacement, the 'new protectionist paradigm' advocates radically restricting resource-use practices employed by people resident in reserves and parks. Such restrictions constitute a form of structural displacement in that, while people have not been geographically moved, the norms and practices with which they have engaged the environment in the process of social reproduction have become so altered as to effectively change their environment from one that is known to one that must be freshly encountered with new norms and new practices if social reproduction is to continue.

Economic Debates: Evaluating Risks and Compensating Losses

If the decisions to displace and resettle people are fundamentally political, the purposes of development projects that displace people are most often economic. In economic terms, DIDR resistance involves a conflict between the needs of a local society and the needs of a regional or national one. Between a project that is justified on purely economic grounds and a community's multifaceted existence, there is a fundamental analytical disjuncture. The data, rationale and basis for projects are generally unidimensionally quantitative and economic. Economic planners and their methods and tools cannot address the multidimensionality that is presented by DIDR. Characteristically, that which economics cannot address is dismissed as external to the problem, statistically insignificant or unimportant. This idea of multidimensionality, so fundamental to any clear understanding of resettlement, is therefore rarely factored into the planning process of projects that will displace people (Cernea 1999: 21, 23), and this inevitably provides the rationale for resistance. The motivation and justification for projects is fundamentally economic, and the nature of the decisions that have been made and the plans that have been drawn up come from a perspective that in most cases has markedly different value orientations and rationalities from those of the people to be displaced, and are almost inevitably going to provoke resistance.

Many of the core disputes fuelling resistance movements are thus economic in nature. There is a close linking of the idea of economic quantification with rationality and science, allegedly allowing for precision and banishing the ambiguity that plagues decision-making in political discourse (Espeland 1999). The means by which such a position is derived is a calculus known as cost-benefit analysis (CBA), which provides policy makers and politicians with a method for making decisions that is purportedly objective, fair and democratic, with the decisions and outcomes being arrived at scientifically. If the value of the benefits outweighs the value of the costs, an objective basis for proceeding with a project is deemed to have been provided to the policy maker. For CBA to be carried out, the costs and benefits in all their diversity have to be conveniently expressed in some uniform, quantitative format, preferably in money prices. Money values or prices are usually arrived at by the modified or unmodified intersection of supply and demand in a marketplace. Using prices thus presents a problem for arriving at the price of costs and benefits from a project that are not the result of the intersection of supply and demand in a market.

Therefore, a method must be devised to access how people would monetarily value nonmarket items. In 'contingent valuation', people are asked how much they would be 'willing to pay' (WTP) for the things the analyst is seeking to value if they were for sale (Adams 1996: 2). WTP works best when people are asked about benefits. However, in cases of DIDR, the question for people who are being impacted is more frequently one of costs. In the case of costs, the question then revolves around how much money a person would be willing to pay to prevent losses or 'willing to accept' (WTA) as compensation for losses. These questions are not simply inversions of each other. They elicit manifestly different responses. On the one hand, asking a person how much they would be willing to pay to prevent a loss is constrained by that person's ability to pay. On the other hand, asking a person how much they would be willing to accept as compensation for a loss elicits what economists have characterised as 'unrealistically high answers' (Adams 1996). WTP is generally preferred, for reasons of sound economy.

As Cernea points out, CBA justifies a project economically on the basis of benefits that are greater than costs in terms of total sums. However, it does not account for the distribution of either costs or benefits. It cannot ask who pays the costs, suffers the losses or reaps the benefits. Moreover, CBA establishes aggregate costs and benefits when it is individuals who incur the costs and absorb the losses (Cernea 1999: 20). It is also inadequate for assessing costs that are real, but difficult to quantify, such as the losses experienced in the breakdown of community or the loss of cultural or spiritual resources. Other critics of CBA (Adams 1996, Espeland 1998, O'Neill 1999) contend that it distorts the values that people attach to both natural and cultural resources.

One of the main points of dispute in DIDR resistance is the appropriate means to measure or account for costs and losses of natural resources. As a feature of the natural environment, land, however altered or enhanced it may be, is here considered a natural resource. Market value for land in the home context may be greater than the market value of land in the region of resettlement, due to both availability and quality. Hence, many people engage in protest and resistance activities to militate for the use of replacement value as the standard for compensation in the case of land.

However, rights in property are rarely completely clear-cut. In many contexts in which DIDR has taken place, formal titles to land are more the exception than the rule. People may depend on resources that exist on land that is considered to be either government or common property. Thus, when people are displaced, the issue of whom to compensate as well as how to compensate is central in the demands resistance movements put forth. The pressure by resistance movements for the recognition of other forms of tenure and ownership has in recent years led to a modification of the position taken by many projects in this regard. Further, a great deal of pressure has been mounted to militate for compensation for other kinds of natural resources such as water and forests.

From an economic standpoint, the basic motivation for resistance lies squarely in the fact that resettlement projects consistently impoverish people (Koenig 2001). A simplistic approach towards this issue is largely responsible for much of the economic injustice, impoverishment and resistance that DIDR projects generate. The loss of access to resources that are fundamental to the maintenance of life, whether in the rural or urban context, can provide the basis for mobilisation of resistance. People are generally not compensated for less tangible assets than land such as access to markets, communal property resources or social networks (Fisher 1995: 32). In urban contexts, a key issue is loss of accessibility to employment. Slum clearance and urban renewal have frequently left resettled people far from sources and sites of employment, and often distant from regular transportation routes and facilities (Perlman 1982). Such losses may be actively resisted because they impoverish people in diverse ways. The shift to a monetised economy from a use-value, reciprocity-based economy has rarely been smooth (Moore 1966), but when those profound cultural changes are coupled with the threat and/or trauma of resettlement, then social disarticulation, cultural disintegration and resistance become more likely.

Cultural resources become particularly problematic to CBA; in order to work, the requirements of CBA oblige a form of commodification of everything. What is the consequence of asking someone what he or she would be willing to pay to prevent the inundation of the burial grounds of their ancestors? The outrage that frequently results from such a query represents an intractable problem known as 'constitutive incommensurability', which increasingly confronts the discourse of CBA (O'Neill 1999). Constitutive incommensurability refers to an unresolvable plurality of values. That is, there are some objects, places, conditions or states of affairs that resist being reduced to a single, uniform measure. They are essentially constituted by particular kinds of shared understandings that are incompatible with market relations on moral or ethical grounds. Appropriate forms and levels of compensation clearly cannot be arrived at by outsiders employing some ostensibly 'objective' method such as CBA, but only in consultation with the affected people (Fisher 1995: 32).

Recent work carried out for the World Commission on Dams points to the overwhelming need for reparations for people displaced by dam construction whose losses have never been appropriately compensated (Johnston 2000). The 1994 Manibeli Declaration also called on the World Bank to establish a fund to provide reparations to the people displaced by Bank-funded dams, arguing that the fund should be managed by an independent, transparent and accountable institution and should include training and assistance for affected communities in the preparation of claims. This demand was reiterated at the first international meeting of dam-affected people in Curitiba, Brazil in 1997. Resistance and opposition movements have made payment of reparations to dam- affected peoples a central issue in their campaigns. Dam reparations call for a variety of remedies, including monetary and such nonmonetary measures as dam decommissioning, official recognition of injustices committed and the restoration of ecosystems (International Rivers Network 2000a).

Some private-sector interests, such as the Rio Tinto Corporation, have developed resettlement policies and attempt to work with the affected people to implement them. Nevertheless, most private-sector development relies on the market mechanism to assess adequate compensation for people displaced by such development. The market mechanism provides the appearance of voluntary relocation by participants. Indeed, private-sector driven DIDR, often involving large numbers of people, frequently simply passes as 'unrecognised' (Appa and Patel 1996). In rural contexts, private-sector expansion, particularly in the developing world, has often adopted informal and even violent methods of expulsion.

The expansion of the private-sector tourist economy has seen the displacement of many traditional residents as well. Private-sector tourism development, often with the complicity of governments, threatens communities around the world. Golf course development in Asia has evoked widespread resistance from threatened communities in several nations seeking to stimulate economic growth through tourism (Ling and Ferrari 1995, Pleumarom 1994, Schradie and De Vries 2000).

Cultural Discourses of Resistance

Although the reasons people resist DIDR are often assumed to be economic in nature, the concerns that people express in resistance movements are generally more complex, embracing economic, social and, particularly, cultural issues. Indeed, project planners frequently err in supposing that people have only economic motives in mind when they undertake resistance to DIDR. While violation of economic rights has proven to be a powerful motivator in resistance, a great deal of the moral content of resistance discourse derives its power from explicitly cultural issues pertaining to the right to persist as cultural entities, as well as to identity, spiritual links to land and the environment, and loyalty to both mythological and historical ancestors. It is reductionist to attribute resistance solely to economics or, for that matter, to cultural concerns. Human motivations in general are complex, and positions and actions in resistance to DIDR are adopted out of many interwoven concerns, rather than one overriding issue.

Two core concepts in resistance to DIDR are power and place. Power includes the ability to move people and things about the landscape in any way you see fit. Place attachment processes involve the behavioural, cognitive and emotional embeddedness of individuals in the relationship between their sociocultural and physical environments, providing a form of ontological stability. A place may become the matrix in which a repository of life experiences becomes embedded and therefore in some sense becomes inseparable from the feelings associated with them (Altman and Low 1992).

Attachment to places may involve the constellation of social relations, and the cultural values that inform them, of entire groups or communities. Places become identified with the genealogy and continuity of families and groups through history. Economic ties of individual or collective ownership, inheritance or other forms of appropriation, are fundamental to many place attachments, and cultural factors such as the intimate connections between environment and religion, cosmology and world-view, play significant roles in the relationship of a society to its land base and general environment. As Rodman notes, 'Place then is both context and content, enacted and material. It is the lived world in physical form' (1992: 650). Resistance to resettlement reveals how important a sense of place is in the creation of an 'environment of trust' in which space, kin relations, local communities, cosmology and tradition are linked (Giddens 1990: 102, cited in Rodman 1992: 648). Threats of removal from these physical and symbolic environments have generally elicited some form of resistance.

In the conflict of resistance, particularly for small, relatively isolated groups, more precise definitions of cultural identity are often worked out and conceptions of the community in broader national and global contexts may be developed. DIDR projects carry with them the potential for a virtually total undermining of local identity. Resettlement imposes forces and conditions on people that may transform their lives, evoking profound changes in environment, in productive activities, in social organisation and interaction, in leadership and political structure, and in world-view and ideology. Resettlement not only relocates a people in space; it may also remake them. DIDR projects may directly or indirectly further two fundamental processes: the expansion of the state and integration into regional and national market systems. In most instances, DIDR projects initiate a restructuring of social, economic and political relationships to resemble those of the larger society. In that sense, resettlement will not necessarily destroy 'local cultures', but it will appropriate them and restructure them in terms of values and goals often originating from far beyond the local context (Garcia Canclini 1993).

Although many small societies face total assimilation and cultural disappearance, or 'ethnocide', as Bartolomé and Barabas (1973) have termed it, others have become conscious of their minority status and have constructed it in terms of an active defence of cultural identity and concerted political action. In effect, development projects can catalyse a shift in cultural consciousness from an ahistorical and acultural sense of identity to that of an ethnic group with a culture and identity to protect, in confrontation with a national society (Waldram 1980). The struggle to resist the Ralco Dam on the Biobio River in Chile has reunited Mapuche Indians, who have come to the region to reconnect with their communities. People who had hidden their indigenous identity began to reclaim their cultural heritage with pride (Evans 2001: 6). Although the damage they inflict can threaten the existence of subaltern groups, development projects can sharpen local identities through the oppositional process and resistance, and further the political development of subaltern groups. As such, development projects can produce inadvertent positive outcomes when they stimulate the development of civil organisations that are able to resist state excesses in their efforts to transform local systems (Smith, C. 1996: 47).

Cultural heritage refers to the historical memory of a community and is constituted in objects, resources, places and practices that locate a people in the universe, giving them a sense of identity through time. Such elements play a signal role in individual and collective identity formation, in the way that time and history are encoded and contextualised, and in interpersonal, community and intracultural relations. If CBA arrives at its conclusions through an objective calculation based on a constructed commensuration of values across a wide spectrum of costs and benefits, the cultural models or values that energise the discourse of those affected come from different sources, as is illustrated in the following.

> You tell us to take compensation. What is the state compensating us for? For our land, for our fields, for the trees along our fields. But we don't live only by this ... Our gods, the support of those who are our kin – what price do you have for these? Our Adivasi [tribal] life: what price do you put on it? (Brava Mahalia, 'Letter from a Tribal Village', Lokayan Bulletin 11/2/3, Sept.-Dec 1994 in O'Neill 2001: 1866)

This is a letter written to the Chief Minister of Gujarat in India by a tribal person who was being displaced by the construction of the Sardar Sarovar Dam, and who clearly differentiates between a set of values in which price is seen as a neutral measuring rod and a set of values that are based in the socially constructed relationship between a community and its environment (O'Neill 1996: 99). Essentially, land is an incommensurable entity. Government establishment of compensation levels for land and for cultural heritage resources settles nothing. The attempt simply sharpens political dispute.

Material compensation or reimbursement may be insufficient to enable people to reconstruct their culture and way of life after resettlement. Central to the ontological basis of many cultures are the notions of time and place. People are linked to places by residence in time as well as space. Long histories in a place in which family and community roots are deeply embedded tie generations to each other in a 'community of memory'. It is through such communities of memory that people come to know themselves 'as members of a people, as inheritors of a history and a culture that we must nurture through memory and hope' (Bellah et al. 1985: 138). The power of memory as a mobilising force for resistance and protest long after resettlement frequently remains strong (Conuel 1981, Greene 1985, Gray 1996: 102, Bilharz 1998, Jing 1999, Jeffrey 2000).

The broad discursive styles associated with the two domains of human rights and science play key roles in the campaigns of resistance movements. Since the discourse of developers relies heavily on a scientific approach and discursive style, resisters are extremely careful about the accuracy of both their data and the factual basis for their arguments. NGOs have developed their own cadres of scientific experts, who often volunteer their services, from a diverse array of scientific fields to research and generate both data and perspectives to confront the arguments offered by developers and their funders. Consistently calling attention to the lack of adequate research, faulty methodology, the shoddiness of actual data collection, and the inconsistency and incompleteness of studies, the NGOs assume a position of scientific rigour as opposed to the politically compromised, biased and inferior science of the developers (McCully 1996).

The discourses developed by local people and their allies in the area of human rights are based on fundamental concepts of sacrifice and justice, and serve to question the morality of development projects that displace people. The listener or reader is called upon to recognise the sacrifice that people are forced to make in the name of development, and the injustice inflicted in inadequate or nonexistent compensation and faulty resettlement. The dishonesty and hypocrisy of governments that call upon the poorest to sacrifice for the benefit of the richest are themes that commonly appear in both the spoken and written discourse of resisters.

Another key theme in the human rights discourse involves an evocation of fidelity to a cultural heritage. Abandoning one's land means separation from, and the loss of the right to express and to practice, one's identity and religion. Accepting resettlement is equated with betraying one's ancestors and everything that one stands for. Persecution, determination, martyrdom and finality are also themes that run through the human rights discourse. People consistently affirm their intentions to perish, either by drowning in reservoirs or at the hands of oppressive authorities, before they abandon their homes. Hunger strikes by both people and leaders of the NBA in India represent another form of this discourse of martyrdom and finality.

The Politics of DIDR Resistance

Although the actual resettlement project may be defined in social or, more commonly, economic terms, the phenomenon of resettlement is fundamentally a political one, involving the use of power by one party to relocate another. These power relations are conditioned by the climate of the various political contexts in which they are engaged. At the broadest level, the assimilation of global norms by states can produce new political spaces for NGOs, GROs and social movements to further their goals by holding states accountable for conformity with their own normative principles and rules. On the other hand, state institutions and practices are also embedded in local structures and are susceptible to pressure from domestic actors such as dominant classes and class coalitions, particular local interest groups or the interests of political élites (Khagram 1999: 29–31).

Local and transnational resistance to large-scale development projects will have the least success in states with authoritarian regimes and local actors with little or no capacity or political space to organise (Khagram 1999: 32). The free flow of information, both nationally and internationally, is absolutely essential for NGOs and their lobbying efforts for changing environmental and development policies (Khagram 1999: 40). In a democratic regime in which political parties vie for the votes of the electorate, DIDR resisters can take advantage of the competition among parties to further their agendas (Khagram 1999: 40–41). However, by the same token, when resisters come from the traditionally marginalised sections of a society, their lack of political power may make them less appealing to politicians (Bilharz 1998). Nevertheless, in regard to dams, Khagram argues persuasively that transnational NGOs, allied with grassroots organisations and social movements, have changed the terms of debate and significantly affected both policy and practice in the political economy of development in the Third World.

Barring immediate, outright and open conflict between people facing DIDR and the state and project authorities, most resistance at some point involves dialogue and negotiation among the various parties over such points as alternative sites, resource valuation methods, compensation levels and quality, timetables and eligibility for benefits, to name only a few key issues. DIDR resistance movements face considerable difficulty in their discussions with state or corporate authorities, due to the great imbalances of power that are usually based in the structure of the national political economic and sociocultural context (Davidheiser 2000). Often, as members of minority groups or the poor who live at the margins of national societies, people facing DIDR lack the economic, social and political capital necessary to affect decisions beyond the local level. The cultural gaps among the parties entering into negotiations, in which participants are not familiar with the cultures, values, norms or conventions of ordinary behaviour regarding issues of conflict and communication, can reduce the possibility of fair and just outcomes.

In some cases overcoming the power differential may be virtually impossible and weak parties should seek recourse in formal legal systems, rather than in modes of negotiation, to achieve just and equitable solutions (Nader 1994, 1997). However, options may also be limited there, since many marginalised groups have customarily been ignored or discriminated against by formal legal systems (Little 1999). Power disparities may actually reduce the likelihood of undertaking negotiations, since there is little to be gained by the stronger party in compromises that substantively address the interests and needs of all participants (Ott 1972).

Fisher and Ury (1981) have argued that good-faith negotiations, employing objective bases in presenting positions and arriving at group decisions, can reduce the role of pure power. If some specific criteria can actually be agreed upon, this can support the position of the weaker party, by bestowing the symbolic power of legitimacy, and can increase the possibility of successful outcomes by establishing some clear measures for making decisions (Davidheiser 2000). The chance of successful negotiations for weaker parties can also be improved if decision-making is relegated from a central bureaucracy to regional or local institutions, thus possibly reducing the social distance between local communities and state representatives (Penzich et al. 1994).

Another way to address the question of power imbalances in negotiations is the formation of alliances (Penzich et al. 1994). Allies provide a variety of significant resources including negotiating experience, material resources and, perhaps most importantly, information. Alliances with national and international NGOs have provided local-level DIDR resisters with leverage to engage administrators and funders of development projects in debate and negotiations (McDonald 1993: 9). The potential of these external parties to offset the great disparities in power, in negotiations between local communities and the national or corporate forces that seek to relocate them, offers resisters some opportunity for gain in such contexts.

Scales of Interaction and Conflict

When resistance movements develop, they tend to generate contacts and linkages with social actors that operate at four levels: the local community; the project; the national political context; and the international or global context. However, it is important to maintain the distinction between internal and external actors in a local DIDR situation. If the focus becomes too trained on external actors and their resources, it becomes easy to see local movements as only the outcome of external resources (Rothman and Oliver 1999: 43). Local activists are anything but passive recipients of external aid. The relationship between internal and external actors is reciprocal, and is composed of exchanges of resources, influence, information and validation.

The Local Scale

The majority of resistance movements emerge in response to a specific project in a specific local context, which may vary in size from one community or even part of a community to a very large region. Early confrontations of varying intensity may result from first encounters between local people and initial project personnel, ranging from puzzled reactions to physical assaults. However, in most cases, responses by local people are quite reasoned and frequently take the form of a request for dialogue and information. The response of project personnel to these requests is often so abrupt or evasive that resistance can move quickly to more activist stances.

When the decision to resist is taken and formalised, such action often evolves into the formation of grass-roots organisations. Furthermore, the speed and intensity of communications linking areas remote from each other establishes contact between groups with similar goals in other regions of the world, creating networks of resistance movements that share information and other resources. The networking and sharing of these experiences by resettled people with those threatened with resettlement resulted in the formation of the Regional Commission of Dam Refugees (CRAB) and eventually the nationwide organisation, Movement of Dam-affected People (MAB), in Brazil (Bartolomé 1992, Serra 1993, Rothman and Oliver 1999).

People may reorient their central cultural symbols to construct interpretations of the threat of resettlement in very traditional forms. The Chinantecs and Mazatecs of Mexico recontextualised the threat of resettlement in mythological symbols, generating a resistance movement expressed largely in Messianic terms (Bartolomé and Barabas 1990:

76–77). Regional levels of social and institutional development in local contexts also affect the action and organisation of DIDR resistance movements. Local DIDR resistance movements, however, risk becoming pawns of local and regional political parties if they tie their fortunes too closely to them (Baviskar 1992). Since resistance in effect constitutes a challenge to the state, the politics of state-local relations, in all their complexity, come to the fore.

Established leaders of the community, if they favour resistance, are frequently chosen to lead local movements. However, if they prove unsatisfactory or unequal to the task, new leadership may emerge in the context of the conflict. For example, the James Bay Cree, in response to the unfair negotiations with Hydro-Quebec, voted out three chiefs who were enthusiastic advocates of discussions with Hydro-Quebec and replaced them with three who were opposed to the proposals (Colchester 1999: 37). Success at leadership in resistance at the local level has led to important leadership roles at national and even international levels. Kayapo leadership, for example, has been composed of both traditional authorities and younger members of communities with greater experience of the outside world, who have been particularly astute in their understanding and use of local, national and international sources of power for resisting the Tucurui Dam and other Brazilian government and private initiatives affecting their land (Fisher 1994, Posey 1996: 125).

The role of 'Gramscian organic intellectuals', those individuals who have left the community for economic or educational purposes and then return to assist with the struggle, has been key in movement leadership (Rothman and Oliver 1999). In one case, a trained anthropologist, who is also a member of one of the Nahuatl communities that were threatened with DIDR by the San Juan Tetelcingo dam, became a spokesperson, activist and analyst of that resistance movement (Celestino 1999).

Women have played important roles in organisational leadership and in spearheading resistance movement activities, and have been at the forefront of voices condemning DIDR. Without question, one of the most notable leaders of a resistance movement today is Medha Patkar, the charismatic leader of the Narmada Bachao Andolan, who has played a major role not only in the development of that organisation, but also in the transnational antidam movement and in the evolution of the discourse on sustainable development. She also became a commissioner when the WCD was established, and in its final report made an independent comment in which she continued to challenge the reigning model of development as leading to the marginalisation of the majority, despite any precautions that might be recommended by the Commission (WCD 2000: 321–22). In many ways, she has come to symbolise resistance to DIDR around the world. The active role taken by many women in the organisation, leadership and action of anti-DIDR resistance movements is both the result of, and a contributing factor to, increasing changes in the status and roles of women in societies all over the world.

The Project Scale

The quality of the resettlement project itself may play a major role in the decision to accept or resist DIDR (Chambers 1970). Many DIDR resisters maintain that adequate and just resettlement is impossible from the outset, leaving total opposition to the project as the only strategic option. Other resisters do admit the possibility of adequate and just resettlement, and commit themselves to achieving that goal. One of the best outcomes that might be imagined for DIDR projects is to work out a system in which people can materially sustain themselves while they themselves begin the process of social reconstruction. However, if the level of impoverishment experienced by most resettled peoples is any indicator, even adequate systems of material reproduction are beyond either the will or the capabilities of most contemporary policy makers and planners. Projects almost inevitably have generated high levels of impoverishment, dissatisfaction and often resistance, even after resettlement has taken place. When national resettlement policy is inferior or nonexistent, DIDR resistance at the project level may become a means to improve policies at a national level. The support of international allies is crucial in such cases (Cernea 1993: 32).

Although difficult to assess exactly, it is not far-fetched to attribute a significant proportion of DIDR resistance to the appallingly bad basic research, planning and implementation of resettlement projects. Here DIDR resistance rejects a poor resettlement project and produces strategies of negotiation to improve the terms and conditions of resettlement, such as better replacement land, increased compensation for losses or increased housing allowances. However, where policy makers are sensitive, DIDR-project protest and resistance can lead to the improvement of poor policy. There is little question that protest over, and resistance to, specific projects are responsible for the increased attention to the deficiencies in resettlement policy by national authorities, and that they have also contributed to the adoption of guidelines for resettlement projects at the World Bank and other multilateral organisations (Morse and Berger 1992, Cernea 1993, Gibson 1993, Guggenheim 1993, Serra 1993). In the final analysis, resettlement projects must be well designed and communicated, affording resettled people some control and understanding of their circumstances, if they are to have any chance of effectively reducing the impacts of DIDR (Cernea 1988: 15). Some, however, argue very convincingly that positive, productive resettlement schemes are extremely difficult to achieve, even under the best of circumstances, and inevitably promote cultural disintegration (Chernela 1988: 20).

The National Scale

The national scale of action involves the two major institutions that develop projects that require DIDR: the state and the private sector. Ethnic or class differences between state and project personnel and local people often complicate the relationship between local contexts and the state in resettlement situations (Colson 1971, Zaman 1982, Wali 1989, Bartolomé and Barabas 1990, Oliver-Smith 1991). In some cases a secondary and somewhat covert goal of resettlement is actually state control and integration of ethnic minorities, and resistance will be expressed in terms of a defense of ethnicity as well as territory (Zaman 1982). However, the state is not a monolithic structure. It is composed of different agencies, departments and ministries, which may have competing agendas. Similarly, the personnel of those state entities are not always of uniform class, ethnic or regional origin. DIDR resisters may find sympathetic individuals and supportive entities within the apparatus of the state. For example, state governments in Brazil supported the resistance to dams to be constructed by ELETROSUL, and the Environmental Ministry Working Group in India sided with the NBA against the states of Maharashtra, Gujarat and Madhya Pradesh.

The availability of political rights, such as that of speech or assembly, condition the possibility and kind of political space for DIDR resistance (Magee 1989, Bartolomé 1992, Robinson 1992). DIDR resistance generally is part of a broad national network of human rights and environmental movements that exert pressure for change in civil and political rights policies. DIDR resistance movements in various locations in Mexico are part of an array of interests that have produced an epochal change in national politics with the defeat of the Partido Revolucionario Institucionalizado (PRI), which had ruled Mexico for more than seventy years.

Increasingly today, national and state governments are giving way to private-sector development interests in the planning, financing and construction of large infrastructural projects. Private-sector driven DIDR presents a different set of challenges to resistance movements because corporations are not subject to the same restraints and guidelines imposed by multilateral lenders that states are. Resistance movements can challenge the state to live up to guidelines for resettlement agreed upon as part of the terms of the loan. With private-sector development, despite apparent attention to guidelines, there is generally little evidence that corporate compliance with international human rights standards and development policies and procedures is forthcoming (Feeney 2000). NGOs and DIDR resistance movements have undertaken selected campaigns to boycott the products of companies involved directly in DIDR projects or indirectly through funding guarantees (International Rivers Network 2000b).

The importance of the media to movements resisting DIDR, in documenting and publicising the processes through which much DIDR is carried out and the impacts that it has on the lives of people, cannot be understated. Accurate and timely information is essential to the struggles of people resisting DIDR to enable them to formulate appropriate strategies and tactics, as well as to communicate the challenges they face, and the conditions they suffer, to others. In this effort, the role of the print and visual media is indispensable.

Whether made by the affected people themselves or by others, film and video in particular have become important tools in the struggles against DIDR around the world. Information technology, greatly facilitating the dissemination of both the printed word and still and moving images, has become an essential feature of DIDR resistance. Thus, Kayapo individuals have become skilled videographers of their own culture and of their interactions with Brazilians in resisting resettlement. The websites of NGOs, social movements and GROs constitute a key feature of struggles of those resisting DIDR. Visitors can find out how to contribute support for these struggles, influence policy, send letters to appropriate authorities, order more information and offer their own ideas through bulletin boards (Weeks 1999: 20).

One of the most significant aspects of information technology for 'electronic politics' (cyberactivism) is the speed with which it transmits information, and consequently the speed and level of organisation of response that the information elicits globally. Indeed, such is the speed with which information is now disseminated that central governments are sometimes among the last to learn of events and are forced into a reactive position by national and international DIDR allies. The links between websites and listservers representing many different interests enable a single individual or group to 'connect with' and inform many thousands of people all over the world with one message.

The International Scale

DIDR resistance movements have participated increasingly in global dialogues on development policy, as well as in discussions about changes in practice in specific institutions. DIDR resistance movements and their NGO allies were among those who pressured successfully for the establishment of the WCD. In this sense, DIDR resistance movements are important contributors to what many see as a fundamental transition in the terms of global development discourse.

Greater interest from the World Bank has arisen in projects addressing the alleviation of rural poverty, and in shifting the emphasis towards social impacts (Shihata 1993). This shift has been due to the intensity of rural protest and resistance as well as the public embarrassment of the

Bank at the catastrophic consequences of resettlement resulting from development projects it had funded. Like national governments, multilateral development banks (MDBs) are complex, internally diverse organisations, composed of individuals and groups with particular specialisms and interests. DIDR resisters at all levels can find sympathisers and allies in their struggles within MDBs. The results of the efforts of individuals within MDBs can be seen in the creation of guidelines for resettlement by such MDBs as the World Bank, the Inter-American Development Bank and the Asian Development Bank. Although these guidelines recommend that DIDR be avoided where possible, they are nevertheless clearly developed within the framework of the model of development that necessitates such large-scale projects as are likely to give rise to resettlement.

The exposure of project failures and their impacts in the media created pressure for the formulation of a set of resettlement policy guidelines within the World Bank (see Rich 1994). The result was 'Operational Directive 4.30: Involuntary Resettlement' (OD 4.30), which called for: minimising resettlement; an improvement in or restoration of living standards, earning capacity and production levels; the participation of people faced with resettlement in project activities; a resettlement plan; and valuation and compensation for assets lost (World Bank 1990: 1–2). When problems with projects continued, the Bank advocated the formulation and implementation of resettlement legislation in borrower nations, producing policy changes in such nations as Brazil, Colombia and Mexico, and in other development agencies such as the Organisation for Economic Co-operation and Development (OECD) and the Inter-American Development Bank (IDB) (Cernea 1993: 32, Shihata 1993). However, a number of nations have seen the OD 4.30 guidelines as an infringement on national sovereignty. Furthermore, adoption of formal policies, either by the World Bank or borrower nations, is no assurance of adequate implementation. In addition, the degree to which projects financed by private capital must adhere to these and subsequently modified guidelines and procedures established by the Bank is far from clear. The World Bank-commissioned independent report on the Narmada Sardar Sarovar project in India (Morse and Berger 1992), which recommended cessation of the project pending major improvements in environmental and social monitoring and implementation, resulted in the rejection of further World Bank funding of the project by the government of India. Recent efforts (World Bank 2001) to alter the OD 4.30 version of the guidelines were seen by human rights and environmental groups as attempts to weaken safeguards, particularly for indigenous peoples, and were responded to with an internet and letter campaign of protest. The new guidelines, glossed as 'operational policies' and 'best practices', are seen by many resisters as a World Bank response to accusations by borrower nations that the guidelines infringe on issues that are properly the domain of state sovereignty.

NGOs have severely criticised the performance of MDBs and other international agencies in DIDR projects, with the aim of reforming their internal guidelines and policies. Of particular concern is the fact that the International Finance Corporation and Multilateral Investment Guarantee Agency guidelines for projects are less strict and comprehensive than the World Bank's Operational Directive (Fox and Brown 1998, Khagram 1999: 307). Grass-roots organisations, NGOs and social movements involved in resistance to DIDR have also acquired or developed legal personnel, expertise and general knowledge that enable them to sue projects for violation of national civil and human rights law, as well as of international accords (Johnston 2000).

Resisters and their allies in NGOs and social movements have succeeded in communicating their position, backed by solid documentation, through declarations at numerous international meetings and conferences over many years, including most recently the Manibeli Declaration of 1994, the Curitiba Declaration at the First International Meeting of Dam Affected Peoples in Curitiba (Brazil) in 1997, and the Walker Creek Declaration at the International Seminar on Strategies for Dam Decommissioning in 1998. NGOs also continue with their Multilateral Development Bank Campaign, putting pressure on national donors of funds and banks to withhold funds for dams and other projects that displace people against their will.

The multiplicity of organisational forms and levels of action inevitably involve tensions and problems of coherence, consistency and contradiction for all participants in the struggles against DIDR. However, thus far, the coherence between grass-roots communities, co-operating NGOs, national social movements and transnational networks has been sufficient to gain the right to sit at the negotiating table for many projects of national scale, and enough political and social power to influence the policies of multilateral development organisations.

The Results of DIDR Resistance

Since DIDR resistance movements frequently confront vastly more powerful forces, there may be considerable costs involved. At the most basic and most profound level, there may be serious personal risks in resisting. In Guatemala in 1982 about four hundred Maya Achi men, women and children from communities resisting resettlement related to the Chixoy Dam were killed by military and paramilitary forces (Colajacomo 1999: 68). Beatings and detentions for indeterminate periods of time without due process are also among the risks of resistance. Ethnic, religious, caste or class prejudices may also buttress the ideological justification for such abuse.

There may also be considerable economic costs to resistance. Resistance has opportunity costs; it requires human and economic resources for organisation, communication and mobilisation, few of which may be actually present in sufficient surpluses in project-affected regions to underwrite the costs of resistance. Where resettlement is already underway, resisters may run the risk of exclusion from benefits that people who have accepted resettlement receive. Resisters can become scapegoats, and may be punished by receiving inadequate state support.

Resistance may create problematic relations with local and regional elements of local power and/or authority structures that might have benefited from the project's success. The defeat of a dam planned for the state of Guerrero in Mexico has assured the Nahuatl people of remaining on their land. However, it would appear that one of the costs of their victory is forgoing future state development assistance. Despite the fact that the resisting communities fall within a zone targeted for federal aid for the marginalised, they have received no federal assistance in ten years (Garcia 2000).

Failure to halt a development project does not always mean that positive outcomes are not forthcoming. Failed resistance efforts can gain a measure of success if they can bring about improvements in the terms and conditions of resettlement. If resistance activities threaten to increase the costs sufficiently, resisters can gain bargaining space to improve the resettlement project. Resistance movements that emerge from local responses and require the participation of local people generate invaluable experience in dealing with outside agencies and institutions. The acquisition of allies may make available other resource pools, injecting new skills, technology and access to specialised economic resources into the local context. Successful resistance constitutes a form of self-affirmation that can serve as a stimulus leading to a florescence of local culture and greater local autonomy. The demands that resistance movements voice for greater citizen participation in decision-making, for access to information and for respect for civil and political liberties, can also signify progress towards a more responsive and representative society.

From the perspective of NGOs, social movement allies and transnational networks, stopping the project is just one battle in a war with many fronts against certain models or approaches to development and the institutions associated with them. The experience of the antidam movement over the last thirty years has proved instructive in the struggle to alter approaches to development. The milestone meetings of dam-affected people from around the world and their Declarations at Manibeli and Curitiba, representing a global mobilisation through networking and external support, as well as the validation of many of its arguments and contentions by the Morse Report and the WCD, will serve as major examples for resistance to other forms of unsustainable and undemocratic development.

Conclusion

Regardless of the specific issues being contested in a given case, people resist DIDR because they recognise that certain basic rights that they consider legitimate are being abridged. Principal among these are the rights to self-determination and the control of one's own life and future. The threat of DIDR amounts to the potential loss of the right of self-determination; in effect, the loss of relative control over self and community (Scudder and Colson 1982). Resistance to DIDR, then, must be considered as a form of legitimate expression of the defence of the right to self-determination, as well as a defence of land, religion or identity. People also reject the loss of autonomy and the extreme form of political domination that resettlement both signifies and enacts, and their resistance questions whether resettlement can ever be development or empowering. Their resistance is, in some fundamental form, an act of self-empowerment, as it constitutes:

- a rejection of the dominant society's cultural construction of the poor, ethnic minorities, and peasants as incapable, powerless and unworthy of consideration;
- part of the effort to democratise their societies;
- an articulation of local needs and priorities;
- an analysis of project deficiencies (project problems do not originate with people and are not the resettled people's fault); and
- a demand for accountability and responsibility from government, development agencies and MDBs for actions taken in the name of social policy and development.

The messages that resisters seek to communicate are not difficult to understand, but do require a perspective that is capable of re-evaluating often deeply embedded suppositions about the nature, quality and scale of the development process, forms of governance and power sharing, and minority-majority relations. DIDR resisters and their allies at a variety of levels insist that if development is to be a truly democratic process that reflects both the interests and participation of all the affected parties, then:

- the legitimacy of the right of the state to relocate people and appropriate property with or without compensation must be re-examined;
- appropriate and just forms and levels of compensation must be determined in consultation with affected people;
- local rights must be recognised because development projects are felt first at the local level;
- development must be defined and evaluated qualitatively as well as quantitatively;

- local knowledge must be mined for predicting DIDR outcomes and as a source for viable, less destructive alternatives;
- the method and focus of decision-making must shift from purely economic criteria to more dialogic forms of participatory decision-making; and
- if it is to be seen as the justification for development projects, then national purpose has to be defined pluralistically and projects have to be demonstratively inclusive – a national purpose that requires only sacrifices from those least able to absorb them for the benefit of those who least need them is authoritarian, regardless of the supposedly democratic character of the regime.

There are obvious points of tension that can occur between a population threatened with resettlement, which resists to gain a better negotiating position for better resettlement conditions, and allies at other levels who may have more systemic goals, reaching beyond the local context to question the dominant models of development. Local resistance dramas 'in the shadow land ... at the outer edge of the realm of politics' may thus become internationalised, the actors becoming participants in the changing arena of global political culture (Falk 1983: 25, as quoted in Wilmer 1993: 39; see also Fisher 1995).

The major challenge within DIDR resistance is maintaining the coherence between the agendas, goals and discourses of the participants at all levels of the struggle. When the local dramas of resistance to resettlement are cast in terms of national debates, attracting the attention of national and international NGOs and multilateral and international institutions, then people under threat of resettlement become active participants in a larger global dialogue. In effect, resistance to resettlement is helping to reframe the entire contemporary debate on development, the environment and human rights – a debate that shows considerable signs of expanding and gaining increasing relevance to both national development and human rights policy, as well as to international standards.

References

Acselrad, H. and M. Da Silva. 2000. 'Social Conflict and Environmental Change at the Amazon Tucurui Dam Region'. Paper presented at the meeting of the International Rural Sociology Association, in Rio de Janeiro, Brazil, 4 August.

Adams, J. 1996. 'Cost-benefit Analysis: The Problem, Not the Solution'. *The Ecologist*, 26(1): 2–4.

Albert, B. 1992. 'Indian Lands, Environmental Policy and Military Geopolitics in the Development of the Brazilian Amazon'. *Development and Change*, 23: 35–70.

Altman, I. and S. Low. 1992. *Place Attachment, Human Behavior and Environment: Advances in Theory and Research*. Vol. 8. New York: Plenum Press.

Appa, G. and G. Patel. 1996. 'Unrecognised, Unnecessary and Unjust Displacement: Case Studies from Gujarat, India'. In C. McDowell (ed.). *Understanding Impoverishment: The Consequences of Development-induced Displacement*, pp. 139–50. New York, Oxford: Berghahn Books.

Bartolomé, L. 1992. 'Fighting Leviathan: The Articulation and Spread of Local Opposition to Hydrodevelopment in Brazil'. Paper presented at the 41st Annual Conference of the Center for Latin American Studies: Involuntary Migration and Resettlement in Latin America, held at the University of Florida, Gainesville, 2–4 April.

Bartolomé, M. and A. Barabas. 1973. *Hydraulic Ethnocide: The Mazatec and Chinantec People of Oaxaca, Mexico.* Copenhagen: IWGIA.

_____ 1990. *La presa Cerro de Oro y el ingeniero El Gran Dios, Tomo II*, Mexico DF: Instituto Nacional Indigenista.

Baviskar, A. 1992. 'Development, Nature and Resistance: The Case of the Bhilala Tribals in the Narmada Valley'. Ph.D. Dissertation, Cornell University, Ithaca, New York.

Beck, U. 1992. *Risk Society: Towards a New Modernity.* Thousand Oaks CA: Sage Publications.

_____ 1995. *Ecological Politics in an Age of Risk.* London: Frank Cass.

Bellah, R.N., R. Madsen, W.M. Sullivan, A. Swidler and S.M. Tipton. 1985. *Habits of the Heart: Individualism and Commitment in American Life.* New York: Harper and Row.

Bilharz, J.A. 1998. *The Allegany Senecas and Kinzua Dam: Forced Relocation Through Two Generations.* Lincoln: University of Nebraska Press.

Brechin, S.R., P.R. Wilshusen, C.L. Fortwangler and P.C. West. 2003. *Contested Nature: Promoting International Biodiversity with Social Justice in the Twenty-first Century.* Albany: University of New York Press.

Celestino, E.S. 1999. 'Nadando Contracorriente en el Balsas'. Paper presented in the Seminar-Workshop on Forced Relocation from Disaster Risk, Universidad Autonoma de Colima, 30 July–1 August.

Cernea, M.M. 1988. *Involuntary Resettlement in Development Projects.* Washington DC: The World Bank.

_____ 1993. 'Anthropological and Sociological Research for Policy Development on Population Resettlement'. In M.M. Cernea and S.E. Guggenheim (eds). *Anthropological Approaches to Resettlement*, pp. 13–38. Boulder CO: Westview Press.

_____ (ed.). 1999. *The Economics of Involuntary Resettlement: Questions and Challenges.* Washington DC: The World Bank.

Chambers, R. (ed.). 1970. *The Volta Resettlement Experience.* New York: Praeger Publishers.

Chernela, J. 1988. 'Potential Impacts of a Proposed Amazon Hydropower Project'. *Cultural Survival*, 12(2): 20–24.

Cleaver, F. 1999. 'Paradoxes of Participation: Questioning Participatory Approaches to Development'. *Journal of International Development*, 11: 597–612.

Colajacomo, J. 1999. 'The Chixoy Dam: The Maya Achi Genocide: The Story of a Forced Resettlement'. *Indigenous Affairs*, 3–4: 64–79.

Colchester, M. 1999. 'Sharing Power: Dams, Indigenous Peoples and Ethnic Minorities'. *Indigenous Affairs*, 3–4: 4–54.

Colson, E. 1971. *The Social Consequences of Resettlement: The Impact of the Kariba Resettlement Upon the Gwembe Tonga*. Manchester: Manchester University Press.

Conuel, T. 1981. *Quabbin: The Accidental Wilderness*. Lincoln MA: Massachusetts Audubon Society.

Davidheiser, M. 2000. 'Negotiations between Unequals: A Review of the Literature'. Unpublished manuscript. Gainesville FL: Department of Anthropology, University of Florida.

Dwivedi, R. 1997. 'Why Some People Resist and Others Do Not: Local Perceptions and Actions over Displacement Risks on the Sardar Sarovar'. *Working Paper Series No. 265*. The Hague: Institute of Social Studies.

———— 1998. 'Resisting Dams and "Development": Contemporary Significance of the Campaign against the Narmada Projects in India'. *European Journal of Development Research*, 10(2): 135–79.

———— 1999. 'Displacement, Risks and Resistance: Local Perceptions and Actions in the Sardar Sarovar'. *Development and Change*, 30: 43–78.

Escobar, A. 2001. 'Culture Sits in Places: Reflections on Globalism and Subaltern Strategies of Localization'. *Political Geography*, 20: 139–74.

Espeland, W. 1998. *The Struggle for Water: Politics, Rationality, and Identity in the American Southwest*. Chicago: University of Chicago Press.

———— 1999. 'Value Matters'. Paper delivered at the Conference entitled 'The Cost-benefit Analysis Dilemma: Strategies and Alternatives', Yale University, 8–10 October.

Evans, W. 2001. '"Women with the Strength of the Earth" Keep Biobio Dam at Bay'. *World Rivers Review*, 16(3): 6–7.

Falk, R. 1983. *The End of World Order*. London: Holmes and Meier.

Fantasia, R. 1988. *Cultures of Solidarity*. Berkeley: University of California Press.

Feeney, P. 2000. 'Globalization and Accountability: The Corporate Sector in Involuntary Displacement and Resettlement'. *Forced Migration Review*, 8: 22–24.

Fisher, J. 1996. 'Grassroots Organisations and Grassroots Support Organisations: Patterns of Interaction'. In E. Moran (ed.). *Transforming Societies, Transforming Anthropology*, pp. 57–102. Ann Arbor MI: University of Michigan Press.

Fisher, R. and W. Ury. 1981. *Getting to Yes: Negotiating Agreement Without Giving In*. New York: Penguin Books.

Fisher, W.F. (ed.). 1995. *Toward Sustainable Development: Struggles Over India's Narmada River*. Armonk NY, London: M.E. Sharpe.

———— 1999. 'Going Under: Indigenous Peoples and the Struggle Against Large Dams: Introduction'. *Cultural Survival Quarterly*, 23(3): 29–32.

Fisher, W.H. 1994. 'Megadevelopment, Environmentalism, and Resistance: The Institutional Context of Kayapo Indigenous Politics in Central Brazil'. *Human Organisation*, 53(3): 220–32.

Foweraker, J. 2001. 'Towards a Political Sociology of Social Mobilization in Latin America'. Presented at the conference 'Latin American Sociology and the Sociology of Latin America'. Gainesville FL: Center for Latin American Studies, University of Florida.

Fox, J.A. and L.D. Brown (eds). 1998. *The Struggle for Accountability: The World Bank, NGOs and Grassroots Movements*. Cambridge MA: MIT Press.

Fried, M. 1963. 'Grieving for a Lost Home'. In L. Duhl (ed.). *The Urban Condition: People and Policy in the Metropolis*, pp. 151–71. New York: Basic Books.

Gans, H.J. 1962. *The Urban Villagers: Group and Class in the Life of Italian Americans.* Glencoe IL: Free Press.

Garcia, M. 2000. 'Alto Balsas, Una decada de lucha indigena'. www.mileniodiario.com.mx/anteriores/ 23102000/te3.htm.

Garcia Canclini, N. 1993. *Transforming Modernity.* Austin: University of Texas Press.

Geisler, C. and R. De Sousa. 2001. 'From Refuge to Refugee: The African Case'. *Journal of Public Administration and Development,* 21: 159–70.

Gibson, D. 1993. *The Politics of Involuntary Resettlement: World Bank Supported Projects in Asia.* Unpublished Ph.D. dissertation, Department of Political Science, Duke University.

Giddens, A. 1990. *The Consequences of Modernity.* Cambridge: Polity Press.

Gray, A. 1996. 'Indigenous Resistance to Involuntary Relocation'. In C. McDowell (ed.). *Understanding Impoverishment: The Consequences of Development-induced Displacement,* pp. 99–122. New York, Oxford: Berghahn Books.

Greene, J.R. 1985. *The Day Four Quabbin Towns Died.* Athol MA: The Transcript Press.

Guggenheim, S.E. 1993. 'Peasants, Planners and Participation: Resettlement in Mexico'. In M.M. Cernea and S.E. Guggenheim (eds). *Anthropological Approaches to Resettlement,* pp. 201–28. Boulder CO: Westview Press.

Harvey, D. 1996. *Justice, Nature and the Geography of Difference.* Oxford: Blackwell Publishers.

International Rivers Network. 2000a. 'When the Rivers Run Dry: The World Bank, Dams and the Quest for Reparations'. International Rivers Network Briefing Paper. Berkeley CA: International Rivers Network.

———— 2000b. 'Discover Three Gorges' (Brochure). Berkeley CA: International Rivers Network.

———— n.d. 'Large Dams, False Promises'. Berkeley CA: International Rivers Network video production.

Jeffrey, J.L. 2000. *The Siege of Zapata: Long Term Consequences of Displacement in a Border Town.* Unpublished Ph.D. Dissertation. Gainesville FL: Department of Anthropology, University of Florida.

Jing, J. 1999. 'Villages Dammed, Villages Repossessed: A Memorial Movement in Northwest China'. *American Anthropologist,* 26(2): 324–43.

Johnston, B.R. 2000. 'Reparations and the Right to Remedy'. Briefing paper prepared for the World Commission on Dams. http://www.dams.org/thematic/contrib._papers.php

Khagram, S. 1999. *Dams, Democracy and Development: Transnational Struggles for Power and Water.* Ph.D. Dissertation, Department of Political Science, Stanford University.

Koenig, D. 2001. *Toward Local Development and Mitigating Impoverishment in Development-induced Displacement and Resettlement.* Unpublished report, Refugee Studies Centre, University of Oxford.

Kumar, C. 1996. 'It's Virtually Politics: Information Technology and Transnational Activism in the Developing World'. Ph.D. Dissertation, Department of Political Science, University of Illinois at Urbana-Champaign.

Ling, C.Y. and M.F. Ferrari. 1995. 'Golf Wars'. *Toward Freedom: A Progressive Perspective on World Events,* June-July, 44(3): 8–9.

Little, P.E. 1999. 'Political Ecology as Ethnography: The Case of Ecuador's Aguarico River Basin'. *Serie Antropologia, 258*. Brazil: Department of Anthropology, University of Brazil.

Magee, P.L. 1989. 'Peasant Political Identity and the Tucurui Dam: A Case Study of the Island Dwellers of Para, Brazil'. *The Latinamericanist*, 24(1): 6–10.

McAdam, D., J.D. McCarthy and M.N. Zald. 1988. 'Social Movements'. In N. Smelser (ed.). *Handbook of Sociology*. Newbury Park CA: Sage Publications.

McCully, P. 1996. *Silenced Rivers: The Ecology and Politics of Large Dams*. London: Zed Books.

McDonald, M.D. 1993. 'Dams, Displacement and Development: A Resistance Movement in Southern Brazil'. In J. Friedmann and H. Rangan (eds). *In Defense of Livelihood: Comparative Studies in Environmental Action*, pp. 79–105. West Hartford CT: Kumarian Press.

Moore, B., Jr. 1966. *Social Origins of Dictatorship and Democracy: Lord and Peasant in the Making of the Modern World*. Boston: Beacon Press.

Morse, B. and T. Berger. 1992. *Sardar Sarovar: Report of the Independent Review*. Ottawa: Resource Futures International, Inc.

Murphy, R. 1994. *Rationality and Nature*. Boulder CO: Westview Press.

Nader, L. 1994. 'Coercive Harmony: The Political Economy of Legal Models'. Unpublished manuscript. Department of Anthropology, University of California, Berkeley.

———— 1997. 'Controlling Processes: Tracing the Dynamic Components of Power'. *Current Anthropology*, 38: 5.

Oates, J.F. 1999. *Myth and Reality in the Rain Forest: How Conservation Strategies are Failing in West Africa*. Berkeley: University of California Press.

Oliver-Smith, A. 1991. 'Involuntary Resettlement, Resistance and Political Empowerment'. *Journal of Refugee Studies*, 4(2): 132–49.

———— 1994. 'Resistance to Resettlement: The Formation and Evolution of Movements'. *Research in Social Movements, Conflict and Change*, 17: 197–219.

———— 1996. 'Fighting for a Place: The Policy Implications of Resistance to Resettlement'. In C. McDowell (ed.). *Understanding Impoverishment: The Consequences of Development-induced Displacement*, pp. 77–98. New York, Oxford: Berghahn Books.

O'Neill, J. 1996. 'Cost-benefit Analysis, Rationality and the Plurality of Values'. *The Ecologist*, 26(3): 98–103.

———— 2001. 'Markets and the Environment: The Solution is the Problem'. *Economic and Political Weekly*, 36: 1865–73.

Ott, M.C. 1972. 'Mediation as a Method of Conflict Resolution'. *International Organisation*, 26: 595–618.

Parasuraman, S. 1999. *The Development Dilemma: Displacement in India*. New York: St. Martin's Press.

Penzich, C., G. Thomas and T. Wohlgenant. 1994. 'The Role of Alternative Conflict Management in Community Forestry'. Working Paper No. 1, Community Forestry Unit: Forests, Trees, and People Programme Phase II, Forestry Division. Rome: Food and Agriculture Organisation of the United Nations.

Perlman, J.E. 1982. 'Favela Removal: The Eradication of a Lifestyle'. In A. Hansen and A. Oliver-Smith (eds). *Involuntary Migration and Resettlement: The Problems and Responses of Dislocated Peoples*, pp. 225–44. Boulder CO: Westview Press.

Pleumarom, A. 1994. 'Sport and Environment: Thailand's Golf Boom Reviewed'. *TEI Quarterly Environment Journal*, 2(4): 1–11.

Posey, D. 1996. 'The Kayapo Indian Protests against Amazonian Dams: Successes, Alliances and Un-ending Battles'. In C. McDowell (ed.). *Understanding Impoverishment: The Consequences of Development-induced Displacement*, pp. 123–38. New York, Oxford: Berghahn Books.

Rapp, K.W. 2000. 'Yacyreta: Affected People's Resistance to Involuntary Resettlement'. *Eastern Anthropologist*, 53(1/2): 223–57.

Rich, B. 1994. *Mortgaging the Earth: The World Bank, Environmental Impoverishment and the Crisis of Development*. Boston: Beacon Press.

Robinson, S. 1992. 'Participation and Accountability: Understanding the Political Culture of Involuntary Resettlement in Mexico'. Paper Presented at the 41st Annual Conference of the Center for Latin American Studies, Involuntary Migration and Resettlement in Latin America, University of Florida, Gainesville, 2–4 April.

Rodman, M.C. 1992. 'Empowering Place: Multilocality and Multivocality'. *American Anthropologist*, 94(3): 640–56.

Rothman, F.D. and P.E. Oliver. 1999. 'From Local to Global: The Anti-dam Movement in Southern Brazil, 1979–1992'. *Mobilization: An International Journal*, 4(1): 41–57.

Schradie, J. and M. DeVries (Directors). 2000. *The Golf War*. Oley PA: Anthill Productions/Bullfrog Films.

Scott, J. 1985. *Weapons of the Weak: Everyday Forms of Peasant Resistance*. New Haven: Yale University Press.

Scudder, T. and E. Colson. 1982. 'From Welfare to Development: A Conceptual Framework for the Analysis of Dislocated People'. In A. Hansen and A. Oliver-Smith (eds). *Involuntary Migration and Resettlement: The Problems and Responses of Dislocated People*, pp. 267–87. Boulder CO: Westview Press.

Serra, M.T.F. 1993. 'Resettlement Planning in the Brazilian Power Sector: Recent Changes in Approach'. In M.M. Cernea and S.E. Guggenheim (eds). *Anthropological Approaches to Resettlement*, pp. 63–86. Boulder CO: Westview Press.

Shihata, I.F.I. 1993. 'Legal Aspects of Involuntary Population Resettlement'. In M.M. Cernea and S.E. Guggenheim (eds). *Anthropological Approaches to Resettlement: Policy, Practice, and Theory*, pp. 39–54. Boulder CO: Westview Press.

Smith, C. 1996. 'Development and the State: Issues for Anthropologists'. In E. Moran (ed.). *Transforming Societies, Transforming Anthropology*, pp. 25–56. Ann Arbor MI: University of Michigan Press.

Smith, N. 1996. *The New Urban Frontier: Gentrification and the Revanchist City*. London: Routledge.

Terborgh, J. 1999. *Requiem for Nature*. Washington DC: Island Press.

Waldram, J. 1980. 'Relocation and Political Change in a Manitoba Native Community'. *Canadian Journal of Anthropology*, 1(2): 173–78.

Wali, A. 1989. *Kilowatts and Crisis: Hydroelectric Power and Social Dislocation in Eastern Panama*. Boulder CO: Westview Press.

Weeks, P. 1999. 'Cyber-activism: World Wildlife Fund's Campaign to Save the Tiger'. *Culture and Agriculture*, 21(3): 19–30.

Williams, P.B. 1997. 'A Historic Overview of IRN's Mission'. Berkeley CA: International Rivers Network, Unpublished manuscript.

Wilmer, F. 1993. *The Indigenous Voice in World Politics*. Newbury Park: Sage Publications.

Wolf, E. 1982. *Europe and the People without History*. Berkeley: University of California Press.

World Bank. 1990. 'Operational Directive 4.30: Involuntary Resettlement'. *The World Bank Operational Manual*. Washington DC: The World Bank.

―――― 2001. *Involuntary Resettlement (OP/BP 4.12)*. Washington DC: The World Bank.

World Commission on Dams (WCD). 2000. *Dams and Development: A New Framework for Decision Making*. London, Sterling VA: Earthscan.

Zaman, M.Q. 1982. 'Crisis in Chittagong Hill Tracts: Ethnicity and Integration'. *Economic and Political Weekly*, 17(3): 75–80.

7

Risk, Complexity and Local Initiative in Forced Resettlement Outcomes

Chris de Wet

Introductory Remarks

The track record shows only too clearly that, in the great majority of cases, things turn out badly for people subjected to forced resettlement (in the sense that they have to move whether they wish to or not) as a result of development projects or political programmes – and often also for others who may not actually have to move, such as host populations and other parties affected by the development project. It is not necessarily true that resettlement will always turn out badly for the affected people, and there have been a number of encouraging cases. But, if we are to do something constructive about it, we have to start with the reality that, on the whole, forced resettlement has not been successful, in the sense that resettled people are both economically better off and socially stable in their new settlements in a manner that has shown itself to be sustainable over time. Why are such positive cases so few and far between, notwithstanding ongoing efforts to develop and improve resettlement guidelines and policy? That needs to be our starting point in trying to reverse the situation.

In this chapter I try to develop a framework to explain why this should be the case. This framework is somewhat different in emphasis from the prevailing 'risks and reconstruction' approach developed by Cernea (2000), seeking to incorporate his important insights into a more comprehensive approach. I argue that we need to locate our understanding of why things go wrong and, consequently, our thinking about how to set about improving matters, in an analysis of the complexity inherent in the resettlement process. After outlining the approach from complexity, I then examine the successes recorded in some Chinese forced resettlement schemes, such as Shuikou and Xiaolangdi, as well as in voluntary settlement schemes, and consider whether their successes are likely to be replicable in forced resettlement schemes in 'developing countries'. In a number of cases, resettlers have taken initiatives and/or capitalised on unplanned for opportunities (in the sense that they were not necessarily planned for by the scheme itself), thereby improving their situation; I examine a number of such cases in the African context, and ask what they teach us. In conclusion, I offer some thoughts on the need to factor considerations of complexity more effectively into the policy process and to capitalise on the initiative shown by resettlers.

Why Forced Resettlement So Often Goes Wrong: The 'Inadequate Inputs' Approach

Why does forced resettlement so often go wrong, and end up leaving the resettled people (and often others as well) economically, socially and psychologically worse off than before? There seem to be two broad approaches to answering this question, which one might call the 'inadequate inputs' and the 'inherent complexities' approaches respectively. These different 'diagnoses' have implications for how we should go about attempting to improve resettlement outcomes.

The 'inadequate inputs' approach, which will be familiar to many of us, is largely associated with the initiatives and policies of the World Bank. This approach can be summarised as arguing that resettlement goes wrong principally because of a lack of the proper inputs: national legal frameworks and policies, political will, funding, preresettlement surveys, planning, consultation, careful implementation and monitoring. Lack of these inputs is what gives rise to what Michael Cernea has conceptualised as eight principal 'impoverishment risks': landlessness; joblessness; homelessness; marginalisation; food insecurity; increased morbidity; loss of access to common property resources; and community disarticulation (Cernea 2000: 20, 22 ff).

Cernea defines 'risk' as follows:

> We use the sociological concept of risk to indicate the *possibility* that a certain course of action will trigger injurious effects – losses and destruction ... Risks are often directly perceptible, and also measurable through science ... as they are an objective reality. The cultural construction of a risk – be it a social or a natural risk – could emphasise or de-emphasise (belittle) its seriousness, or could also ignore it, but this does not change the objective nature of risks. (Cernea 2000: 19)

> Risk may be defined as the possibility embedded in a certain course of social action to trigger adverse events. (Cernea 2000: 19, footnote 5)

For Cernea, risks thus have an objective nature, independently of how they are subjectively understood. Without the proper inputs, the risks of landlessness and homelessness *will almost certainly* be actualised.

This approach is, however, basically optimistic in tenor, as Cernea argues that 'the general risk pattern inherent in displacement *can be controlled through a policy response* that mandates and finances integrated problem resolution' (Cernea 2000: 34, emphasis in original). Proper policy, political will and provision (particularly funding) can overcome the problem of inadequacy of inputs, and the impoverishment risks can then be turned into opportunities for reconstruction, such that resettlement becomes resettlement with development, leaving the resettled people better off than before (Cernea 2000: 35 ff).

The approach is broadly economic (Koenig 2001) and technical in character. Most of the impoverishment risks relate to economic resources, with Cernea emphasising the importance of the risk to people's livelihoods, and the centrality of reconstructing livelihoods (Cernea 2000: 35). The key problems confronting resettlement are seen as essentially operationalisable – as problems that can be dealt with through the reform of policy and procedures, and the provision of the necessary resources. The complexity of the resettlement process can thus, in principle, be mastered, to good effect.

In contrast to this, is what I call the 'inherent complexities' approach. I argue that, because of the nature of forced resettlement, it is characterised by a complexity, which gives rise to a range of problems that are more difficult to deal with than, and the resolution of which involves more than the provision of, the kind of inputs mentioned above. I develop this approach in more detail as the substance of this chapter.

Why Forced Resettlement So Often Go Wrong: The 'Inherent Complexities' Approach

This is an exploratory exposition, and by no means a final formulation. I will try to identify what I consider to be some of the main characteristics of forced resettlement, and show how they generate a complexity around resettlement, which gives rise to a range of risks which, while not necessarily all equally threatening in all instances, seem to me to be all but inherent in the process of forced resettlement as such. These risks seem to operate at different levels of comprehensiveness or incorporation, and I will suggest a schema for analysing risks in this way. Where we locate risks and their source will have implications for how we go about attempting to deal with them. I refer to some African cases in my exposition, but cannot go into any great detail.

The Main Characteristics of Forced Resettlement

Forced resettlement involves imposed spatial change, in the sense that it involves people having to move from one settlement and area to another. This has cultural, social, political and economic implications. Particularly in small scale rural settings – but also in urban working-class settings (Western 1981 and Whisson 1976, for Cape Town, where 'Coloured' communities were relocated because of the Group Areas Act of 1950, during the apartheid era) – social relationships have a strong territorial component, and are in this sense to a considerable degree spatially based. The spatial change thus requires people to develop new sets of relationships. Depending on the scope of the spatial change, and the speed and degree of participation with which it takes place, people may experience serious social disruption, or 'dislocation', in Cernea's terms. In one of the more extreme cases, the Sudanese Nubians were moved about eight hundred kilometres from their original homes, and away from the banks of the Nile River (Fahim 1973: 43), while in the case of the Akosombo Dam on the Volta River, the formation of Lake Volta started more than a year ahead of the originally planned date, which put tremendous pressure on the planning and preparation for resettlement (Lumsden 1973: 119).

Spatial change usually involves a change in the patterns of people's access to resources. Typically, resettlement and the agricultural plans accompanying it in rural cases involve a change in land use and often also in land tenure. In the case of a number of villagisation schemes in South Africa, and elsewhere in Africa (de Wet 1995: 26–38), people have often found themselves with less arable and / or grazing land, further from their land, and (except where piped water supplies have not broken down) further from resources such as water and wood. Resettled people in urban areas often have found themselves further from sources of work and shops, and having to bear the additional cost of transport and higher prices (for Cape Town, see Western 1981; for East London, see Mayer and Mayer 1971; for Lagos, see Marris 1961). Compensation for lost lands or other resources has, certainly in the case of dam-related resettlement in Africa, typically been inadequate and / or late in being paid (e.g. Nangbeto Dam in Togo – see World Bank 1998: 8ff; Manantali Dam in Mali – see Grimm 1991: 136).

Resettled people usually find themselves in larger and more heterogeneous settlements than previously. Thus, in the cases of the Aswan Dam and the Volta River Project, people found themselves in settlements from ten to thirty times larger than they had been accustomed to (Butcher 1970: 89, Fahim 1981: 55–57). Not only have new settlements usually been larger, but also more ethnically diverse. This tends to give rise to problems around competition for resources (with access having been altered and often diminished, as above), and around the negotiation of political leadership within new settlements. While such tensions are usually most acute in the early years after resettlement, easing off with time, in some cases, such as some new settlements in the Volta situation (Diaw and Schmidt-Kallert 1990: 120), twenty-five years on, divisions have persisted and even worsened. The day-to-day handling of cultural diversity in new settlements remains a sensitive issue, with new procedures having to be worked out for such delicate matters as to how to conduct funerals. Christians and Muslims were unable to sustain combined burial societies in the Qeto resettlement area in Wellega in Ethiopia after they had been moved there with the massive drought and politically related resettlement of the mid 1980s (Pankhurst 1992: 185–92). Tensions and even conflict have characterised many new settlements.

Resettlement involves people in wider structures. They are drawn into the structure of the resettlement scheme and its administration, as well as of the development project of which the resettlement scheme is part. They are also drawn into provincial/regional type administrative and political structures, and economic marketing networks, into which the resettlement scheme becomes incorporated (see Thiele 1985 and 1986 for the Ujamaa villages in Tanzania; Pankhurst 1992 for Ethiopia). People are also brought into the domain of national- and international- level structures. This is because resettlement-inducing development projects are usually part of national-level development-cum-political/ideological programmes (as was the case with the Aswan Dam in Egypt – see Fahim 1981: 15, and the Akosombo Dam in Ghana – see Lumsden 1973: 117), which bring the affected people under the influence of the relevant government department. Projects are often funded by international banks or aid agencies, which then also exercise their influence upon the resettlement area and its people. In most cases, these various kinds of incorporation involve a lessening of the political and economic autonomy enjoyed by the resettled people.

Resettlement involves accelerated socio-economic change. Development-induced displacement and resettlement (DIDR), as a planned intervention by an outside agency powerful enough to foist its will upon the 'receiving' community, takes place largely in terms of the agenda and timetable of that agency (e.g. a government agency or a private development company). Our concern here is that such agendas and timetables will artificially speed up and telescope the ongoing processes of change at the local level. This is because certain physical changes, such as the new land use-plan and the actual relocation, have to take place within the agency's project cycle. DIDR also speeds up the process of local communities' increasing involvement with, and often dependence upon, their wider political and economic setting. The fact that DIDR often results in diminished access to agricultural land, or disrupts local means of livelihood, makes resettled people more dependent upon cash sources of income, driving them outwards to the regional or national labour market. The changed balance between subsistence and cash sources of income tends to lead to changes in patterns of consumption, and to a more urban-oriented focus (e.g. villagisation schemes, particularly in South Africa, but also elsewhere in Africa – see de Wet 1995: Ch. 4). The resettlement projects also involve new types of leadership, geared to the new type of community (e.g. agricultural scheme, party cell or bulwark against guerrillas, as in the socialist villages in Tanzania in the 1970s and in Ethiopia in the 1980s – see Hyden 1980; Pankhurst 1992) that the outsiders wish to establish via the resettlement scheme, and again speeds up this new community's involvement in the wider political and administrative structures of which it is seen as part. Such accelerated change usually impacts negatively upon the already disrupted communities' capacity to control their own socio-economic situation, and the terms of their interaction with their wider context/situation. Their diminished capacity to influence the terms of that wider interaction, in turn, further serves to accelerate the process of social change.

The combination of the above factors in resettlement tends to lessen people's material well-being, limit their choices and control over their circumstances, and increase the presence of social tension and conflict within new settlements. The involuntary nature of both the resettlement and the conditions under which they are resettled, the frequent loss of resources, the incorporation into wider, more powerful, more directive and more remote structures, and the dislocation involved, as well as the accelerated fashion in which it all happens, all serve to limit the choices open to people and, accordingly, the degree of control they have over, and the degree of harmony in, their day-to-day circumstances.

The Resettlement Project as a Problematic Institutional Process

A number of factors at the level of the resettlement project as an institutional process combine, usually in such a way that the goals of the resettlement component of the overall project are not realised, resettlement with development does not happen and people are left socio-economically worse off than before.

Alan Rew (Rew et al. 2000) has coined the term 'policy practice' to suggest that policy and its implementation should not be seen as two separate phases, but as part of one process. He suggests that policy is significantly transformed in the process of implementation. Policy is usually a negotiated outcome, which has to accommodate the concerns of various interest groups: it thus tends to be fairly general and may even embody contradictory elements. It is implemented in a context characterised by poor communication and co-ordination between the various agencies, by work pressure and by capacity and resource shortages – all of which allow considerable discretion to local-level resettlement officials, who cut corners and develop their own operational routines in order to cope with the demands of their situation. Resettlement policy thus effectively becomes what local-level officials make of it on the ground.

The above situation seems to be a direct outcome of the fact that many countries or regions needing infrastructure projects are faced with a number of mutually reinforcing critical shortages. They usually lack the very things needed to make resettlement work, such as money, staff, skills and, critically, time, since lack of the other resources tends to result in resettlement planning and schedules progressively falling behind other project schedules, such as construction schedules (as in the case of the Akosombo Dam in Ghana, mentioned earlier). This is made worse by the fact that, with the exception of countries like Brazil, China and India, the lessons learned and the skills acquired are not usually transferable across resettlement situations. Projects such as Kariba (Zambia), Nangbeto (Togo) and Volta (Ghana) were firsts for those countries, and each country accordingly has had to build up its resettlement administrative structures and experience pretty much from scratch. Expert missions or 'helicopter anthropology' cannot close that gap, as there is no substitute for the local development of institutional capacity – which takes time and includes making what could become very expensive mistakes.

Development projects are about infrastructure and about generating revenue from that infrastructure. As a result, in some cases, resettlement is seen as an external cost, as a hassle that has to be accommodated if the overall project is to go ahead. Thus, an official on the Volta River Project referred to the eighty thousand people who would have to move to make way for the project as 'the fly in the ointment' (quoted in Chambers 1970). Officials seconded to resettlement administration do not necessarily have the appropriate social training, and accordingly are unlikely to have either the social understanding or the commitment necessary to make resettlement work. Resettlement accordingly often has to make do with an allocation of less than 10 percent of the overall project budget – and at times, money is taken from resettlement to pay towards cost overruns in other parts of the project, such as construction (Scudder 1997: 688–89). Resettlement is thus often treated as a subordinate consideration, a necessary cost, in situations where it is seen as economically rational (in the short term) to allocate as few resources as possible to it.

Given that resettlement projects in Africa have often been part of wider political agendas and programmes (see below), and have been conducted in the context of critical shortages by officials and technicians who have seen infrastructure provision as a key to economic progress, it is not surprising that many African resettlement projects have been characterised by inadequate consultation and participation. Where there has been participation, inadequate attention has been paid to the complexities and problems that it involves. This has been the case in Africa for resettlement arising out of dams, drought relief, political programmes and villagisation. Although actual participation has varied across schemes, and although officials have listened to what affected people had to say, by and large resettlement schemes have been planned and implemented on behalf of and for, rather than by and with, the affected people. Following on from this, resettlement is usually not consciously planned as a development exercise, intended to leave the resettled people better off.

The result of the above factors is that, by default, resettlement all too often becomes reduced to relocation. For project officials, the priority becomes to get people out of the area where the infrastructure is to be placed and to have an effect (as with the rising waters of a dam), as well as making sure that they are relocated to the new resettlement area, or wherever else they are to go. Once resettlement has taken place, the development of those new areas often goes largely by the board, with the resettled people being left to find ways of generating their own livelihoods in the new context. The predictable result is impoverishment.

Aspects of the Resettlement Process That Are Potentially Not Amenable to Rational Planning and Procedures

Certain aspects of the resettlement process do not seem to be readily amenable to the essentially rational, technical planning type of approach preferred by officials, which seems to characterise the 'inadequate inputs' approach discussed earlier. If certain issues are beyond the reach of rational planning, then that has implications for the way in which we should go about resettlement. Four of these issues are detailed below.

Large-scale infrastructure projects, such as dams, irrigation schemes or highways, are often seen by the authorities as part of national, and even nationalistic, projects (the Akosombo Dam in Ghana; the Aswan Dam in Egypt; the (then) Hendrik Verwoerd / (now) Gariep Dam in South Africa). Such projects – and the resulting resettlement – have to fit in with essentially political objectives and time frames, regardless of whether these are compatible with sound planning, financing and implementation. Resettlement thus has to adjust to 'national priorities', with predictably negative results.

Everything happens all at once, a whole range of things, of different orders. Cernea (2000: 31) argues that the impoverishment risks he identifies hit affected people all at once, and that they 'must deal with these risks virtually simultaneously, as a patterned situation, not just one at a time. The result is a crisis'. The same problem confronts those officials administering and implementing resettlement, who must handle all at once a host of legal, administrative, institutional, financial and personnel demands, as well as having to deal with the people to be resettled. The result, for both affected people and for officials, is ad hoc crisis management, rather than rational procedure – with unanticipated and unintended outcomes, which further feed into the ongoing situation of crisis and ad hoc way of doing things.

Development-induced displacement and resettlement embodies conflicting time frames, which further work against the likelihood of a rational approach. First, the time frames of the infrastructural and the social aspects of the overall project are often out of synch and pulling in different directions, which tends to lead to resettlement being rushed. Second, the time frames for change held by the project, and by the affected people, are often also at odds, making for conflict, which further messes up time frames and other aspects of resettlement planning.

Competing visions of the nature and process of development are involved in DIDR. Outsider government and development agencies usually have a very different view of *what constitutes development* (e.g. infrastructure development), who the key constituencies are and how to go about achieving development, from people at the local level, who tend to have a much more localised, territorially based view of such issues and who may feel themselves deeply threatened by outsider perspectives. Local people also tend to see the *process of development* very differently, particularly the role and importance of dialogue and negotiation, and how that relates to matters such as autonomy and self-respect. They may respond to these differences with resistance, as a means of keeping the dialogue going and of keeping their vision of development in the public eye (Oliver-Smith 2002). Actors' responses feed back into the way a resettlement project develops. Actors, whether the affected people, or those implementing resettlement, respond to the situations in which they find themselves (e.g. by resisting, by taking initiatives, by changing plans, or by changing allocations of resources). These actions feed back into the way things unfold, and often cannot be predicted or planned for. In combination, these factors reinforce each other, making the resettlement process even less amenable to a rational, technical approach.

Ethical Complexity in Forced Resettlement

While ethical issues are also not readily amenable to strictly rational considerations, in the sense that they usually cannot be resolved simply by a direct appeal to reason, I wish to mention them as an issue in their own right, so as to draw attention to their central role in any development undertaking. There is not space to go into issues in detail here, so I am merely going to list some of the more difficult questions, which I see as 'conundrums' – precisely because, while they make for more inclusive decision-making, procedures such as options assessment relating to development projects cannot resolve ethical problems by themselves.

- Is it acceptable to transpose a culturally specific view of development upon other people?
- Can one argue that, if there is no other way, some should suffer for the greater good?
- What should happen if negotiation does not reach a stage where the parties agree on a course of action? Should any party have the power to impose or veto a project? Can one decide how much negotiation is 'enough'?
- How are we to decide between the rights of various parties and interest groups? Should the fact that some have to move or suffer disadvantage for the benefit of others give them a kind of 'extra vote'? Surely a number of different parties are suffering in different ways?
- What should be done when there appears to be a conflict between fairness and equality of treatment of different categories of affected people?
- How should cultural loss/damage be evaluated for purposes of compensation? Distasteful as cost-benefit analysis may be, is there any realistic alternative?
- Is compulsion ever acceptable? If so, under what conditions?

Ethical issues add to the complexity of something like resettlement, precisely because of the human rights issues involved in resettlement and particularly in light of the fact that it is often of a forced nature and often gives rise to unexpected outcomes. Policy needs clarity in issues such as criteria for making decisions and allocating resources. Uncertain outcomes (both in terms of overall project goals as well as of resettlers' postresettlement fortunes) render problematic a utilitarian approach to deciding whether resettlement is ethically justifiable. The kind of openness that respecting other people and taking ethical issues seriously requires, can only compound the problems confronting policy makers, who need clear criteria, rather than intransigent dilemmas.

Complexity as a Possible Opportunity in Situations of Forced Resettlement

Although in many ways the complexity, that I argue is inherent in forced resettlement, seems to work against the achieving of successful outcomes, there may also be another side to the story, contributing to some more positive, albeit unintended, outcomes. That same complexity limits officials' ability to control the resettlement process and to implement resettlement as planned. Officials are thus limited in the degree of control that they can exercise over resettlers, in the extent to which they can make resettlers conform to externally imposed crop and marketing regimes, keep livestock off irrigation schemes, etc. This leaves room, more in some situations than in others, for resettlers to take the initiative to utilise the resources and opportunities provided by the resettlement project and the regional economy in ways perhaps other than intended by the project, for their own benefit.

Later on in the chapter I look at some African cases where resettlers have taken this initiative and improved their circumstances.

The 'inherent complexities' position thus argues that there is a complexity in resettlement, which arises from the interrelatedness of a range of factors of different orders: cultural, social, environmental, economic, institutional and political – all of which are taking place in the context of imposed spatial change and of local-level responses and initiatives. Interlinked and mutually influencing transformations are taking place simultaneously, as ongoing (preresettlement) processes of change interface, with changes initiated by the imposition from outside of a development project and the resultant resettlement to which it gives rise. Understanding this complexity, attempting to come to terms with it, and utilising the opportunities it may create seems to require a more comprehensive and open-ended approach than the predominantly economic and operational perspective that characterises the 'inadequate inputs' approach.

Levels At Which Risks Operate in Forced Resettlement

I submit that the complexities sketched above give rise to a number of risks within the resettlement process. Although this may seem to suggest some kind of causality, I do not here propose to try and map out a set of mechanical, one-to-one type, causal correspondences between particular kinds of complexity and particular risks – not least because its very integration is what characterises and powers the kind of complexity I have been trying to describe. The resulting risks do, however, seem to operate at various levels of comprehensiveness and incorporation, and I would here like to try and develop the outlines of a framework for understanding how this might work. This will hopefully assist us in trying to understand and counter such threats.

The Individual/Household Level

Most of Cernea's risks, with the exception of social disarticulation, seem to operate at this level, as do risks suggested by other authors, such as psychological marginalisation (Fernandes 2000: 212), loss of access to services (Mathur 1998: 70), loss of access to schooling (Mahapatra 1998: 218) and certain aspects of the loss of civil/human rights (Downing 1996). This level relates to the risk of the loss of natural, man-made and human capital (Cernea 2000: 32).

The Community Level

Here we find Cernea's 'social disarticulation', which relates to the disruption of 'the existing social fabric: ... patterns of social organization and interpersonal ties, ... kinship groups, ... informal networks, ... local voluntary organizations' – i.e. 'social capital' (Cernea 2000: 30). Linked to social disarticulation, there is what one might similarly term the risk of 'cultural disarticulation', or what Downing calls 'disruption of the spatial-temporal order' or 'social geometry' (1996: 33–34). This would include risks to the cultural integrity and autonomy of a group, which could arise out of a disregard for affected people's human rights. Economic impoverishment can take place at a collective, community level, as in the loss or lessening of access to communal property resources, community services and/or schooling.

Different sections of the resettled group, such as rich and poor, young and old, men and women, healthy and ill, will experience the risks inherent in resettlement with differential intensities and correspondingly be more or less likely to succumb to them.

Resettlement fundamentally alters the institutional context in which people find themselves (McDowell 2002: 183). Rapid change poses the risk of institutional instability, as new local-level institutions struggle to establish themselves in relation to their new setting and wider context. This, in turn, negatively affects their ability to negotiate access to resources. Linked to this is what one might call the risk of 'political disarticulation'. Koenig (2001: 17) suggests that 'involuntary resettlement is also impoverishing because it takes away political power, most dramatically the power to decide about where and how to live'. Groups find themselves displaced, with less political autonomy and rights, with less command over resources in their area, and being more tightly controlled by wider political and administrative structures. They lose resources and autonomy because they did not have the sociopolitical 'capital' to take an effective stand against the intruding outsiders (Koenig 2001). The conjunction of territorial, economic, administrative and political change leads to crises of leadership, which may result in factionalism and intracommunity conflict. The interaction between resettlers and the local host community is a fault line along which such conflict often crystallises, as between the Gumuz hosts and their new Highland neighbours in the Metekel region of Ethiopia (Wolde-Selassie Abbute 2002: Part Four).

The cumulative result of the interaction of the above factors is a risk of a sense of fatalism and dependency developing in resettled communities. This would characterise situations where settlements were unable to achieve what Scudder (1993) calls the stage of economic development and social formation. Cernea and others rightly emphasise that we should not overlook the problems facing host communities; most of the risks confronting resettlers at the individual and community levels can also apply to their host populations.

The Level of the Resettlement Project as Institutional Process

At this level, risks come into play that relate to issues raised above (in the section on The Resettlement Project as a Problematic Institutional Process), i.e. policy practice; mutually reinforcing critical shortages; resettlement being seen as an external cost; and, as a result, the very real risk of resettlement becoming reduced to relocation, with any plans for resettlement as development effectively falling by the wayside.

The fact that the resettlement component of a development project often runs out of time in relation to the other aspects of the project, coupled with the co-ordination problems discussed earlier, gives rise to the risk that the resettlement component will be unable to meet its goals, and accordingly the actualisation of Cernea's impoverishment risks.

Limited participation by resettlers raises the real possibility of the way they see the risks and opportunities with which resettlement confronts them (i.e. where Dwivedi (1999: 46) would argue that, for them, risk is precisely about the *uncertainty* of outcomes) not being taken into account, with the risk of planning and subsequent action being not only inappropriate, but actively damaging to the welfare of the resettlers.

Not seeing the resettlement project, with all its different constituencies, as an integrated whole, carries the risk of the problems facing parties other than the resettlers (such as officials) not being taken into account – which raises the spectre of even further alienation of local resettlement officials, who are already overworked and short on capacity and resources, and of the local-level institutional process becoming increasingly unworkable.

A risk that seems to apply at the three previous levels of individual/household, community and resettlement project, is what one might call the risk of *loss of flexibility*. When people's social structures, their 'social geometry' (Downing 1996: 34) and their sources of livelihood are disrupted, this tends to lead to an undermining of tried and trusted ways of doing things, lessening of resources and options, anxiety or stress, and therefore loss of flexibility and adaptability. When the risks (discussed earlier) that threaten a resettlement project come into play, this likewise lessens flexibility and adaptability at project level – which will surely impact negatively upon attempts to achieve successful resettlement.

The National/Regional Level

The absence, in most cases, of proper legal and policy frameworks at national level, of sufficient political will, commitment and fiscal restraint, and of functional co-ordination between the various agencies responsible for different aspects of resettlement, creates the risks of resettlement projects not being properly planned, funded or implemented, of the rights and wishes of the affected people not being respected, and of socio-economic failure.

Where the wider context within which a resettlement scheme finds itself is characterised by political and economic weakness and instability (such as with the Akosombo Dam in the Ghanaian context), this creates the risk, not only that the scheme will not become effectively integrated, but that the wider context will function in a way that is actively disabling for the scheme, leading to its social and economic decline.

The same state that initiates and enforces resettlement is also the author and supposed upholder of the laws that are supposed to offer protection to people billed for resettlement (Barutciski 2000). The state is thus effectively both player and referee, and there is thus the real risk of affected people having little, if any, effective recourse to the law to protect themselves against the state.

The International Level

The fact that international law does not appear to provide adequate or effective protection for DIDR resettlers (Barutciski 2000), together with the fact that the resettlement guidelines of funding agencies such as the World Bank are not always observed or properly policed, and that a number of financing institutions in the private sector are seemingly happy to lend money without worrying too much about the niceties of resettlement, all increase the risk of resettlers effectively having no protection when they are the victims of unjust laws and action on the part of their national government.

There is no 'free lunch', and aid and assistance, whether from funding agencies or from NGOs and activists, increases the risk of resettlers who need outside help in their struggles becoming vehicles or puppets for other groups to advance their agendas – yet again having their autonomy further eroded.

These various levels of risk – and how they are dealt with, or not dealt with – are clearly interrelated and impact upon each other.

What Lessons Do Cases of Successful Resettlement Have to Teach Us?

Before moving on to consider some broader policy implications in the last chapter of the book, it may be useful to consider examples where resettlement has enjoyed some success, in order to see what lessons can be learned from them.

Some Chinese Successes: Is China an Exception, or Does it Have the Formula for Successful Resettlement?

In recent years, China has achieved what would seem to be successful resettlement in a number of cases, most notably at Shuikou and Xiaolangdi, where there was a significant degree of resettler participation, and there has been a substantial improvement in household incomes, housing and services, as well as a high degree of settler satisfaction with the postresettlement situation (Trembath et al. 1999, Shi, Su and Yuan 2000, Picciotto et al. 2001). These schemes have been characterised by comprehensive planning, involvement of the project-affected people, a commitment to job creation as a vehicle of income restoration, and a high degree of flexibility in dealing with problems as they arose (Picciotto et al. 2001: 41).

What has led to these successes? In the 1980s China developed a progressive new legal, policy and administrative framework, designed to achieve 'resettlement with development', and with a strong commitment to income restoration. This approach, regarded by some resettlement scholars and practitioners as the most progressive in the world, includes pioneering work in developing benefit sharing as a means of facilitating local development, for resettlers as well as for their host areas (Van Wicklin 1999).

Resettlement in the post-Mao period has benefited from 'the persistence of planning elements in the Chinese economy' (Travers and Kimura 1993: xii), with an effective and decentralised resettlement bureaucracy. It has also benefited – at least in the case of the more successful schemes – from considerable financial assistance from government. The Chinese commitment to successful resettlement is epitomised by the fact that it is probably the country in the world with government machinery most dedicated to resettlement. All the necessary ingredients seem to be there: political will, legal framework, policy, adequate financing and an effective bureaucracy.

However, to what extent are the success stories such as Shuikou and Xiaolangdi representative of Chinese resettlement since the new approach was adopted? Shuikou and Xiaolangdi have enjoyed high resettlement budgets, with Jing (1999: 26) claiming that 'the Xiaolangdi Project has the highest resettlement budget per person of any project in China ... [and that] moreover, a separate [World] Bank credit was created, distinct from the dam project and loan, to ensure a high level of attention, staff inputs and budgetary resources'. Income restoration at Shuikou was greatly assisted by significant regional economic development (independent of Shuikou), 'that provided jobs and markets for the displacees' (Picciotto et al. 2001: 48). In addition, 'a major contributor to the success of the resettlement, which was not planned or financed by the Shuikou project, was the highway paralleling the reservoir, which considerably boosted the opportunities for economic development' (Trembath et al. 1999: 7). Other projects, which have been less high profile and less favourably situated, have been less successful. At Yantan (like Shuikou and Xiaolangdi, also a World Bank funded project), which is in an economically more isolated area than Shuikou, the negative income gap between resettlers and other people in the area has widened (Picciotto et al. 2001: 55). The less successful projects in China seem to have been characterised by problems similar to those discussed in the African situation, such as problems relating to inadequate planning, budget management, compensation, experienced staff, income generation and monitoring and evaluation, as well as corruption (Travers and Kimura 1993, Shi, Su and Yuan 2000, Shi, Wu, Chan and Zhu 2000).

Will China be able to continue with its progressive policies and achieve resettlement with development? Economic changes resulting from globalisation and the move to a 'socialist market economy' have led to an increasing 'disengagement of the state' (Meikle and Zhu 2000: 131), with the result that the Government increasingly no longer underwrites financial shortfalls in relation to resettlement nor guarantees employment or social welfare support. Difficulties with finding land or jobs to replace livelihoods (whether rural or urban) that have been lost to resettlement are seemingly making it increasingly difficult for China's undoubtedly progressive resettlement policy to be implemented in practice, and for livelihoods to be guaranteed for resettlers (Meikle and Zhu 2000).

How replicable are the Chinese success stories likely to be in countries without the strong economy, the progressive legal and policy framework, the efficient bureaucracy, the longstanding experience of resettlement, and the apparent political will necessary to make resettlement with development a reality? China would appear to be something of a special case – and, even then, with all the right inputs, the successes in income restoration would appear to have been significantly aided by unusual financial inputs by the state and/or the World Bank, and/or by proximity to the economically stronger eastern seaboard, thereby 'easing the difficulty of job creation' (Travers and Kimura 1993: xii). Although the right inputs are clearly a necessary condition for successful resettlement, they are not by themselves a sufficient condition. In the Chinese case, successful resettlement also seems to depend upon factors external to the project, such as a strong regional or national economy, as well as (what strikes an outsider visitor as) a sense of resettlement as a vehicle of national pride vis-à-vis the West, leading people to identify with and participate in resettlement projects seen as in the national interest.

What Can We Learn from Voluntary Resettlement Schemes?

Voluntary resettlement programmes enjoy 'greater success' than their enforced counterparts (Eriksen 1999: 94). There appear to be a number of common-sense reasons as to why this should be the case. With voluntary resettlement, scheme managers can decide what qualities they want settlers to have, whereas with forced resettlement, those who are being resettled have to be taken in, whether they have the disposition or capabilities to make a success of the new agricultural situation or not (Eriksen 1999: 111). Voluntary resettlers are self-selected, more likely to be positively oriented towards the new situation and more likely to have the necessary skills to succeed than forced resettlers, who have no choice in the matter (Eriksen 1999: 112). Voluntary resettlers can sometimes keep their premove assets or decide when to sell them to best advantage, whereas forced resettlers usually lose their former assets and are all too often poorly compensated for them (Eriksen 1999: 117). Voluntary resettlers can return to their area of origin if the new venture does not succeed, whereas this option is usually not open to forced resettlers (Eriksen 1999: 117).

In addition to these differences mentioned by Eriksen, it seems to me that there is likely to be much more flexibility in the voluntary resettlement situation, for two reasons: first, because there should be less of a time constraint than in the enforced situation, where resettlement has to be co-ordinated with, and often compromised with, a range of other project schedules, such as construction deadlines, sluice gates being closed, etc. Second, because the voluntary scheme is a single-purpose venture, scheme staff are likely to be more skilled and more experienced in the relevant areas, such as settlement planning and agriculture – which again allows for more flexibility and adaptability.

Because the voluntary scheme has been designed as a single-purpose venture, which must succeed on its own terms, resettlement and income regeneration will be the central focus of the project to a greater extent than with forced resettlement, where those factors are (all too often) thought of as a necessary burden and additional cost to what is seen essentially as an infrastructure project. As a project that must succeed on its own terms, a voluntary resettlement project is more likely to be located and designed so as to have links to its regional economy and marketing networks and to provide its settlers with the necessary training to achieve this integration.

One would expect scheme staff and settlers to be more skilled, committed and entrepreneurial, with a common interest in communication and consultation, in the voluntary situation than in its enforced counterpart, where both staff and resettlers are often there against their will, not necessarily qualified to be doing what is expected of them, and more likely to see one another in adversarial terms.

Voluntary resettlement schemes are thus characterised by a greater degree of commitment, skills, entrepreneurial ability, focus, integration and flexibility than enforced schemes. It is in this light that I suggest we should best understand the much better track record of voluntary resettlement schemes, in relation to criteria such as presettlement surveys, participation, planning, budgeting, funding and implementation etc. – all of which are necessary to successful resettlement (Eriksen 1999). We need to find ways to transfer the positive qualities that characterise successful voluntary schemes to forced resettlement situations – in spite of what appear to be significant comparative disadvantages on the part of forced resettlement.

Some African Cases: Local Initiative and Unexpected Opportunities Result in an Improvement of Resettlers' Circumstances

In spite of what seems to be a situation loaded more towards failure than success in relation to forced resettlement, a number of African cases show how local initiative, including the capacity to capitalise on unexpected opportunities that present themselves, has resulted in people improving their circumstances in a postresettlement situation. At Kainji, in Nigeria, some people made use of small, petrol-powered pumps to draw water from the dam to irrigate lands above the water line, and also utilised the drawdown area for grazing livestock (Roder 1994: 57). At Kariba, on the Zambian side, a fishery was established as part of the resettlement project. Initially successful, it did not, however, last more than a few years. What is significant for our purposes is that people used the earnings gained from fishing to diversify into cotton as a cash crop, build up their livestock holdings and invest in enterprises and education (Scudder 1985: 29; Scudder, personal communication May 2003). Elders at Kariba with large landholdings, able to command labour through having additional wives and children before resettlement, were able to turn this to good effect in the new areas, and also able to direct their compensation money and general income into various kinds of local investment opportunities. A number of people capitalised on various government loans and marketing outlets, diversifying the range of crops planted and venturing into cash cropping, with pig farming and small, hand-watered gardens also becoming widespread. The better roads and the increase in job opportunities arising from the construction of Kariba and the independence of Zambia resulted in an increase in the circulation of both money and goods, raising the general standard of living in the new areas (Colson 1971: Ch. 6). At the New Halfa scheme on the Sudanese side of the Aswan High Dam project, pastoralists who had joined the scheme continued to run their livestock off the scheme, as well as having access to cultivable land on the scheme. In a number of cases, their off-scheme income enabled them to balance the books (Sorbo 1985: 15).

After it seemed for a decade or more as if resettlement at Kom Ombo on the Egyptian side of the Aswan Dam was doomed to failure, there was a dramatic turnaround in the fortunes of the settlers, because they were able to capitalise on what were mainly unexpected opportunities and plain good fortune, arising out of the construction of the Aswan Dam.

Nubians found an unexpected patron in President Anwar Sadat, who had a Nubian grandmother and so used his influence to ensure an improved delivery of infrastructure and services to the affected people. Nubians had already had long-standing experience of migration and working in urban areas. This, together with the fact that schools were plentiful in New Nubia (a direct outcome of the establishment of resettlement areas), enabled them to obtain white-collar and other jobs that became available in Aswan City (which developed as part of the larger Aswan High Dam project) – as well as to continue their migrant jobs further afield. By letting out or sharecropping their tenancies on the scheme, they were able to benefit from both on- as well as off-scheme income-generating opportunities. The area from which Nubians moved included Abu Simbel, the site of some of the world's major archaeological treasures. The pending flooding and rescue of these treasures attracted worldwide interest, giving the Nubians, who previously had low status as an ethnic group, a new sense of history, identity and pride. The fact that the scheme at Kom Ombo has been able to maintain the viability of service provision to a much greater extent than many other African resettlement schemes seems to relate to greater economic and administrative capacity at a regional level, which, in turn, seems to reflect the importance of the Aswan High Dam project in its regional political context in Egypt. In combination, these factors made for a positive turnaround in the socio-economic position of Nubian resettlers, as well as giving them a much more prominent place in the national Egyptian political scene (Fahim 1981: 63, Fernea and Fernea 1991: Chs 16, 17, Fernea 1998).

Such initiatives and utilisation of opportunities feed back into the way a resettlement scheme unfolds, acting as a positive stimulus to the creation of further opportunities. To capitalise on this kind of entrepreneurial energy, it is essential that project plans and time frames, as well as scheme staff and structures, are adaptable and innovative enough to accommodate and encourage initiative and innovation, and to make the most of good fortune when it arises.

The Need to Factor Considerations of Complexity More Effectively into the Policy Process

People working with policy matters usually prefer clarity of criteria for making evaluations and decisions, and clearly mapped out and accountable procedures to accounts of complexity, of the kind that anthropologists tend to regard as the measure of their worth. However, if there is a complexity inherent in resettlement that does in fact give rise to risks and consequences in the way I have tried to outline, and if we are to come up with a policy approach that is able to counter those risks, it is going to have to be able to accommodate and deal with that complexity. So, the challenge is to find a new, creative way of accommodating complexity within the requirements of effective policy, incorporating the qualities that characterise the more successful instances of resettlement.

This appeal to complexity is in no way an attempt to do away with either existing policy initiatives or Cernea's risks and reconstruction analysis. Unless we deal with the risks that Cernea has identified and explored, there will be no successful resettlement. And unless we secure the proper 'inputs', such as national-level legal frameworks and policies, political will, funding, preresettlement surveys, planning, participation, careful implementation and monitoring, we will not be able to turn those risks into reconstruction opportunities. Where Cernea and I perhaps see things differently is that, whereas I understand him to believe that getting the above inputs right can in principle overcome the complexities in resettlement, I do not believe that this is sufficient. As I have tried to argue, however necessary 'adequate inputs' are, there are complexities and therefore risks in resettlement that cannot be dealt with in this manner; and this is not simply a matter of getting better legal frameworks, policies, funding, planning etc. Dealing with complexity – as opposed to complicatedness – requires us to find a way to build open-endedness and flexibility into the more structured frameworks and procedures that are an inescapable part of policy formulation and application, and to find ways of capitalising on and incorporating the creativity and entrepreneurial talent to be found among resettlers. Trade-offs will have to be negotiated and lessons learned on an ongoing basis, project by project. Like any development project, policy reform is a process, with its ups and downs.

The challenge is thus to develop policy that enables a genuinely more participatory and open-ended approach to planning and decision making, and that is better able to accommodate the complexity inherent in resettlement. This may, in turn, increase the subjective risks for planners, implementers and funders, all of whom might wish to draw clearer boundaries, budgets and time frames in relation to projects. But the case material repeatedly shows us that this is false economy. An unrealistically constrained process generates problems, resistance and unanticipated outcomes of its own, usually in a very costly manner. Genuine open-ended participatory planning brings people on board, identifies real problems and potentially practicable solutions, makes for more realistic budgeting and plans, enhances local capacity, agency and leadership, and reduces conflict (Koenig 2001).

In the end, it comes down to a question of *respect*: respect for the people we presume to put through resettlement for the 'greater good', and respect for the complexity of what such resettlement involves. *That* critical shortage (i.e. a lack of such respect, not understanding what it involves and not following through on its implications) results in a lot of the necessary detail being overlooked and is a significant part of why things so often go wrong in resettlement projects. How are we to translate the more general issue of respect, so as to take account of both the risks incurred and rights held on the part of all the stakeholders involved in a development project, and particularly those to be displaced (World Commission on Dams 2000: 206ff), into the specifics of policy and planning? That is the challenge, and policy reform, like anything else worthwhile, is a risky business. Trying to find ways of developing criteria and procedures that allow us to keep people's choices open and cater for complexity in the process, for as long as possible, seems a good place to start.

Acknowledgement

I would like to thank Simon Bekker, Thayer Scudder and Cornelis van der Waal for their very constructive comments on earlier drafts of this chapter.

References

Barutciski, M. 2000. *Addressing Legal Constraints and Improving Outcomes in Development-induced Resettlement Projects*. Unpublished report, Refugee Studies Centre, University of Oxford.

Butcher, D.A.P. 1970. 'The Social Survey'. In R. Chambers (ed.). *The Volta Resettlement Experience*, pp. 78–102. London: Pall Mall Press.

Cernea, M.M. 2000. 'Risks, Safeguards and Reconstruction: A Model for Population Displacement and Resettlement'. In M.M. Cernea and C. McDowell (eds). *Risks and Reconstruction: Experiences of Resettlers and Refugees*, pp. 11–55. Washington DC: The World Bank.

Chambers, R. (ed.). 1970. *The Volta Resettlement Experience*. London: Pall Mall Press.

Colson, E. 1971. *The Social Consequences of Resettlement: The Impact of the Kariba Resettlement upon the Gwembe Tonga*. Manchester: Manchester University Press.

de Wet, C.J. 1995. *Moving Together, Drifting Apart: Resettlement Planning and Villagisation in a South African Homeland*. Johannesburg: Witwatersrand University Press.

Diaw, K. and E. Schmidt-Kallert. 1990. *Effects of Volta Lake Resettlement in Ghana: A Reappraisal after 25 Years*. Hamburg: Institut fur Afrika-kunde.

Downing, T. 1996. 'Mitigating Social Impoverishment when People are Involuntarily Displaced'. In C. McDowell (ed.). *Understanding Impoverishment: The Consequences of Development-induced Displacement*, pp. 33–48. Oxford: Berghahn Books.

Dwivedi, R. 1999. 'Displacement, Risks and Resistance: Local Perceptions and Actions in the Sardar Sarovar'. *Development and Change*, 30: 43–78.

Eriksen, J.H. 1999. 'Comparing the Economic Planning for Voluntary and Involuntary Resettlement'. In M.M. Cernea (ed.). *The Economic of Involuntary Resettlement: Questions and Challenges*, pp. 83–146. Series on Directions in Development. Washington DC: The World Bank.

Fahim, H. 1973. 'Nubian Resettlement in the Sudan'. *Ekistics*, 212: 42–49.

———— 1981. *Dams, People and Development: The Aswan High Dam Case.* New York: Pergamon Press.

Fernandes, W. 2000. 'From Marginalisation to Sharing the Project Benefits'. In M.M. Cernea and C. McDowell (eds). *Risks and Reconstruction: Experiences of Resettlers and Refugees*, pp. 205–25. Washington DC: The World Bank.

Fernea, E.M. and R.A. Fernea. 1991. *Nubian Ethnographies.* Prospect Heights IL: Waveland Press.

Fernea, R.A. 1998. *Including Minorities in Development: The Nubian Case.* Unpublished report. Washington DC: The World Bank.

Grimm, C.D. 1991. *Turmoil and Transformation: A Study of Population Relocation at Manantali, Mali.* Unpublished Ph.D. thesis, State University of New York, Binghamton.

Hyden, G. 1980. *Beyond Ujamaa in Tanzania.* London: Heinemann.

Jing, J. 1999. *Displacement, Resettlement, Rehabilitation, Reparation and Development: China Report.* Unpublished report. Cape Town: World Commission on Dams.

Koenig, D. 2001. *Toward Local Development and Mitigating Impoverishment in Development-induced Displacement and Resettlement.* Unpublished report. Refugee Studies Centre, University of Oxford.

Lumsden, P. 1973. 'The Volta River Project Village Resettlement and Attempted Rural Animation'. *Canadian Journal of African Studies*, 7(1): 115–32.

Mahapatra, L.K. 1998. 'Good Intentions or Policies are Not Enough: Reducing Impoverishment Risks for the Tribal Oustees'. In H.M. Mathur and D. Marsden (eds). *Development Projects and Impoverishment Risks: Resettling Project-affected People in India.* pp. 216–36. Delhi: Oxford University Press.

Marris, P. 1961. *Family and Rehousing in an African City.* London: Routledge and Kegan Paul.

Mathur, H.M. 1998. 'The Impoverishment Risk Model and its Use as a Planning Tool'. In H.M. Mathur and D. Marsden (eds). *Development Projects and Impoverishment Risks: Resettling Project-affected People in India*, pp. 67–78. Delhi: Oxford University Press.

Mayer, P. and I. Mayer. 1971. *Townsmen or Tribesmen* (2nd edn). Cape Town: Oxford University Press.

McDowell, C. 2002. *Impoverishment Risks and Livelihoods: Towards a Framework for Research.* Unpublished conference paper, International Symposium on Resettlement and Social Development, Nanjing, May.

Meikle, S. and Y. Zhu. 2000. 'Employment of Displacees in the Socialist Market Economy of China'. In M.M. Cernea and C. McDowell (eds). *Risks and Reconstruction: Experiences of Resettlers and Refugees*, pp. 127–43. Washington DC: The World Bank.

Oliver-Smith, A. 2002. *Displacement, Resistance and the Critique of Development: From the Grass-roots to the Global.* University of Oxford, Refugee Studies Centre, RSC Working Paper No.9.

Pankhurst, A. 1992. *Resettlement and Famine in Ethiopia: The Villagers' Experience.* Manchester: Manchester University Press.

Picciotto, R., W. Van Wicklin and E. Rice (eds). 2001. *Involuntary Resettlement: Comparative Perspectives.* New Brunswick: Transaction Publishers.

Rew, A., E. Fisher and B. Pandey. 2000. *Addressing Policy Constraints and Improving Outcomes in Development-induced Displacement and Resettlement Projects.* Unpublished report, Refugee Studies Centre, University of Oxford.

Roder, W. 1994. *Human Adjustments to Kainji Reservoir in Nigeria*. New York, London: University Press of America.

Scudder, T. 1985. *A History of Development in the Twentieth Century: The Zambian Portion of the Middle Zambezi and the Lake Kariba Basin*. Unpublished report.

————— 1993. 'Development-induced Relocation and Refugee Studies: 37 Years of Change and Continuity among Zambia's Gwembe Tonga'. *Journal of Refugee Studies*, 6(2): 123–52.

————— 1997. 'Resettlement'. In A.K. Biswas (ed.). *Water Resources: Environmental Planning, Management and Development*, pp. 667–710. New York: McGraw-Hill.

Shi, G., Q. Su and S. Yuan. 2000. *Risk Control and the Design of a Social Security System for Resettlers: A Case Study of Xiaolangdi Reservoir Resettlement in China*. Unpublished conference paper, Tenth Conference of the International Rural Sociology Association, Rio de Janeiro, August.

Shi, G., Z. Wu, S. Chen and W. Zhu. 2000. *Policy, Planning and Implementation of Resettlement and Rehabilitation of Reservoir Projects in China*. Unpublished conference paper, Tenth Conference of the International Rural Sociology Association, Rio de Janeiro, August.

Sorbo, G. 1985. *Tenants and Nomads in Eastern Sudan: A Study of Economic Adaptations in the New Halfa Scheme*. Uppsala: Scandinavian Institute of African Studies.

Thiele, G.P.C. 1985. 'Villages as Economic Agents: The Accident of Social Reproduction'. In R. Abrahams (ed.). *Villagers, Villages and the State in Modern Tanzania*, pp. 81–109. Cambridge African Monographs No. 4. Cambridge: African Studies Centre, University of Cambridge.

————— 1986. 'The Tanzanian Villagisation Programme: Its Impact on Household Production in Dodoma'. *Canadian Journal of African Studies*, 20(2): 243–58.

Travers, L. and Y. Kimura. 1993. *China: Involuntary Resettlement*. Washington DC: The World Bank.

Trembath, B., M. Ter Woordt and Y. Zhu. 1999. *The Shuikou Hydroelectric Project in China: A Case Study of Successful Resettlement*. Washington DC: The World Bank. (This report is a summary of a larger report entitled 'Successful Reservoir Resettlement in China: Shuikou Hydroelectric Project'; EASES Discussion Paper Series.)

Van Wicklin, W.A. 1999. 'Sharing Project Benefits to Improve Resettlers' Livelihoods'. In M.M. Cernea (ed.). *The Economics of Involuntary Resettlement: Questions and Challenges*, 231–56. Series on Directions in Development. Washington DC: The World Bank.

Western, J. 1981. *Outcast Cape Town*. Pretoria: Human and Rousseau.

Whisson, M.G. 1976. 'The Significance of Kinship in a Cape Peninsula Township'. *African Studies*, 35(3/4): 253–71.

Wolde-Selassie Abbute. 2002. *Gumuz and Highland Resettlers: Differing Strategies of Livelihood and Ethnic Relations in Metekel, Northwestern Ethiopia*. Unpublished D.Soc.Sci. dissertation, University of Göttingen.

World Bank. 1998. *Recent Experience with Involuntary Resettlement: Togo-Nangbeto*. Operations Evaluation Department, Report No. 17543. Washington DC: The World Bank.

World Commission on Dams. 2000. *Dams and Development: A New Framework for Decision-making*. London: Earthscan.

8

Policy Recommendations and Suggestions for Further Research

Chris de Wet

Policy Recommendations

International-level legal frameworks, funding institutions and pressure groups can exert some pressure on national-level resettlement policy, administration and funding, which in turn strongly influence the way in which resettlement actually takes place at the project level. However, it is at the project level that resettlement ultimately either succeeds or fails. I will therefore start by considering some recommendations for improving outcomes at project level and work back up the system, considering what needs to happen at the national and international levels to make those improvements at project level possible.

If impoverishment risks are to be dealt with, and resettlement outcomes to be improved, the complexities of resettlement need to be taken into account and an integrated set of improvements need to take place. Recommendations, synthesised from the individual chapters, are presented below for such changes at project, national and international levels.

Project-level Recommendations

As argued in several chapters of this book, resettlement projects need to adopt a democratic, participatory approach to planning and implementation. This requires authentic participation by the affected people in all phases of the resettlement project, such that they have the ability to influence decisions concerning

- whether a specific development project is the best way to achieve development for that particular area;

- if so, whether displacement is unavoidable if the overall development project is to achieve its goals;
- and if so, how little resettlement can be got away with – as well as
  the details of the actual resettlement itself, and changes that may
  need to be considered once things are in process.

Koenig argues that for such genuine and open-ended negotiation to be
possible, all parties must have the skills to be able to participate as equal
partners and approach negotiation as a process of accommodating differences and handling conflict, rather than as a one-off showdown. This will
require officials and local law-enforcement officers to be able and willing
to recognise resistance as something much more complex than a simple
veto activity and incorporate it as part of the negotiation process. For this
all parties will need to have the necessary skills training. Equal participation also requires that there is a free flow of information at all stages of a
development project that may cause displacement. So, participation
requires all parties to recognise each other as full voting members, and to
all have the necessary skills, information and values to be able to negotiate effectively and respect the outcomes of such negotiation.

Linked to the need for a democratic, participatory approach is the need
for a flexible, learning-oriented approach at project level. Unexpected
developments occur, such as policy changes once the project is already
underway, budgets shrink, schedules fall behind, the rains come early or
resistance occurs. The way the various parties involved in the resettlement project respond to such events also affects the way the project
unfolds, and projects need to be designed so as to be able to adapt as they
go along. This requires the necessary range of technical, economic, social,
planning and other skills in the implementation team, as well as sufficient
funding, a project plan that allows for various options, and a time frame
that contains sufficient slack to allow for such flexibility.

Such participation and flexibility can be enhanced by developing a
range of both resettlement options and compensation options in consultation with the affected people and consciously building these into the
resettlement plan. Local people are more likely to know what is likely to
go wrong in the area, and a multi-option approach gives one more of a
chance of dealing with unexpected developments and problems. Such an
approach also caters for the fact that people occupy different socio-economic positions, and that some would stand to benefit or lose more from
one particular resettlement or compensation option than another, or may
want to change options as circumstances change.

A resettlement project's economic success will be significantly determined by the relationship it has with the larger development project of
which it is a part, as well as by its relationship with the regional economy.
One reason why resettlement is not properly implemented is that the

budget for resettlement is often eaten into by other aspects of the larger project as they experience overruns. One way of dealing with this problem is to ensure that the resettlement component is seen as a budget item in its own right, i.e. that it has its own separate budget, negotiated and approved at the start of the overall project. Ongoing income generation and development for resettlers can be facilitated by a percentage of the project's overall profits being ploughed back into the resettlement area, in perpetuity, with this percentage being established in a contract as part of the negotiations around resettlement. Ultimately, a new community will only remain economically viable if it is integrated into its regional economy, and care should be taken to plan resettlement projects so that they can be integrated into already existing development programmes, allowing for greater efficiency and synergy.

Rew, Fisher and Pandey (Chapter 3) remind us of the considerable discretion exercised by officials implementing resettlement on the ground. While such discretion is unavoidable – not least in the interests of adaptability and flexibility – it can also lead to inefficiency, social insensitivity and corruption. Fine policies do not mean much if they are not properly employed, and staff need to be trained to be socially sensitive and adaptable, as well as held accountable. This is where the role of senior managers at project level is crucial. They must have a clear understanding and appreciation of both the social and the economic aspects of resettlement and a commitment to upholding the rights of development-induced displaced persons (DIDPs). While they themselves will need to be closely monitored, they must also be given the political room to be allowed to appoint their own people, so that jobs will be filled by appropriately qualified and experienced staff, rather than simply having to accept staff seconded from the regional capital, with engineers appointed as resettlement officers. To be able to hold staff accountable, managers need to have the freedom to dismiss unsatisfactory officials – without having to answer for their job every time they hold someone accountable after due procedure has been followed. One project manager whom I interviewed in 2001 claimed that he had cut corruption drastically on the scheme by simply turning suspects over to the police. In his words: 'We had a couple of suicides, but since then corruption has dropped dramatically'.

National-level Recommendations

Rew, Fisher and Pandey (Chapter 3) argue that part of the problem with policy is that it is often ambiguous and general, involving political trade-offs between various departments and interests within government. It also falls foul of weak chains of decision making, poor communication, multi-agency involvement and 'organisational dependency', as it works its way down the administrative ladder.

At the national level, effective policy reform therefore requires greater clarity in the formulation of policy goals, as well as a stronger focus on implementation, and on the setting and upholding of achievable and ethically acceptable standards in this regard. To achieve this would seem to necessitate the development and enforcement of a coherent and shared policy framework, clearly stipulating requirements for resettlement to be undertaken as development, and addressing the issues of inalienable human rights, sustainable development and the elimination of poverty. Clarification of lines of authority and compliance with this framework would help to address the problems of decision making, communication and co-ordination mentioned above. This framework also needs to be extended to resettlement involving the private sector, with a clarification of its role and obligations.

Specific issues to be directly addressed within the scope of this policy framework include:

- that the affected people should be persuaded of the necessity of the development project in the first place and the inevitability of displacement if it is to be implemented;
- that development projects should consciously be planned so as to minimise such displacement;
- that effective legal mechanisms should be put in place to guarantee the rights of those affected to representation, complaint and redress;
- that resettlement should consciously be planned so as to be resettlement with development, and that sufficient funding to enable this should be a non-negotiable criterion for the development project happening in the first place; and
- that resettlement should be planned and implemented in accordance with internationally accepted guidelines, such as those of the World Bank.

To develop and consistently enforce a coherent framework and set of procedures based on the idea of development as a human right requires political will at the higher and medium levels of the resettlement administrative hierarchy. Political will usually responds to political pressure, and whether the policy framework is in fact applied consistently may well hinge on the ability of civil society groupings to monitor resettlement and apply such pressure where necessary.

International-level Recommendations

Barutciski shows (in Chapter 4) that international provisions for upholding the rights of DIDPs have only limited applicability and effectiveness. The more effective promotion of the rights of DIDPs requires accessible mechanisms that allow for the lodging and following up of individual complaints. Governments making bilateral loans seem to be better placed to establish such mechanisms, as they are not limited by nonpolitical mandates, as are the international banks. If an international alliance of funding and other organisations (such as UN groupings) could be formed, that spoke with one voice about displacement and resettlement, and that underwrote an independent and international monitoring mechanism (which could include inspection panels), it could provide the political and economic leverage necessary to ensure the consistent adoption and implementation of internationally accepted guidelines – in the private sector as well. In this regard, support should be given to the European Parliament's recommendation for such mechanisms in relation to a code of conduct for European enterprises operating in developing countries (see Chapter 4, fn. 33). Development agencies, such as the U.K. Department for International Development (DfID), could also assist in obtaining compliance with international standards in the countries to which they provide assistance, by providing support for NGOs and other civil society groupings working in those countries to monitor events and provide human rights and legal support to their citizens.

However, we also need to 'guard the guardians': these NGOs and other groupings need to be monitored to ensure that they do not co-opt or manipulate affected local groupings for their wider agendas.

In the great majority of cases, forced resettlement has worked in such a way as to restrict the number of choices open to the affected people, to impoverish them and to compromise their autonomy as communities. Those who plan and implement resettlement therefore need consciously to do so in such a way as to create choices and options; they must view resettlement as an upfront development initiative in its own right and go about it in such a way as to empower those involved. We, as members of the wider community of people who in any way exercise any influence over the resettlement phenomenon (whether as funders, politicians, officials, implementers, consultants, academics or activists), should in the first instance use all our skills, influence and contacts to push as hard as possible for development *without* resettlement and be more selective as to which resettlement projects we support or facilitate. If we do support a project we need to do everything we can to ensure genuine participation and negotiation, and for resettlement-as-development, and to make these conditions for our support. If we are agreed that a number of attributes (such as proper planning, participation, political will, administrative capacity, funding, skills, implementation etc.) are necessary in order for a resettlement project in principle to stand any chance of success, and if it is clear that those attributes are not present, then we have a dilemma. Should we have nothing to do with it and even contemplate resisting it, or should we use our influence and our experience of resettlement to try and keep options open for DIDPs and minimise the damage that we almost certainly know is going to happen? That is a judgement call, and an ethical decision, that each of us must make for ourselves – but if we have been arguing for a human rights approach to development and resettlement, then we must apply that same standard to our own intervention (or nonintervention): it must be done with the human rights and best interests of those who are to be affected in mind.

Some Suggestions for Further Research

I will here briefly mention for consideration some issues that have been suggested by the various authors in this volume as requiring further research, rather than developing a more detailed agenda as to how this might be done.

Understanding Forced Migration

If sound policy needs to be based on sound sociology, then we need further to develop our understanding of what we have argued are the complexities inherent in the resettlement process, as well as of the similarities and differences between different kinds of forced migration.

Learning From General Development Theory

Although resettlement is in some ways a unique phenomenon, we should perhaps not overemphasise its singularity. If we are looking to achieve sustainable livelihood restoration after resettlement, we would do well to look to other kinds of development initiatives, to see what we can learn from their successes and failures.

Understanding Income Restoration as a Socio-economic Issue

If we are to achieve sustainable income generation after resettlement, we need to understand more of what is involved in trying to reconstitute socio-economic systems, in all their complexity, in a transformed situation. When income generation fails, this is in significant measure because we have not catered for the complexity of the socio-economic system that we are changing through resettlement. We need a better grasp of the diversity of income-generating strategies in a community up for resettlement, and their interrelationships, as well as of the way they are embedded in the wider social and institutional fabric of such communities.

Dealing with Conflict and Differentiation

In the same way as we need to understand the complexity of socio-economic systems if we are to achieve economic recovery, we must also do so if we are to achieve political stability in a postresettlement community. We need to understand more closely the nature of inequality, differentiation and conflict in the preresettlement community, if we are to be able to find a way of managing competition for leadership and resources, as well as constructively bringing the élite on board in the interests of the new settlement as a whole – while yet seeking to achieve a greater measure of empowerment and equity in the new situation.

Confronting the Problematic Nature of Participation

The fact that affected communities are not cohesive or undifferentiated means that participation, which is meant to enhance democratic participation and empowerment, may have the opposite effect (Cooke and Kothari 2002). We need better to understand ways in which participation can be manipulated for the purposes of particular interest groups, both in the immediately affected communities and beyond, as well as how participation may work against an effective and informed decision-taking process.

Securing the Human Rights of Those Displaced.

We probably all agree that resettlement policy needs to respect the human rights of those affected, and to regard development as their right, inasmuch as they have had to give up their homes and territory in the greater interest. However, we need to develop a clearer understanding of the issues and obstacles involved in integrating a human rights and entitlements approach into resettlement policy and procedures. We also need to consider in greater detail why it is that both national and international law provide relatively little protection for DIDPs, and what is needed if we are to achieve greater enforcement of rights provisions.

Learning From Resistance

Oliver-Smith tells us (Chapter 6) that people resist when they feel that the risks of displacement and consequent resettlement exceed what is regarded as culturally acceptable. We need to understand more about the way in which people's 'risk calculus' operates, how it varies by e.g. age, gender, income etc., and how it influences whether people resist or not. We also need to know more about the impact of resistance on the way the resettlement process unfolds: what factors determine whether it simply dies, or influences project design and implementation and possibly even policy formulation. This includes developing feedback mechanisms into project planning such that the lessons from resistance can be incorporated in an iterative and positive manner.

Refining the Concept of Risk

While the concept of risk is a valuable tool for helping us to develop a policy response to the problems of displacement and resettlement, we need to refine it. Following on from Cernea's (1999) path-breaking matrix of objective impoverishment risks (i.e. risks that exist regardless of whether they are perceived to be risks or not), Dwivedi (1999) has argued for taking subjective perceptions of risk more actively into account, and de Wet (see Chapter 7) has attempted to develop a typology of (objective) risks. We need to develop a more comprehensive and systematic understanding of the different kinds and levels of risk involved in resettlement, and particularly of the interaction between people's behaviour in terms of their subjective perception of risk, and objective risks.

Refining Our Understanding of Resettlement as a Process

With the recent focus on impoverishment risks and income restoration, we have perhaps lost sight somewhat of the fact that resettlement is a process, which unfolds over time. The most developed model of resettlement as a process is that advanced by Scudder (1993), which focuses predominantly on the path taken by successful resettlement schemes. We need to ask ourselves what kinds of process emerge in schemes that may not count as successful in Scudder's terms; whether different kinds of risk emerge at different stages of the process; and how factors such as resistance, or responsiveness on the part of officials, or changes in the national political or economic situation, influence the way a resettlement project unfolds – as well as its outcomes.

Developing a Moral Framework in Relation to Resettlement

By its very nature, forced resettlement raises a number of ethical issues, not least of which are: under what conditions it might be considered acceptable to compel people to move against their will, and how we are to adjudicate between the rights and interests of the various parties involved. These are questions to which there do not appear to be any clear answers based on rational criteria, because a rationally based moral argument requires both a starting assumption as to what constitutes the moral good to be upheld, as well as its application in a logically valid argument. But those of us who are concerned with or working in resettlement are not necessarily agreed amongst ourselves about what the primary moral good is that is to be upheld in the case of resettlement. Is it the public interest, self-determination, equality (Pentz 2002) or the restoration of livelihoods? How should we try to balance the claims of utilitarianism and 'the greater good' against those of the Kantian imperative always to treat people as ends and never as means (Sterba 2000)? There are always trade-offs, and hence choices, to be made. The temptation is to say that these are questions of conscience. But this does not help us very much in trying to develop ethically responsible and coherent policy. We need to think seriously about how to develop a coherent moral framework within which to make decisions about the moral acceptability or otherwise of particular resettlement projects, as well as about matters such as how to decide when/whether there has been 'sufficient negotiation' and sufficient demonstration of the public good, such that there is moral justification for going ahead with the project, although some people may not want it, and about how one decides what constitutes 'acceptable levels' of compensation. To develop such a framework, we need to ask ourselves what is particular to the moral issues that arise when the right is presumed to move some people against their will, in what is claimed to be the greater public interest.

The Bottom Line

We need to think of alternatives to the combination involved in forced resettlement as such. That is the bottom line. Having to move away from one's home area need not necessarily guarantee socio-economic disaster; neither need moving to a planned resettlement area. It is the combination of (i) having to move to (ii) an externally designated and planned resettlement area, in (iii) a context where resettlement with development is realistically not a possibility, that guarantees socio-economic disaster and is morally indefensible. If we are honest, in the light of all the arguments and evidence advanced in this book, we need to recognise that most countries, even with foreign aid, are not able to provide the minimum conditions or capacity to achieve forced resettlement with development. So, if it has been fairly agreed that a project is genuinely in the public interest, and that there is no way around the fact that people are going to have to move to make this possible, then every effort must be made by all parties concerned, working together, to counteract the otherwise disastrous combination of factors referred to above. This requires the affected people participating as genuine partners in every stage of the project cycle, with the aim of keeping their options as open as possible, so as to i) minimise displacement, ii) provide a range of settlement and compensation options, and iii) create livelihood improvement opportunities (e.g. through benefit-sharing). To generate responsible and viable policy and its effective implementation, requires the optimum combination of our experience of the resettlement record, a coherent and defensible moral framework, and the imagination, creativity and empathy that enable officials both to 'stand in the shoes' of the affected people and, together with them, to generate new options.

In the words of the anthropologist Kirsten Hastrup,

> If there is anything common to humanity, it is that we are imaginable to one another ... To perceive and understand different worlds of whatever scale, we must extend our imaginative powers as far as possible, and make more events of understanding happen. (Hastrup 1995: 76)

Development (and, for our immediate purposes, resettlement) involves other people, and as such, development/resettlement failures are failures of the imagination. Imagination – in the sense of putting ourselves in the position and perspective of other people – is at the heart of the social sciences, whether 'pure' or 'applied': it is the sine qua non of any successful intellectual, moral, and therefore development-oriented, activity.

References

Cernea, M.M. 1997. 'The Risks and Reconstruction Model for Resettling Displaced Populations'. *World Development*, 25(10): 1569–88.

Cooke, B. and U. Kothari (eds). 2002. *Participation: The New Tyranny?*. London, New York: Zed Books.

Dwivedi, R. 1999. 'Displacement, Risks and Resistance: Local Perceptions and Actions in the Sardar Sarovar'. *Development and Change*, 30: 43–78.

Hastrup, K. 1995. *A Passage to Anthropology*. London: Routledge.

Pentz, P. 2002. 'Development, Displacement and Ethics'. *Forced Migration Review*, 12: 4–5.

Scudder, T. 1993. 'Development-induced Relocation and Refugee Studies: 37 Years of Change and Continuity among Zambia's Gwembe Tonga'. *Journal of Refugee Studies*, 6(2): 123–52.

Sterba, J.P. 2000. 'Towards Reconciliation in Ethics'. In H. La Follette (ed.). *The Blackwell Guide to Ethical Theory*, pp. 420–41. Oxford: Blackwell Publishers.

Index